COUNTER
INSTITUTION

COUNTER INSTITUTION

ACTIVIST ESTATES OF THE LOWER EAST SIDE

NANDINI BAGCHEE

EMPIRE STATE EDITIONS
AN IMPRINT OF FORDHAM UNIVERSITY PRESS
NEW YORK 2018

All drawings, timelines, and illustrations by author Nandini Bagchee unless otherwise noted.

This project was made possible through support from the Independent Projects category of the Architecture + Design Program at the New York State Council on the Arts with the support of Governor Andrew M. Cuomo and the New York State Legislature. Van Alen Institute served as the fiscal sponsor.

Visit us online:
www.empirestateeditions.com
www.fordhampress.com

Library of Congress Control Number: 2018933429

Printed in Canada
20 19 18   5 4 3 2 1
First edition

CONTENTS

The bibliography for this book can be found on the web at
https://fordham.bepress.com/nysh/3.

INTRODUCTION

In recent years, questions about the importance of public space have surfaced as demonstrations and occupations have visibly reentered the civic imagination. Current debates about public space in cities, or the lack thereof, focus mainly on open and accessible places of assembly—that is, parks, squares, and streets. The concept of a physical commons in short supply and highly monitored by police and cameras is undoubtedly problematic to the formation of discursive practices. However, there is another kind of space that is just as critical to democracy—one in which the nature of public participation is negotiated, coordinated, sustained, and developed into productive propositions for political action. This space is the office, workshop, or building where activist groups meet to organize and plan what often appear to be impromptu acts of political dissent and collective participation. In the many debates about the public sphere, this less visible domain of participation has not yet garnered adequate attention. *Counter Institution: Activist Estates of the Lower East Side* explores the history and potential of such private-public spaces through a study of select buildings that have been appropriated and adapted by politically oriented citizens and nonprofit organizations in New York City.

COUNTER INSTITUTION

Public institutions play a critical role in the way cities are structured. In the '70s and '80s, as federal funding for public programs was systematically dismantled, New York City's civic infrastructure was seriously compromised. The closing of schools, hospitals, parks, and playgrounds; the end of the federally funded public housing programs; the deinstitutionalization of mentally ill patients; and the cutbacks in funding for the arts adversely affected life in the city. To compensate for the retreating welfare state, many New Yorkers organized to pursue alternative types of collective action. This activity took many forms. Artist collectives, guerrilla gardeners, social activists, and various advocacy groups converted city-owned and semi-abandoned properties into places that fostered civic participation and encouraged self-organization. The term *counter institution* refers to these insurgent, grassroots efforts that provided direct deliverables and generated alternative forums of empowerment to communities under pressure from an unfortunate set of circumstances. The concept of an "institution" encompasses an organization with a set of covenants and the building that houses such an entity. This book examines the dual identification of institutions as both administrative and physical structures by underscoring the history of actions and activity within the buildings. In doing so, *Counter Institution: Activist Estates of the Lower East Side* aims to highlight the importance of such physical space not simply as a backdrop but as a crucial aspect of social movements within the city.

ACTIVIST ESTATES

Within the Lower East Side, networks of counter-institutions, although not precisely linked, form an association through activism. An examination of political activism around war, housing, and social justice that have informed social reform efforts in New York City provides the context for analyzing three activist-run buildings selected for this study. These three structures are an office building used by anti-war and social justice advocates, a large abandoned schoolhouse run as a Puerto Rican community center, and a tenement building that was converted to a collectively run art center. These three case studies represent three different but overlapping political constituencies that emerged in New York City in the '70s. Fiscal crisis and the temporary devaluation of real estate during this period allowed ad hoc citizen undertakings and social advocacy groups to establish control over semi-abandoned buildings and properties.

This book argues that the use of these buildings by activists over the past five decades is tied to the flux of political and economic events affecting the city and the nation. The provocation of the philosopher Henri Lefebvre that the city is an oeuvre, a work, a collective creation, is extended here to apply to buildings that act as repositories of the collaborative actions of its inhabitants. By examining how properties and buildings have been used as a base by social movements to launch a critique of the city and the nation, this book explores the important and often unrecognized ways in which "activist estates" have contributed to the civic realm. While the buildings are not in themselves agentic, there is, within social movements, a practice to co-opt space and ascribe to it a symbolic charge by naming a building or a place. The three buildings discussed in this book were each named accordingly: the Peace Pentagon was the headquarters of the anti-war movement; El Bohio was a metaphoric "hut" that envisioned the

Activist Estates: Three Buildings in the Lower East Side.

Illustration by Nandini Bagchee.

Puerto Rican community as a steward of the environment; and ABC No Rio, with its name appropriated from a storefront sign with missing letters, was a playful punk move that appealed to the anarchistic sensibility of the artists that ran a storefront gallery in a run-down tenement. These names activated the spaces and ascribed to them an aspirational charge and thereby created an agency that is discussed and envisioned here in this book as *Activist Estates*.

LOWER EAST SIDE

In discussing the past, present, and future of these three institutions, it is important to define the geographical area in which they emerged. The Lower East Side traditionally refers to an area east of the Bowery, extending from Fourteenth Street in the north to the Brooklyn Bridge in the south. This area is designated as Community Board 3 by the city, and the neighborhoods within this jurisdiction have historically been defined by the different migrant groups that have brought varying cultural and economic perspectives to the area. There is a wealth of multidisciplinary urban histories and social studies of the Lower East Side going back to the legendary photo-essay by Jacob A. Riis, *How the Other Half Lives*, a book published in 1890 that described the living conditions of the immigrant poor (Jewish, Italian, and Chinese) in the lower wards of nineteenth-century Manhattan. Since then, this neighborhood, with its mix of ethnicities, cultures, and countercultures, has been examined by various urban practitioners and scholars as a microcosm of a city with all its dialectical potentials and pitfalls.

The first of a series of more critical studies, *From Urban Village to East Village: The Battle for New York's Lower East Side* (1994), edited by Janet L. Abu-Lughod, brought together the research and insights of sociologists, geographers, planners, and historians to examine the contestation of space in this multivalent neighborhood. This narrative of competing interests in a socially diverse neighborhood, which dates to 1994, has since been expanded by other scholars, and recorded in films, oral histories, novels, poems, and essays written by residents of the neighborhood. Of these, Christopher Mele's *Selling the Lower East Side: Culture, Real Estate, and Resistance in New York City* (2000); Malve von Hassell's *Homesteading in New York City, 1978–1993: The Divided Heart of Loisaida* (1996); and *Resistance: A Radical Social and Political History of the Lower East Side* (2007), edited by Clayton Patterson, have been instrumental in shaping my understanding of a contentious history of development in the Lower East Side.

While drawing on these multidisciplinary perspectives, the point of departure for this book is to examine how *buildings* structure the social lives of people and generate an alternative forum for civic participation. *Counter Institution: Activist Estates of the Lower East Side* examines the tension between the impermanence of the insurgent activist practices and the permanent but maintenance-heavy aspects of architecture. The three buildings considered here are part of a larger network of properties that have historically been used to house, aid, and abet social movements in the city. While acknowledging the parallels between many other spaces with similar intentional communities and spaces for activism, this book remains closely focused on the case-study approach. Theoretically, this method of looking at geopolitically specific social movements builds upon the framework set up by Manuel Castells in his seminal 1983 work *The City and the Grassroots: A Cross-Cultural Theory of Urban Social Movements*. Using the case-study method, as opposed to a comparative analysis, this book looks at the transformation of each "counter institution" over an extended period of time.

By remaining within a limited urban context—the Lower East Side—the narrative emphasizes the trajectories of people in between buildings and adjacent sites to construct ideological networks that run as a historic thread through the neighborhood over time. The first chapter pulls together the larger history of social organization in lower Manhattan and, in doing so, moves beyond the Lower East Side to examine actions around City Hall, Washington Square, Union Square, and the former manufacturing districts north and south of Houston Street. The map of the Lower East Side is sometimes stretched, such as in the second chapter, to include a triangular area extending west of the Bowery to Lafayette Street now designated as the NoHo (North of Houston) Historic District. In the third chapter, the actions of the Puerto Rican "Loisaida" movement concentrates on the neighborhood east of Avenue A, between Fourteenth Street in the north and Houston Street in the south. The fourth chapter locates the praxis within the terrain south of Houston Street, within what was once the Jewish immigrant enclave of the Lower East Side. The actions and activities of the three constituencies discussed in the book create a patchwork of links and affinities that present the neighborhood as not merely bound by streets and districts but rather as an interconnected network of actions and possibilities.

While grounding the narrative firmly in a few selected blocks of New York City, the book contextualizes the micronarratives of activism in larger, more geographically dispersed collective undercurrents. The buildings in question are anchors, but the sociopolitical aspirations of grassroots organizing take the project outside these physical spaces as individuals connect to events that intersect with the larger jurisdictions of municipal and federal policy. While exploring the global identities of some of the actors involved in this telling, the book remains confined to the spatial practices and political activism of the Lower East Side. A comparison of anti-war/anti-corporate movements in Latin America, related self-determination movements in Puerto Rico, and a broader understanding of global anarchic spaces is hinted at but beyond the scope of this book. By remaining "location based," this book is an invitation to other scholars and practitioners to study the overlapping constituencies of urban social movements and to expand the research further by examining the global aspects of local movements.

METHOD

The history of organizing and the activities of groups and individuals within the different buildings are culled from various primary sources including newspapers, reports, meeting notes, photographs, and documents from private and public archives. This broad research was enriched by interviews with people involved with the buildings, many of whom are still dedicated to these movements. The history of these spaces as presented here is therefore by no means comprehensive but rather selective and informed by the observations of those interviewed by the author. The placement of the Activist Estates, that is, the buildings, at the center of larger questions of social equity, war, and cultural production, yields a different perspective of the instrumentality of space. The book consciously aims to highlight this point of view. To parse out the reciprocity between urban space and global events, between people and buildings, this work uses a hybrid method of combining words with images. The project of mapping and drawing is integral to the writing of this book. Drawings, photographs, time lines, and collages do not merely complement the text. Rather, they serve to explore the relationships between geography, politics, architecture, and history. The efficacy of envisioning spatial and political practices in relation to time is central to this investigation. As part of this approach, archival photographs of past events are presented along with current documentation and questions about the future of such buildings. This method of analysis is seldom applied to a historic reading of buildings and the way memory and action become a component of a functional space.

Although there is considerable research and writing on alternative spaces formed by artists in New York City from the '70s to the present, there are few attempts to see these spaces as part of a larger network of collective undertakings. By comparing how various social groups use space to establish themselves through the occupation of buildings, this book seeks to provide a more inclusive concept of citizenship and, by extension, readership. Exposition through the mapping of information has long been a part of the lexicon of protest tactics. By borrowing from this tradition, this work hopes to generate new ways to imagine buildings as vital resources for the future and a critical part of the civic infrastructure. This book charts out territorial occupations at different scales and simultaneously builds upon the use and symbolic value of these buildings. This method of research and representation will be of interest to academics and students working at the intersection of art and design with history, the social sciences, preservation, and community organization.

As self-organized spaces disappear from the city center but continue to mushroom in more economically conducive environments, this book can provide a critical perspective on the possibilities of structuring collective resistance. This social and visual history book is addressed to practitioners, activists, artists, architects, policy makers, and others who are interested in how the city can inspire and encourage political engagement. With the continuing thrust of speculative development in cities such as New York, it is essential to ask what alternate forms of participation exist for the many groups who depend on the availability of space to organize movements. This book is about the appropriation of built spaces and the short- and long-term experiments in collectivity forged through the actions of these counter-institutions. In taking over a few dilapidated buildings and breathing social purpose into them, people deliberately countered the rapidly growing commodification of real estate. The fact that many of these ventures began as ad hoc experiments in a grassroots democracy, persisted over the years, and spawned other initiatives attests to the power and promise of this mode of space-based organizing. In trying to memorialize, interpret, and politicize the buildings in question, this book hopes to empower a new generation of activists, architects, artists, and urbanists to engage in the built environment.

1

ACTIVIST ESTATES

CHAPTER 1: ACTIVIST ESTATES

The "long nineteenth century," a phrase used by the historian Eric Hobsbawm to describe the extended period of political and economic change in Europe between the French Revolution and World War I, was also a dramatic period of growth and revolutionary change for the industrial cities of North America. Successive waves of immigrants from Europe—Germans, Italians, Irish, and, later, Eastern European Jews—arriving in New York settled close to points of disembarkation and available work in the industrial districts of Lower Manhattan. A dense landscape of cheaply built tenement housing on the Lower East Side, situated to the east of the Bowery, and the manufacturing warehouses to the west of the Bowery, in neighborhoods today known as SoHo and NoHo, expanded to accommodate and provide work opportunities to the newcomers. Within these neighborhoods, which historians often describe as a "gateway" or "portal" to America, the newcomers shared the common fate of being dislocated from their homeland by political persecution or economic adversity.[1] After traveling across the Atlantic Ocean and disembarking in Lower Manhattan, many of the new arrivals were, at first, faced with more poverty, exploitative working conditions, and substandard living accommodations. The city government, which was dominated by Tammany Hall in the nineteenth century, did little to run the city for the good of the larger population. Instead, it controlled the electorate with bribes and favors. It was through this shared experience of having to fight for basic subsistence and communal dignity that many social and political organizations emerged in the Lower East Side. Widespread corruption within the municipal government and the actions of profiteering landlords and callous employers were gradually met by an organized resistance from unionized workers, tenant associations, and an assortment of neighborhood clubs. Local religious and ethnic societies formed with the intention of helping residents gain a social footing in the chaotic milieu of linguistic and cultural multiplicity. Within the working-class poverty of the lower wards of New York City, an ensemble of institutions—religious, secular, and anarchistic—shaped the political and spatial discourse of the Lower East Side.

This legacy of social action, designed to provide a platform for immigrants and to reform the city from the ground up, was expressed in the built environment in the form of settlement houses, clubs, libraries, bathhouses, playgrounds, and all manner of charitable institutions. Following the two world wars, the Lower East Side's demographics shifted as new immigrants from the Ukraine, Poland, and the Dominican Republic, along with migrants from Puerto Rico and the wave of African Americans moving north, brought different cultural perspectives into this historically immigrant enclave. By the middle of the twentieth century, with a declining economy that was based on shipping and manufacturing and a dwindling job market, it was the large stock of affordable tenement housing and the established network of social support that continued to attract newcomers. The influx of politically marginalized arrivals caught in the cycles of investment and disinvestment[2] in the physical fabric of this neighborhood decidedly shaped the countercultural spaces of a grassroots activism.

In the 1990s, amidst the fast-paced gentrification of the city at large, evidenced by the proliferation of luxury housing, pricey restaurants, and high-end shops, there remained the remnants of the previous era of social organization. On the Lower East Side, the soup kitchens, boys' and girls' clubs, settlement houses, radical churches, arts facilities, libraries, community centers, and gardens are a shared resource. With the engine of real estate driving the development of the neighborhood toward new levels of unaffordability, these vital public amenities hang on, precariously providing a much-needed territory for education, play, and political mobilization.

This chapter provides a selective inventory of properties claimed by sociopolitical advocates over a 150-year period of organizing in Downtown New York City. In a deliberate opposition to the concept of commodified real estate, the accounting of non-commodified property here allows for the assemblage of *activist estates*. I argue that these aggregated properties can be viewed as an outcome of the different political constituencies that have produced three different types of activist estates. The first set of properties, *Progressive Estates*, are institutions initiated by Progressive Era reformers in the late nineteenth century to engage with the social issues of employment, education, and housing in what was then a poor immigrant neighborhood. The second set of properties, *Radical Estates*, dates back to the early twentieth century and combines the Marxist aspirations of labor movement organizing with the more utopian dimensions of the pacifist movement. The third set, *Artists Estates*, is about a creative approach to living and working by repurposing the underutilized infrastructure of the postindustrial city into new types of experimental cultural spaces within New York City.

The list of activist estates examined here is by no means exhaustive or inclusive, but rather lays out the themes addressed in the chapters of this book—anti-war activism, housing, and the arts. These three types of activism that informed the larger political consciousness of the nation are examined in the aftermath of the civil rights, anti–Vietnam War, and right to city movements. This chapter makes the point that the buildings and the institutions set up in the nineteenth century to promote social change constituted a network of physical spaces and generated a continuum of participatory democracy and advocacy in the Lower East Side. The term "activist estates," in this context, refers to the buildings and landscapes as they acquired meaning through the actions of the people involved in social organizing.

PROGRESSIVE ESTATES

SETTLEMENT HOUSES (1886–1918)

The overcrowded municipal wards[3] described in vivid detail in the late nineteenth century by social reformers and journalists brought the Lower East Side and its burgeoning immigrant population to the attention of the middle-class and well-to-do New Yorkers who lived north of Fourteenth Street (**Figure 1.1**). Writers such as Jacob A. Riis [4] rendered the populous living quarters of the neighborhood, with the resulting unsanitary conditions, as cause for concern for the more established inhabitants of the city. The settlement house movement was born out of the desire of the educated and well-to-do citizens to not only advocate for but also socialize the poor to a more middle-class norm.[5] The impoverished slums of the East End of London were the original site of an experiment in social reform that espoused a form of charity whereby a more privileged class of volunteers lived within the impoverished community to better learn about and subsequently change the situation from within rather than remotely. These progressive ideas soon found their way across the Atlantic and had an impact in cities across the United States, notably in low-income immigrant neighborhoods such as the Lower East Side.[6]

The Neighborhood Guild, founded in 1886 and later renamed the University Settlement, was the first of many such organizations formed to help residents of the notorious Tenth Ward in Manhattan.[7] Stanton Coit, a young student at Columbia University, along with other colleagues—mainly university students and young writers—moved to live in this neighborhood and thought of ways to engage with the struggling families in this part of the city. They formed clubs for the residents with the goal of providing both education and

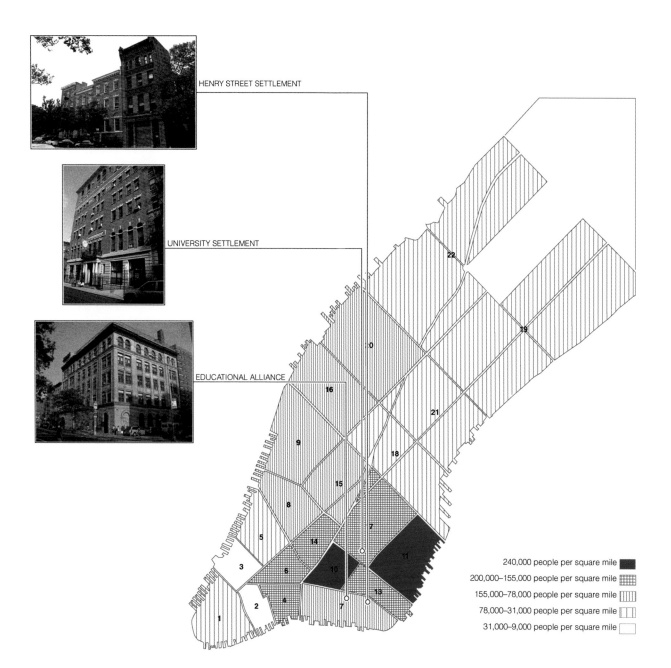

HENRY STREET SETTLEMENT

UNIVERSITY SETTLEMENT

EDUCATIONAL ALLIANCE

240,000 people per square mile
200,000–155,000 people per square mile
155,000–78,000 people per square mile
78,000–31,000 people per square mile
31,000–9,000 people per square mile

1.1
A map of population density of New York's wards in 1900.
The three prominent settlements—Educational Alliance,
University Settlement, and Henry Street Settlement—
retain their original buildings, and these are operational
in 2017.
Illustration by Nandini Bagchee.

The U.S. Census Bureau calibrates the population density of the Tenth
Ward in 1900 at 314,931 people per square mile. This means that three
times as many people lived in this neighborhood as compared to the
rest of Lower Manhattan, which at the turn of the century, held 80 percent of the city's population.

1.2

University Settlement, 1900s.

Photograph courtesy of the New York Public
Library Archives.

recreation.[8] The educational role of the settlement volunteers expanded as they came to understand that the problems of work, housing, health, and environment were intertwined and endemic to the neighborhood.[9]

The settlement house became a nexus of progressive reform, a place to organize socially, politically, and economically. As the membership and support for the University Settlement grew, the volunteer staff raised money to buy property and build a five-story building at the corner of Rivington and Eldridge Streets in the heart of the neighborhood (**Figure 1.2**). It included large public rooms on the lower floors and smaller residential quarters for the settlement workers at the upper levels. A grand staircase, flooded with light from an interior courtyard, occupied the center of the building and connected the boarding rooms of the settlement workers above to the spaces for public gatherings below. Living rooms shared by the settlement workers, known as "settlers," provided the communal link between private and public space. The rooftop was capped with an open steel-framed trellis and served as a gym for local youth. The building provided much needed space for a kindergarten during the day. In the early evening, after-school programs for children were conducted, and later in the day the settlement became a meeting place for social clubs and political organizations.[10]

The investment in a permanent base within a low-income neighborhood brought a level of outside financial and political support that stabilized the institution. This structure was inaugurated by the New York Police Commissioner, Theodore Roosevelt, in 1898.[11] Other settlements were established along similar and complementary lines, often distinguished by a specific approach rather than the goal of simply providing a variety of services to the needy. By 1911 over twenty settlements were located on the Lower East Side (**Figure 1.3**).[12] Each was directed by "headworkers" and emphasized teaching and learning pedagogy. The young, educated volunteer workers hoped to learn more about the conditions and disposition of their neighbors to educate them and transform them into model citizens. Embedded in the goal of reform of the physical environment was a desire to cultivate a Victorian morality in what Jacob A. Riis memorably called the "other half" while providing the needed relief and institutional support. In looking back upon this period, historians both admire and criticize the reformist agenda of the settlement workers in their desire to superimpose their own middle- and upper-class standards of morality upon the newcomers.[13]

EDUCATIONAL ALLIANCE

HENRY STREET SETTLEMENT

UNIVERSITY SETTLEMENT

SETTLEMENTS FROM 1889

1911	
1910	WAGE-EARNERS' BRANCH
1909	HOMEMAKING SETTLEMENT
	RECREATION CENTER AND NEIGHBORHOOD ROOMS
1908	PEOPLE'S THREE ART SCHOOL
1907	THE TEACHERS' HOUSE
1906	
1905	
1904	MUSIC SCHOOL SETTLEMENT	WELCOME HOUSE SETTLEMENT	DOE YE NEXTE THYNGE SOCIETY
1903	EMANU-EL BROTHERHOOD SOCIAL HOUSE
1902	GREENWICH HOUSE
1901	HAMILTON HOUSE
1900	
1899	ALFRED CORNING CLARK NEIGHBORHOOD HOUSE	THE COLLEGE SETTLEMENT
1898	DOWNTOWN ETHICAL SOCIETY
1897	CHRISTODORA HOUSE	THE GOSPEL SETTLEMENT
1896	GRACE CHURCH SETTLEMENT
1895	
1894	
1893	HENRY STREET SETTLEMENT
1892	JACOB A. RIIS NEIGHBORHOOD SETTLEMENT
1891	
1890	
1889	HEBREW INSTITUTE/ EDUCATIONAL ALLIANCE
1888	
1887	
1886	UNIVERSITY SETTLEMENT
1885	
1884	
1883	
1882	
1881	
1880	
1879	
1878	
1877	
1876	

1.3

Reconstituted 1910 map of the Lower East Side with the location and time line of settlements. The three
prominent settlements—Educational Alliance, University Settlement, and Henry Street Settlement—
retain their original buildings, and these are operational in 2017.

Illustration by Nandini Bagchee.
Settlement Data Source: Robert A. Woods and Albert J. Kennedy, eds., *Handbook of Settlements*, 1911.
Map collaged from the G. W. Bromley Map (1911), New York Public Library Digital Archives.

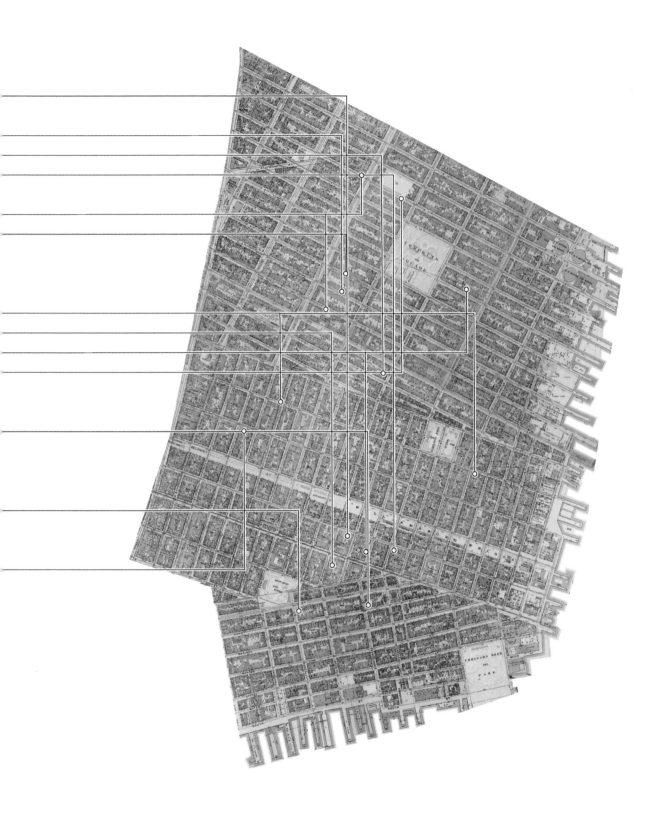

The Henry Street Settlement opened in 1893 as a volunteer nursing service that provided home care to a community that had little access to health care. Trained nurses, organized as the Visiting Nurse Service, visited the homes of ailing residents and, through this intimate contact with them, built trust and acquired knowledge of the living conditions of the women, the children, and the elderly. The trajectory of this settlement expanded to provide day care, play centers, and art instruction for children. Later, as the reputation of the settlement grew, they helped establish women's clubs that fought for legislation to ensure equity within the workplace and to institute laws prohibiting the use of child labor. The initial success of this settlement was in no small part due to the philanthropic interest of Jacob Schiff, a banker who bought two existing townhouses for the nurses at 265 and 267 Henry Street. Lillian Wald, the founder and headworker of the Henry Street Settlement, lived here for forty years, along with a group of settler nurses and volunteers. These houses, the first in a series of real estate holdings of the Henry Street Settlement, became the bedrock of an established community facility on the Lower East Side's Seventh Ward. In 1915 Alice and Irene Lewisohn, two sisters from a wealthy German-Jewish family, founded the Neighborhood Playhouse on the corner of Grand and Pitt Streets as part of the Henry Street Settlement. This three-story playhouse, with a 350-seat theater capacity, became a nucleus of another type of arts-oriented programming associated with the Henry Street Settlement (**Figure 1.4**).

The early settlement houses, thus financed through private philanthropy, enjoyed a level of autonomy and knowledge of the inner city that they leveraged to critique the corruption within the municipal government. The dining table of the Henry Street Settlement became a launching pad for labor organizing, developing legislation on sanitary reform, implementing safety codes in tenement buildings, and regulating labor practices in sweatshops.[14] The ambitions of the settlers were not simply to provide services to the neighborhood but to influence policy and to build civic institutions that would ultimately be integrated into the municipal and national bureaucracy. The goal of settlers was not to challenge and disrupt existing governmental institutions but to improve them. They saw the settlement house research work and community outreach as a first step in providing a Progressive Era model for political reform.[15]

The outbreak of the First World War in Europe revealed a point of disagreement within the progressive ranks. In opposition to national policy, many leaders within the settlement movement across the country were very vocal about their anti-war position. Henry Street Settlement became a gathering place for people opposed to the war, and it was here that Lillian Wald and Jane Addams, founder of the renowned Hull House of Chicago, organized a conference to discuss the adverse effects that United States involvement in the war would have on the communities they served.[16] Politicized by their involvement in the settlement work, the organizing of workers' unions, and their role as suffragists, women were at the forefront of this anti-war movement. On September 28, 1914, a solemn group of fifteen hundred women marched down Fifth Avenue wearing mourning attire and carrying

1.5
The all-women anti-war demonstration parade down Fifth Avenue, 1914.
Photograph courtesy of the New York Public Library Digital Archives.

peace banners (**Figure 1.5**).[17] Lillian Wald and a delegation of nurses from Henry Street Settlement were among the marchers. Along with labor unionists, socialists, and religious and secular pacifists, Wald founded the popular but short-lived American Union Against Militarism (AUAM) in 1916.[18]

The United States entered the conflict in 1917 and subsequently retaliated against the anti-war activists. The settlement community whose members had actively condemned the war were labeled radicals and put on a national blacklist.[19] The war, followed by an economic depression and changes in national immigration policy,[20] resulted in a dramatic decline in the population of the Lower East Side in the mid-'20s. As the country faced growing unemployment and food shortages, the burgeoning culture of unions and self-organized neighborhood clubs was strained. The social institutions that weathered this crisis had to rethink their organizational strategy as the political climate changed. Private benefactors that had supported the settlements grew more fiscally and politically conservative. Henry Street Settlement continued its work but refocused its attention on nonpoliticized issues, such as adding programs in music and art for the neighborhood children to its list of offerings. The Neighborhood Playhouse became a nucleus for this activity, along with a music school in a second building on Grand Street. Connecting back to the concerns of community health, Lillian Wald began summer camps for the children outside the city and built a playground within the block. This recreation and child-focused programming formed the basis of the new fund-raising initiatives at Henry Street Settlement.

HOUSING ESTATES (1930–1950)

In part due to the collective efforts of the settlements working in tandem across the country, the field of social work became increasingly specialized and professional. The National Federation of Settlements,[21] a coalition of settlements nationwide, organized conferences and sponsored studies that created a body of research that was used to prove and leverage government policy. During the Great Depression this more professionalized approach to social reform shifted the role of the settlement volunteers and, by extension, the use of the settlement houses as a place to administrate programs rather than live amongst the poor. While the main building on Henry Street continued to house the organization's main administrators well into the '60s, the rest of the settlement houses, including University Settlement, converted their live-in facilities for the settlers into more extensive program space for the community.

By the 1930s the Henry Street Settlement was run by a mixture of paid and volunteer staff, and although it was still funded by private donations, it increasingly depended on public money as well. Helen Hall, the headworker who took over for Lillian Wald in 1933, represented the second generation of this more professionalized attitude toward social work. Hall worked in a Philadelphia settlement house before coming to the Lower East Side and helped conduct a study on chronic unemployment. Her reports and testimony were a part of Senate hearings in 1934, in support of an unemployment insurance bill put forth by Senator Robert Wagner.[22] Her pragmatic thrust in creating a more responsive government made her well suited for the job at Henry Street Settlement during the Great Depression, when the settlements, along with the city, turned increasingly to the federal government to fund rising unemployment. In the winter of 1933–1934 Henry Street Settlement opened its doors to the Civil Works Administration (CWA) program as men and women from the neighborhood registered to apply for federally sanctioned work relief. Henry Street Settlement made the playhouse available for over four hundred applicants as they waited to register for jobs.[23]

In the '30s, the settlement houses of the Lower East Side became active participants in New Deal Works Progress Administration programs. Workers hired through these programs provided the next generation of social workers, developed new criteria for social service programs, and helped the government connect to grassroots citizens' initiatives.[24] The federal and municipal bureaucracies benefited from the assistance of the entrenched progressives in localities such as the Lower East Side to help negotiate and interface with the local neighborhood unions, clubs, tenants, and block associations. The settlements raised awareness of local campaigns for equity and helped consolidate them into larger national processes.

During this time, no single issue galvanized the various groups working toward a radically transformed Lower East Side landscape more than the question of housing. In 1933, the year that Helen Hall took over the leadership at Henry Street Settlement, Fiorello La Guardia was elected mayor of New York City on a strong housing platform. A year later he directed the New York City Housing Authority (NYCHA) to begin working on proposals to build new low-income housing for various sites in New York City. A majority of these projects executed in the neighborhoods of the Lower East Side, East Harlem, the Bronx, and Brooklyn between 1935 and 1965 were financed by leveraging grants through federal programs created during the New Deal. The proposals for slum clearance and urban renewal in New York, initially recommended by the Regional Plan-

1.6

A photograph from Helen Hall's book, *Unfinished Business* (1971), shows neighborhood housing advocates with Henry Street Settlement director Helen Hall waiting to board a bus from the Henry Street Settlement Neighborhood Playhouse to Washington, D.C., to canvas for low-income housing on the Lower East Side.

Photograph courtesy of the Social Welfare History Archives, University of Minnesota Libraries.

ning Association in 1929 to make room for roadways, bridges, and higher-end housing, were adapted a decade later and led to the low-income housing built along the East River waterfront.[25]

This shift in perspective from for-profit to low-income was viewed positively by the leaders of the settlement movement, who for years had protested the poor light, air, and sanitation in the Old Law tenements and were eager to see these buildings replaced by newer, more up-to-date housing. The Henry Street Settlement provided a staging ground for coalition building that brought the other settlements—the Educational Alliance and the Union Settlement House—into agreement with the local tenant organizations, such as the League of Mothers Club and the United Neighborhood Houses. These local groups boarded buses to Washington, D.C., and canvassed for new low-income housing in the neighborhood (**Figure 1.6**). Within the neighborhood, teams of volunteers led by the settlement houses surveyed local opinion and prepared reports arguing on behalf of demolishing the tenements and building new high-rise, low-income housing along the East River from the Brooklyn Bridge on the south to Fourteenth Street on the north.[26] The interest, expertise, first-hand observation, and familiarity of the on-ground social reformers were harnessed by Mayor La Guardia in the formation of the first NYCHA board.[27]

The modernist tower in the park housing typology, with the playgrounds in between, was implemented as the perfect antidote to the lack of light and air in the tenement housing. One of the earliest blocks of federally funded NYCHA houses, Vladeck I and II, was built in the '40s, directly across the street from the Henry Street Settlement. The demolition of more than 170 buildings, mainly Old Law tenements, allowed for the construction of the 24 six-story Vladeck buildings as well as the construction of a section of the East River Drive along the river. The work was efficiently completed within a year, and many of the residents from the old tenements were resettled into the more spacious housing (**Figure 1.7**).[28] As the new residents moved into the Vladeck Houses, workers from the Henry Street Settlement imagined that they would have a similar role to the one they had played in the tenements—taking care of the residents' social needs and being a part of the social life of the community. The Henry Street Settlement had been integral in the resettlement and planning of this specific project, and as a result, the spaces allocated for community rooms, the "home planning workshop and craft room" at street level, were to be managed by the Henry Street Settlement. This old-school patriarchal approach to tenant organizing, it seemed, was out of touch with the aspirations of the new NYCHA tenants. To the surprise of Helen Hall, the tenants, with the support of a citywide tenants' council, had self-organized into various committees and subcommittees.[29] NYCHA, in its anxiety to quash the independent tenant organizing, saw the settlements, in this case, as a potential ally and preferred to hand over the administration of the lower-level common areas to the progressive settlement workers rather than the self-organized tenants.

Major shifts in the social landscape of the Lower East Side occurred over the next thirty years as swathes of tenements and defunct

1.7
Relocation of families within the neighborhood and citywide was well documented by NYCHA. Interviews with dislocated residents and the applicants for the new housing were often conducted with help from the settlement houses. Photo sequence shows the Bariera family in the tenement quarters on First Street, and then settled into the new Vladeck II Houses, 1940.

Photographs courtesy of NYCHA and the La Guardia and Wagner Archives, La Guardia Community College, CUNY.

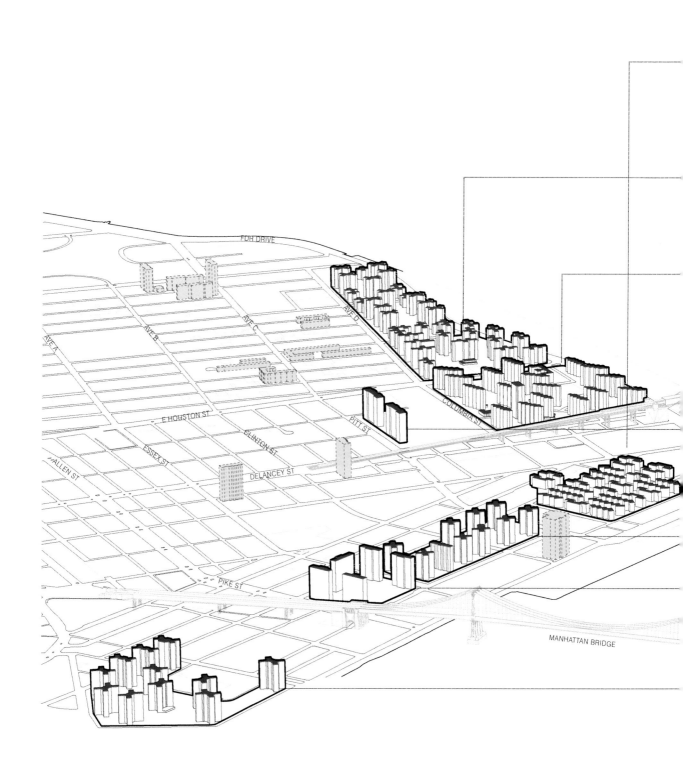

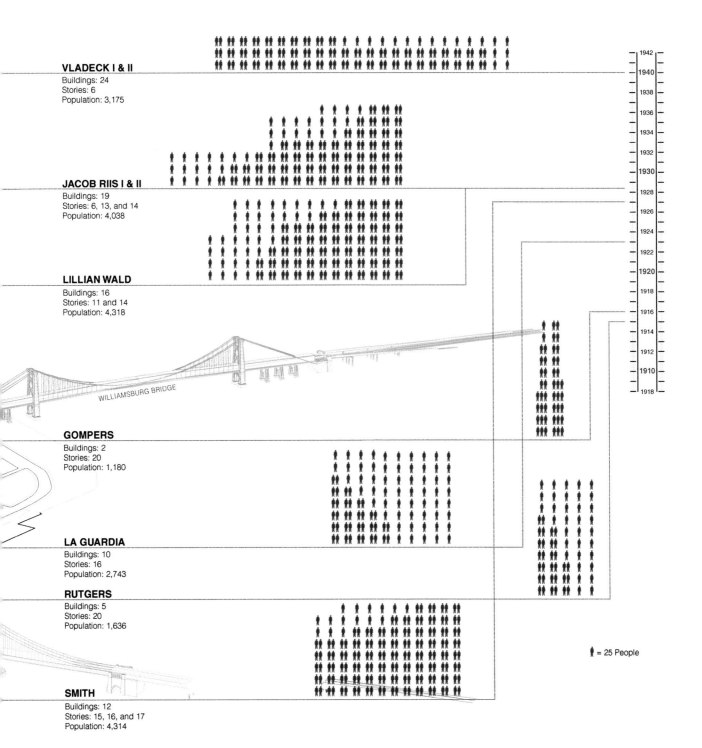

VLADECK I & II
Buildings: 24
Stories: 6
Population: 3,175

JACOB RIIS I & II
Buildings: 19
Stories: 6, 13, and 14
Population: 4,038

LILLIAN WALD
Buildings: 16
Stories: 11 and 14
Population: 4,318

WILLIAMSBURG BRIDGE

GOMPERS
Buildings: 2
Stories: 20
Population: 1,180

LA GUARDIA
Buildings: 10
Stories: 16
Population: 2,743

RUTGERS
Buildings: 5
Stories: 20
Population: 1,636

SMITH
Buildings: 12
Stories: 15, 16, and 17
Population: 4,314

1942
1940
1938
1936
1934
1932
1930
1928
1926
1924
1922
1920
1918
1916
1914
1912
1910
1918

🚶 = 25 People

1.8
**New York City Housing Authority (NYCHA) blocks of housing along the
East River, built between 1940 and 1965; showing occupancy in 2016.**
Illustration by Nandini Bagchee.
Data collected from the web-based NYCHA Interactive Map. Accessed February 2016.

Photo sequence shows the
Catheras family moving from a
temporary veteran's shelter in
Jamaica, Queens, to the new
Jacob Riis Houses, 1947.

Photographs courtesy of NYCHA and
the La Guardia and Wagner Archives,
La Guardia Community College, CUNY.

industrial waterfront infrastructures made way for an extension of the
East River Drive and additional towers of public housing along the
river. These towers, named after settlement reformers, mayors, and
other public figures, brought over twenty-five thousand low-income
residents to the neighborhood. The waiting lists for the apartments
were long, and the process of tenant relocation from slum clearance
in other neighborhoods and the eligibility criteria proved immensely
complicated for public housing residents. The isolated towers, most
twelve to seventeen stories high, stood in sharp contrast to the older
tenements of four to six stories, and inscribed a long-term physical
and social divide into the neighborhood[30] (**Figure 1.8**).[31] The recipients
of this subsidized housing were mainly World War II veterans, African Americans, and Puerto Ricans who began moving to New York
City in the '50s (**Figure 1.9**).[32] With this new demographic, race in
addition to ethnicity became a defining aspect of discrimination in
the postwar Lower East Side. The deindustrializing East River waterfront provided affordable housing but few jobs to the droves of
people migrating into the city. With slim prospects of employment,
welfare-dependent households became a norm in inner-city neighborhoods across the country. The Lower East Side was no exception, and
the settlements once intimately involved in the daily lives of immigrants in a manufacturing district repositioned themselves to deal
with the emergent landscape of welfare alienation. [33]

SETTLEMENT AS ESTABLISHMENT AND COMMUNITY
PARTICIPATION (1948–1965)

In 1948, through the generous endowment of Herbert Lehman,
former governor of New York, and wife Edith, Henry Street Settlement

was able to build a new facility—a youth center at 301 Henry Street, a few doors down from the first settlement townhouses. Pete's House, named in memory of the Lehmans' son, who was killed in World War II, catered to boys and young men in the neighborhood. Through this institution, the settlement became engaged in what was seen, by the '50s, as a crisis of juvenile delinquency among the neighborhood youth.[34] The racial tensions among the community, the increased police violence, and the gradual incursion of drugs into the neighborhood impacted the youth. The matter was discussed at a board meeting at Henry Street Settlement in June 1957, and a federally funded program, Mobilization for Youth (MFY), was conceived in response to this situation.[35] The goal of the settlement workers was to create a series of neighborhood-wide programs to keep teenagers off the streets and engage them in productive workshops that would potentially lead to employment opportunities (**Figure 1.10**). A coalition of

1.10
Photograph from Helen Hall's book, *Unfinished Business*, 1971, shows the group of boys and organizers in front of a Mobilization for Youth Project. Winslow Carlton (bottom right) was on the board of Henry Street Settlement and the founder and chairman of Mobilization for Youth in New York.
Photograph courtesy of the Social Welfare History Archives, University of Minnesota Libraries.

the settlements and neighborhood-based societies jointly participated in this program. However, it was the direct involvement of faculty from the sociology department at Columbia University that brought a different, more nuanced political dimension to the project. Trained in new research methods, this group of MFY administrators insisted on direct democracy that challenged the traditional organizational approaches deployed by the previous generation of settlement social workers. The "we know what's best" approach of the old-school settlement house liberals was seen by the academic sociologists of the MFY as patriarchal and obsolete. The MFY approach encouraged citizen empowerment through grassroots action and self-organization.[36] In dealing with the youth, they provided opportunities for counseling and discussion as opposed to instruction, and they believed in creating an environment that would lead to youth empowerment. Between 1963 and 1965, MFY opened a storefront on East Fourth Street, between Avenues B and C. Additionally, it initiated two coffee shops—Club 169 and The Hideout—designed to create a more informal venue, mainly for young men between fourteen and twenty-two to meet with counselors as well as to socialize. The coffee shops were "inspired by a social-cultural movement developed in the 1950s among college students, artists and intellectuals, who tried to recreate in New York, San Francisco, and other large cities of the United States, the European café as a center of intellectual, social and cultural activities."[37] MFY invited gang members to form peer groups. This well-intended desire to create a democratic forum for the youth was short-lived, as the experimental methods of creating much needed common space met with targeted opposition. The difficulty of dealing with the volume of the youth that needed direction on all fronts with a small staff of mainly settlement workers created an imbalance. The coffee shops failed as safe spaces when drugs, alcohol, and violence permeated the good intentions of the over-extended organizers. Added to this was the criticism by the more mainstream bureaucrats of what was perceived as a "communist" agenda in an era of McCarthyism.[38] Despite its institutional failure, MFY's efforts to achieve greater youth participation and its challenge to the conventional methods of social welfare in low-income neighborhoods were a precedent to the War on Poverty and Great Society Programs adopted countrywide in the '60s.

These later programs had a direct impact on some of the young men that were actively sought out by the program administrators from within the leadership of the youth gangs in cities across the country. The work of transformed gang youth collectives such as the Real Great Society and CHARAS in New York City to consequently shape their own environment through bottom-up initiatives, a decade later, was impacted by the early MFY programs in the Lower East Side. The focus on youth education and spaces of cultural exploration such as the storefronts, theaters, and community centers, discussed in Chapter 3, were indebted to the storefront/café-concept initiated by the MFY. The emphasis on the creation of an alternative, self-organized space resonated positively with the youth within a neighborhood that was increasingly disinvested by the municipal authorities.

RADICAL ESTATES

GERMAN HALLS AND LABOR UNIONS (1840S–1920S)

Long before the establishment of the settlement houses and coexistence within the charitable landscape of the neighborhood, religious institutions, clubs, and mutual aid societies were set up by the immigrant communities to take care of their own. These self-organized entities were often affiliated with specific places of origin in the homeland of the neighborhood's residents and offered a source of community cohesion in the immigrant enclaves of the Lower East Side.[39]

In the 1840s Germans fleeing the recriminations resulting from political revolutions in Europe settled in pockets of New York City. Within the Lower East Side, in an area that came to be known as *Kleindeutschland*, the socially motivated Germans brought a working-class solidarity.[40] They organized a network of voluntary societies that provided charitable support and an avenue of social engagement to compatriots. This culture of participation was expressed in the organization of temporal events—parades, funerals, festivals, and sporting events—but also registered more permanently in the architecture of the neighborhood. The skilled German masons and carpenters were responsible for the construction of the many multistory tenements and working lofts in the Seventeenth Ward of Manhattan. The beer halls, corner saloons, gymnasiums, and theaters along the Bowery and the main avenues of Kleindeutschland provided entertainment to the working-class residents. As the immigrant German community grew more affluent, they added purpose-built halls and clubs to house the many collective undertakings of the community.[41] Larger halls available for rent provided a place to host weddings, large social events, and political rallies. It was in such places of public gathering, in 1850s New York, that the German-American unions of carpenters, cabinetmakers, weavers, the labor party socialists, and the more anti-institutional anarchists organized what are seen to be the beginnings of the American radical left.[42]

In the last decade of the nineteenth century, as the well-to-do German community moved away from this neighborhood, a different contingent of immigrants—Eastern European Jews escaping persecution in pogroms and labor camps—brought with them a different revolutionary perspective. They organized via mutual aid societies and gradually joined the organized labor unions to demand better wages and working conditions. A series of successful strikes from 1908 to 1914 was a collaborative undertaking of the socialist intelligentsia with a more heterogeneous blue-collar Jewish immigrant workforce.[43] The involvement in local organizing gave the marginalized labor class a means to enter the political arena and advance within the city's social hierarchy. Membership within the unions created ties to emergent political parties such as the Jewish Labor Party, the Socialist Party, and the American Labor Party, each of which made some headway within mainstream electoral politics in 1920s New York.[44]

This type of ground-up organizing adopted a more oppositional approach toward the establishment that was different from the steady lobbying and institutional change being proposed by the settlement progressives in early-twentieth-century New York. The beer gardens, meeting halls, and theaters on the Lower East Side—the scourge of the settlement workers—provided places for people to meet, participate in mass culture, and create a space for autonomous political expression. In a report produced by the University Settlement in 1899, different authors criticized the existing "saloons" and "public halls" of the Lower East Side as disreputable places.[45] While recognizing the need for public halls, particularly in the winter months, settlement house workers regarded the culture of drinking within them with disapproval. They advocated, instead, for a large gathering space within the settlement, sans alcohol, to alleviate the problem.

The political potency of the saloons and beer halls, as Tom Goyens explains in *Beer and Revolution*, was not to be underestimated. Commerce and public political life freely associated in these venues, which were decorated with photographs of respected speakers and advertisements of events. Anarchists, socialists, and unionists favored their preferred establishments, each setting up an insider understanding of these places that gained a reputation over time.[46] Enterprising proprietors built purpose-built street level halls with residential quarters all along major commercial thoroughfares. On East Eleventh Street between Third and Fourth Avenues, Charles Goldstein, a Polish-born German émigré, built one such establishment, Webster Hall, in 1886. The grand rental hall included the owner's living quarters in an annex and became a center for the public gatherings of a working-class population, providing a space for dances, receptions, lectures, meetings, conventions, political rallies, military functions, concerts, performances, festivities, and sporting and fund-raising events. All the way up to the Second World War, this hall was the preferred venue for leftist rallies with speakers such as Margaret Sanger, Samuel Gompers, and, later, Emma Goldman drawing large crowds.[47]

LABOR, CHURCH, AND THE INTERWAR YEARS (1910–1940)

With the rise of the organized labor movement and the changing demographic of immigration, the churches, which were long supporters of immigrant life on the Lower East Side, struggled to find relevance. St. Mark's Church on East Tenth Street and Judson Church to the south of Washington Square expanded their parishes to provide amenities such as hospitals, parish halls, and schoolhouses to meet the demands of an Eastern European and Italian immigrant community respectively. These socially responsive religious establishments thus integrated themselves into the twentieth-century landscape of the city by expanding their programs to address the immediate needs of a working-class congregation.[48]

Charles Stelzle, a Presbyterian missionary and onetime union machinist, had a different vision for the future of the religious establishment in an era of labor organizing. In 1910, at a time and place when other churches were closing, he took over a chapel on Fourteenth Street at Second Avenue and transformed it into the "Labor Temple" on behalf of the Second Presbyterian Church. His experience as a minister in the labor movement and roots in the Lower East Side made him keen to breach the growing divide between the church and the working men and women within the neighborhood.[49] As the name suggests, the Labor Temple was meant to attract union members, socialists, and religious thinkers in equal measure. Despite the formidable competition from the many entertainment establishments in the neighborhood (**Figure 1.11**), the sermons and lectures at the Labor Temple were well attended. The "highlight of the Labor Temple's Program," wrote historian Richard Poethig, was the open forum where "radicals of all stripes, labor leaders, social gospellers" were invited to speak.[50]

It was at this church, in 1915, that Jessie Wallace Hughan—a devout Christian, a suffragist, and a member of the Socialist Party—addressed the congregation and urged them to join the "Anti-Enlistment League." Hughan, along with others of the interwar generation, came to the pacifist platform from a religious perspective that was reinforced with a political belief that the root causes of war lay in the

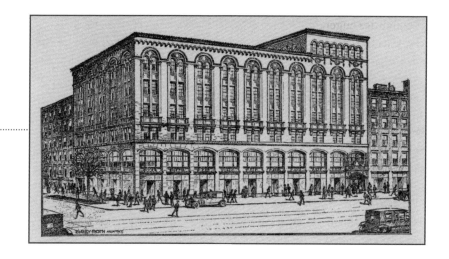

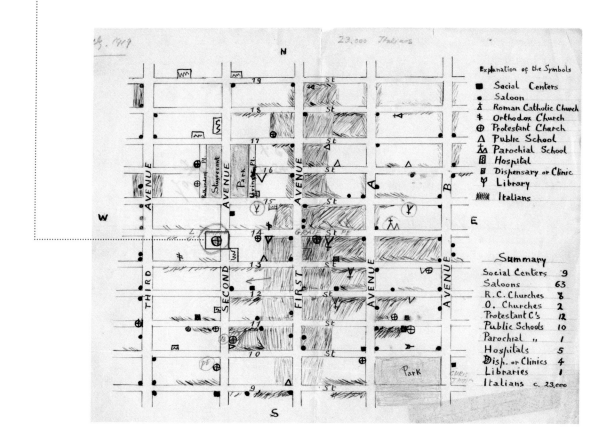

1.11

"Sketch of a neighborhood map around the location of the Labor Temple, at Second Avenue Fourteenth Street in New York City, 1919." The Labor Temple is encircled in blue. The inventory shows the community services around the church. Of note are the sixty-three saloons that provided competition to the social and communal gatherings at the labor church.

Illustration of the Labor Temple from the Edmund B. Chaffee Papers in the Arents Library, courtesy of Syracuse Special Collection Archives. Map of the neighborhood courtesy of the Presbyterian Historical Society.

inequalities engendered by a capitalist economy. In 1923 she founded the War Resisters League (WRL) in New York as the first secular pacifist organization whose membership was not restricted by sex, religion, or political affiliations.[51] While motivated by a religious belief in nonviolence, Hughan recognized the importance of a broad-based secular and socialist anti-war movement. The WRL slogan attributed to Hughan, "Wars Will Cease When Men Refuse to Fight," was instrumental in the later development of the personalist politics of a small but committed cadre of men and women that became a key strategy of the anti-war resistance during World War II.

In 1937, as Japan attacked China and triggered a chain of global reactions that headed toward World War II, the new minister at the head of the Labor Temple, Abraham Johannes Muste, articulated an explicit theological position that forged a link between the peace, labor, and social justice movements within the nation.[52] A. J. Muste, a Quaker, an ordained minister of the Presbyterian Church, and a former member of the Trotskyist party, spent a lifetime reconciling his vested interest in labor organizing with his theological calling. As general secretary of the Amalgamated Textile Workers of America (1919–1921), Muste was a dedicated Marxist union organizer. In his later life he rejected the rigid economic bias of Marxism while maintaining his faith in its proposition of a radical political revolution.[53]

PERSONALIST ESTATES (1941–1955)

> *The Communitarian Revolution is basically a personal revolution.*
> *It starts with I, not with They.*
> *One I plus one I makes two I's and two I's make We.*
> *We is a community, while "they" is a crowd.*
> —Peter Maurin, *Easy Essays, Catholic Worker*

Opposition to World War II, the so-called good war against Fascism, was an unpopular position in the United States. The peace churches— the Quakers, Mennonites, and the Brethren—that had historically refused to participate in wars were officially granted the position of conscientious objectors (COs) in past wars. During World War II, those who qualified as COs were sent to civilian camps to work in some indirect way to support the war effort. Secular pacifists who failed the religious test or religious pacifists who refused to work in these civilian camps were denied conscientious objector status and were incarcerated in federal prisons as traitors.[54] It was in these prisons that the COs protesting the Jim Crow separation of black inmates in the prison dining halls initiated a series of hunger and work strikes.

The first of these began in a correctional facility in Danbury, Connecticut, and generated a chain reaction in prisons across the country where COs were being held.[55]

In 1943 Danbury prison became the first federal prison in the country to be desegregated and proved to the war-resisters that a small handful of people could bring about reform within the system through nonviolent direct action.[56] The civil disobedience doctrine of Gandhi, long admired by the members of the American pacifist left, was thus implemented with success in these prison strikes. The WRL and Fellowship of Reconciliation (FOR) members were key participants in the prison strikes. For WRL members Jim Peck, William Sutherland, Bayard Rustin, David Dellinger, and Ralph DiGia, this experience was formative and initiated a new direction within the pacifist movement upon their return to a small WRL office in New York.[57] The isolation within the prisons created a strategic shift in the anti-war activism, where the broader agenda of social injustice was experienced firsthand by the COs. The focus on individual perseverance and a call to brotherhood and action-based pacifism emerged as the new form of left-wing activism in Cold War America.

The personalist politics of the American left was a reaction to the global events and shift in national perspective that challenged the organized labor and socialist movements within the United States. For Peter Maurin and Dorothy Day, self-proclaimed anarchists and co-founders of the Catholic Worker movement, the "gentle personalism of traditional Catholicism" was the basis for a political and spiritual activism.[58] In 1933 they launched the *Catholic Worker*, a newspaper directed toward the unemployed during the Great Depression, and distributed in Union Square for one cent (**Figure 1.12**). This newspaper reported on human rights, labor unions, and other non-cooperation movements dedicated to nonviolent direct action. Differentiating itself from other labor newspapers, the *Catholic Worker* extolled the idea of "work" as a "gift from God" that rightfully needed to be re-gifted back to the community.[59] This co-option of work back to serve society was an innovative meshing of a Catholic dogma with Marxist labor theory.

The successful sales of the newspaper allowed the Catholic Worker to expand its movement. It set up communal Catholic Worker houses in cities across the country. In 1939, Dorothy Day set up houses of hospitality in two buildings on Mott Street in downtown Manhattan. In these houses, volunteers lived in self-imposed poverty, caring for those in need of food and shelter. The combination of Catholic solidarity with the less fortunate combined with a radical anti-capitalist critique

1.12
People reading the *Catholic Worker*, **Union Square, New York City, 1940.**
Courtesy of the Department of Special Collections and University Archives, Marquette University Archives.

of the nation was fiercely debated at Friday night meetings and lectures by invited speakers. Fourteen years later, Day purchased a five-story red brick building on Chrystie Street, just south of Houston, and organized the St. Joseph's Catholic Workers House. In 1957 this building was demolished as part of a large urban renewal scheme and the operation relocated further east to a smaller building on First Street.[60] In this volunteer-run soup kitchen and boarding house, each Catholic worker lived and served the community by an ethical code that was based on personal conviction. In contrast to the earlier model of the settlement house worker living with the urban poor, the reciprocal relationship between the "worker" and the "poor" in the Catholic House was a blurred and less didactic vision of charity. Furthermore, unlike the settlement houses, the Catholic Worker was staunchly opposed to government assistance and accepted no tax breaks, subsidies, or government aid. This radical, anarchic philosophy of the Catholic Worker was however tempered by a deep humanity and personal empathy toward its fellow men and women.

In the aftermath of the Second World War, FOR, under the leadership of A. J. Muste and the WRL, regrouped in Downtown Manhattan at a rented office at 5 Beekman Street, directly opposite City Hall. The handsome nine-story brick and terra-cotta structure, which was built in 1889, had seen better days. At the time, when the WRL moved into one of the top-floor spaces, the grand atrium court extending through the entire height of the building was boarded up and closed. The poorly maintained and mostly vacant office building provided a well-hidden and affordable working zone for the political dissidents. By the end of the Second World War, it was here that a new left pacifism, influenced by the personalism, was shaped.[61] The building became the peace movement's headquarters, as the generation of activists forged through the CO camp and prison experience, emphasizing civil disobedience and direct action as the way forward. This militant stance put the younger generation at odds with some in the older guard that saw in their actions a violation of some core principles of pacifism.[62] Critical of both the United States and the Soviet Union, the WRL and related pacifist groups, such as the Catholic Worker, FOR, and the Peacemakers, distanced themselves from American Exceptionalism and Soviet Communism in equal measure. The historian James J. Farrell describes this new form of leftist formation as "a third way between capitalism and communism, between radical individualism and collective radicalism."[63]

Internationally, with the specter of the bombings at Hiroshima and Nagasaki heavy on the American conscience, the anti-war activists organized street actions and public forums. They also built ties with global and national justice movements and sent emissaries to Africa and Asia to connect anti-apartheid and anti-colonial struggles abroad to racial struggles back at home. In the '50s the WRL sponsored Bill Sutherland, a pan-Africanist who spoke to audiences in Birmingham, London, Paris, and the Gold Coast.[64] At home, Bayard Rustin, the WRL secretary, was "released" to work and advise Martin Luther King, Jr., on the many nonviolent direct actions that marked the beginnings of the civil rights movement in the United States.[65]

The office's location in Downtown Manhattan allowed for lunch meetings on Wall Street and protests at City Hall (**Figure 1.13**). On June 15, 1955, the various peace and justice activists at 5 Beekman Street protested the civil defense drill enforced by the U.S. government to

1.13
Starting on June 15, 1955, anti-nuclear pacifists gathered in City Hall Park and refused to take cover every year when there was a drill. The demonstrators brought attention to the fact that the shelter was not going to save lives in the event of a nuclear attack. Disarmament, they pointed out, was the only way.

Flyer from Records of SANE Inc., 1957–1987, DG 58. Courtesy of the Swarthmore College Peace Collection.

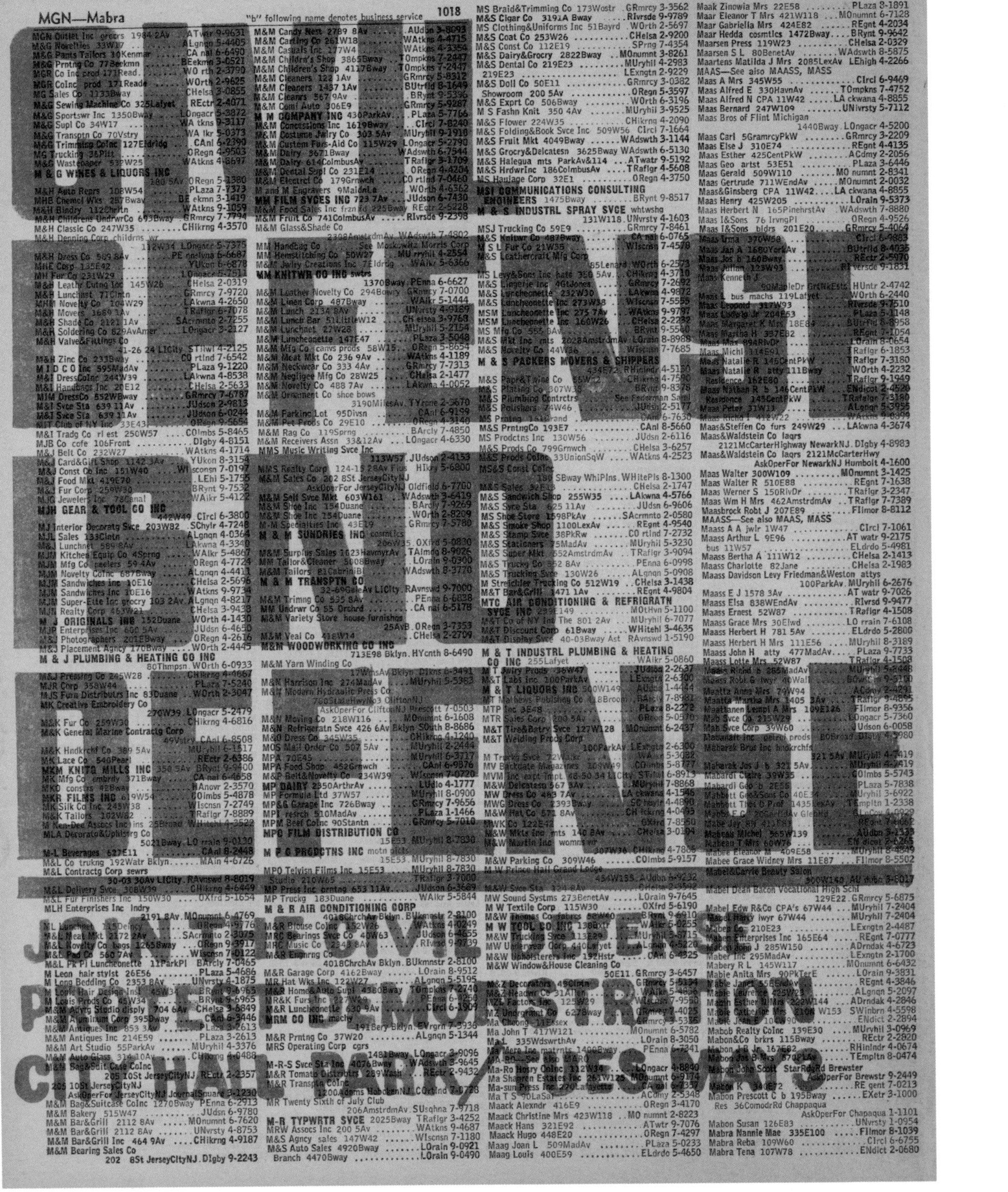

MGN—Mabra "b" following name denotes business service 1018

MGN Outlet Inc grocrs 1984 2Av ....ATwtr 9-9631
M&G Novelties 33W17 ....ALgnqn 5-4405
M&G Pants Tailors 10Kenmar ....CA nal 6-6490
M&G Prntng Co 77Beekmn ....BEekmn 3-0521
MGR Co Inc prod 171Read ....WO rth 2-3790
MGR CoInc prod 171Reade ....WOrth 2-9625
MG Sales Co 1133Bway ....CHelsa 3-0855
M&G Sewing Machine Co 325Lafyet ....REctr 2-4071
M&G Sportswr Inc 1350Bway ....LOngacr 5-3872
M&G Supl Co 34W17 ....WA tkns 9-3117
M&G Transptn Co 70Vstry ....WA lkr 5-0373
M&G Trimming CoInc 127Eldridg ....CAnl 6-2390
MG Trucking 36Pitt ....ORegn 4-9503
M&G Wastepaper 532W25 ....WAtkns 4-8697
M & G WINES & LIQUORS INC
180 5Av ORegn 5-1380
M&H Auto Reprs 108W54 ....PLaza 7-7373
MHB Chemcl Wks 287Bway ....BE ekmn 3-1419
M&H Bindry 112Chrltn ....WAtkns 9-1059
M&H Childrens UndrwrCo 693Bway ....GRmrcy 7-7794
M&H Classic Co 247W35 ....CHikrng 4-3570
M&H Denning Corp childrns wr
112W34 LOngacr 5-7375
M&H Dress Co 589 8Av ....PE nnslvna 6-6687
MHE Corp 135E42 ....YUkon 6-6878
MH Fur Co 231W29 ....LOngacr 5-7511
M&H Leathr Cutng Inc 145W26 ....CHelsa 2-0319
M&H Lunchnet 71Clntn ....GRmrcy 7-9720
MHM Novelty Co 104W29 ....LAkwna 4-2650
M&H Movers 1669 1Av ....TRaflgr 6-7078
M&H Shade Co 2121 1Av ....SAcrmnto 2-7255
M&H Soldering Co 829AvAmer ....LOngacr 3-2127
M&H Valve&Fittings Co
41-26 24 LICity STilwl 4-2125
M&H Zinc Co 233Bway ....CO rtlnd 7-6542
M I D C O Inc 595MadAv ....PLaza 9-1220
M&I DressCoInc 244W39 ....LAkwna 4-8538
M&I Handbags Inc 20E12 ....CHelsa 2-5633
MIM DressCo 552WBway ....GRmrcy 7-6787
M&I Svce Sta 639 11Av ....JUdson 2-9813
M&I Svce Sta 639 11Av ....JUdson 6-0244
MIT Club of NY Inc 33E43 ....ORegn 9-5654
M&I Tradg Co rl est 250W57 ....COlmbs 5-8465
MJB Co cofe 106Front ....DIgby 4-8151
M&J Belt Co 232W27 ....WAtkns 4-1714
M&J Card&Gift Shop 1142 3Av ....YUkon 8-3154
M&J Const Co Inc 151W40 ....WIsconsn 7-0197
M&J Food Mkt 419E70 ....LEhi 5-1755
M&J Fur Corp 259W30 ....BRynt 9-7532
MJG Jewelers Inc 78Canal ....WAlkr 5-4122
MJH GEAR & TOOL CO INC
442W49 CIrcl 6-3800
MJ Interior Decoratg Svce 203W82 ....SChylr 4-7248
MJL Sales 133Clntn ....ALgnqn 4-0364
M&J Lunchnet 584 8Av ....LAkwna 4-3340
MJM Kitchen Equip Co 4Sprng ....WAlkr 5-4867
MJM Mfg Co peelers 59 4Av ....ORegn 4-7724
MJM Novelty CoInc 687Bway ....ALgnqn 4-4411
MJM Sandwiches Inc 10E16 ....CHelsa 2-5696
MJM Sandwiches Inc 10E16 ....WAtkns 9-9734
MJM Super-Ette Inc grocry 103 2Av ALgnqn 4-8217
MJM Realty Corp 463W21 ....CHelsa 3-9438
M J ORIGINALS INC 152Duane ....WOrth 4-1430
MJP Enterprises Inc 600 5Av ....JUdsn 6-4650
M&J Photographers 201EBway ....ORegn 4-2616
M&J Placement Agncy 170Bway ....WOrth 2-4445
M & J PLUMBING & HEATING CO INC
80Thmpsn WOrth 6-0933
M&J Pressing Co 245W28 ....CHikrng 4-0667
MJR Corp 358W44 ....PLaza 7-5240
MJS Furn Distributrs Inc 83Duane ....WOrth 2-3047
MK Creative Embroidery Co
270W39 LOngacr 5-2479
M&K Fur Co 259W30 ....CHikrng 4-6816
M&K General Marine Contractg Corp
49Vstry CAnl 6-8508
M&K Hndkrchf Co 389 5Av ....MUryhil 6-1517
MK Lace Co 540Pearl ....REctr 2-6386
MKM KNITG MILLS INC 350 5Av BRynt 9-9400
MK Mfg Co embrdy 371Bway ....CA nal 6-4658
MKO constrs 42Bway ....HAnovr 2-3570
MKR FILMS INC 619W54 ....COlmbs 5-4878
MK Silk Co Inc 245W38 ....WIscnsn 7-2749
M&K Tailors 102W82 ....TRaflgr 7-8889
M Ken-Dee Assocs Inc ins 25Broad WHitehl 4-3522
MLA Decoratg&Uphlstrg Co
5021Bway LO rrain 9-0130
M-L Beverages 627E11 ....CAnl 8-2448
M&L Co trukng 192Watr Bklyn ....MAin 4-6726
M&L Contractg Corp sewrs
30-03 30Av LICity RAvnswd 8-8019
M&L Delivery Svce 308W39 ....CHikrng 4-6449
M&L Fur Finishers Inc 150W30 ....OXfrd 5-1654
MLH Enterprises Inc lndry
2191 8Av MOnumnt 6-4769
ML Lunchnet 115Delncy ....ORegn 4-9776
M&L Meat Mkt 2172 2Av ....SAcrmnto 2-3075
M&L Novelty Co bags 1265Bway ....ORegn 9-3917
M&L Pad Co 560 7Av ....WIscnsn 7-0122
M&L Pk Pl Luncheonette 11ParkPl ....BArcly 7-0465
M Leon hair stylst 26E56 ....PLaza 5-4686
M Long Bedding Co 2353 8Av ....UNvrsty 4-1875
M Louis Hair Design Inst 45W34 ....BRynt 9-6965
M Louis Prods Co 45W34 ....BRynt 9-6965
M&M Advrg Studio disply 704 6Av ....CHelsa 3-6849
M&M Aluminum Corp 395Bway ....CAnl 6-3446
M&M Antiques Inc 853 3Av ....PLaza 3-2613
M&M Antiques Inc 214E59 ....PLaza 3-2613
M&M Art Studio 55ParkAv ....MUryhil 4-3376
M&M Auto Glass 314 10Av ....CHikrng 4-0488
M&M Bag&Suit Case CoInc
205 10St JerseyCityNJ REctr 2-2357
205 10St JerseyCityNJ
AskOperFor JerseyCityNJ JournalSquare 3-1230
M&M Bag&Suitcase CoInc 1270Bway ....PEnna 6-2913
M&M Bakery 515W47 ....JUdsn 6-9780
M&M Bar&Grill 2112 8Av ....MOnumnt 6-7620
M&M Bar&Grill 2112 8Av ....UNvrsty 4-8753
M&M Bar&Grill Inc 464 9Av ....CHikrng 4-9187
M&M Bearing Sales Co
202 8St JerseyCityNJ DIgby 9-2243

M&M Candy Nest 2789 8Av ....AUdbn 3-8093
M&M Carting Co 261W18 ....WAtkns 4-4715
M&M Casuals Inc 177W4 ....WAtkns 4-3354
M&M Childrn's Shop 3865Bway ....TOmpkns 7-2447
M&M Children's Shop 4117Bway ....TOmpkns 7-2447
M&M Cleaners 122 1Av ....GRmrcy 5-8312
M&M Cleaners 1437 1Av ....BUtrfld 8-1649
M&M Cleanrs 567 9Av ....BRynt 9-5396
M&M Coml Auto 306E9 ....GRmrcy 5-9287
M M COMPANY INC 430ParkAv ....PLaza 5-7766
M&M Concessions Inc 1619Bway ....CIrcl 7-8240
M&M Costume Jwlry Co 303 5Av ....MUryhil 9-1910
M&M Custom Furs-Aid Co 115W29 ....LOngacr 5-2790
M&M Dairy 3671Bway ....WAdswth 6-7544
M&M Dairy 614ColmbusAv ....TRaflgr 3-1709
M&M Dental Supl Co 231E14 ....ORegn 4-4204
M&M Electrcl Co 179Grnwch ....CO rtlnd 7-0460
M and M Engravers 9MaidnLa ....WOrth 4-6362
MM FILM SVCES INC 723 7Av ....JUdson 6-7430
M&M Food Sales Inc frzn fd 225Bway ....REctr 2-5228
M&M Fruit Co 741ColmbusAv ....RIvrsde 9-2398
M&M Glass&Shade Co
2308AmstrdmAv WAdswth 7-4802
MM Handbag Co ....See Moskowitz Morris Corp
MM Hemstitching Co 50W27 ....MU rryhil 4-2554
M&M Jwlry Creations Inc 7Eldrdg ....WAlkr 5-6366
MM KNITWR CO INC swtrs
1370Bway PEnna 6-6627
M&M Leather Novelty Co 294Bowry ....GRmrcy 7-0700
M&M Linen Corp 487Bway ....WAlkr 5-1444
M&M Lunch 2134 8Av ....UNvrsty 4-9189
M&M Lunch Bar 51LittleW12 ....CH elsea 3-9768
M&M Lunchnet 27W28 ....MUryhil 5-2154
M&M Luncheonette 147E47 ....PLaza 3-5048
M&M Mfg Co canvs prods 58W15 ....ORegn 5-8654
M&M Meat Mkt Co 236 9Av ....WAtkns 4-1189
M&M Neckwear Co 333 4Av ....GRmrcy 7-7313
M&M Negligee Mfg Co 28W25 ....CHelsa 2-1477
M&M Novelty Co 488 7Av ....LAkwna 4-0052
M&M Ornament Co shoe bows
3190MilesAv TYrone 2-3670
M&M Parking Lot 95Divsn ....CAnl 6-9199
M&M Pet Prods Co 29E10 ....ORegn 4-3140
M&M Rag Co 119Sprng ....BArcly 7-4850
M&M Receivers Assn 33&12Av ....LOngacr 4-6330
MMS Music Writing Svce Inc
113W57 JUdson 2-4153
MMS Realty Corp 124-15 28Av Flus ....HIkry 5-6800
M&M Sales Co 202 8St JerseyCityNJ
AskOperFor JerseyCityNJ Oldfield 6-7700
M&M Self Svce Mkt 603W161 ....WAdswth 3-6419
M&M Shoe Inc 154Duane ....BArcly 7-9269
M&M Shoe Inc 154Duane ....WOrth 2-8209
M-M Specialties Inc 43E19 ....GRmrcy 7-5780
M & M SUNDRIES INC cosmtics
206W35 OXfrd 5-0830
M&M Surplus Sales 1623HavmyrAv ....TAlmdg 8-9026
MM Tailor&Cleaner 5008Bway ....LOrain 9-0300
M&M Tailors 81CabriniBl ....WAdswth 8-3770
M & M TRANSPTN CO
32-69GaleAv LICity RAvnswd 9-7000
M&M Trimng Co 535 8Av ....PEnna 6-6038
MM Undrwr Co 55 Orchrd ....CA nal 6-5178
M&M Variety Store house furnishgs
25AvB ORegn 3-7353
M&M Veal Co 416W14 ....CHelsa 2-2709
M&M WOODWORKING CO INC
713E98 Bklyn HYcnth 8-6490
M&M Yarn Winding Co
17WinsAv Bklyn DIkns 6-3491
M&N Harrison Inc 274MadAv ....MUryhil 5-5363
M&N Modern Hydraulic Press Co
760StateHwyNo3 CliftonNJ
AskOperFor CliftonNJ Prescott 7-0503
M&N Moving Co 218W116 ....MOnumnt 6-1608
M&N Refrigeratn Svce 426 6Av Bklyn SOuth 8-8686
M&O Dress Co 345W35 ....CHikrng 4-1240
MOS Mail Order Co 507 5Av ....MUryhil 2-2444
MPA 70E45 ....MUryhil 6-3717
MPA Food Shop 452Grnwch ....CAnl 6-9876
M&P Belt&Novelty Co 234W39 ....WIscnsn 7-0720
MP DAIRY 2350ArthrAv ....LUdlo 4-1777
MP Formula Ltd 37W57 ....MUryhil 8-0900
MP&G Garage Inc 726Bway ....GRmrcy 7-9656
MPI resrch 510MadAv ....PLaza 1-1466
MPM Beef CoInc 90Stantn ....GRmrcy 5-7010
MPO FILM DISTRIBUTION CO
15E53 MUryhil 8-7830
M P O PRODCTNS INC motn picts
15E53 MUryhil 8-7830
MPO Telvisn Films Inc 15E53 ....MUryhil 8-7830
Studio 210W65 ....TRaflgr 3-7000
MP Press Inc prntng 653 11Av ....JUdson 6-3689
MP Truckg 183Duane ....WAlkr 5-5844
M & R AIR CONDITIONING CORP
4018ChrchAv Bklyn BUkmnstr 2-8100
M&R Blouse CoInc 152W26 ....WAtkns 4-0249
MRC Bearings Svce Co 40W63 ....JUdson 6-4655
MRC Music Co 2343 8Av ....RIvrsd 9-0739
M&R Enginrng Co
4018ChrchAv Bklyn BUkmnstr 2-8100
M&R Garage Corp 4162Bway ....LOrain 8-9512
MR Hat Wks Inc 122W27 ....ALgnqn 5-5195
M&R Home&Auto Supl 4360Bway ....TOmpkns 7-2740
MR&K Furs Inc 227W29 ....PEnna 6-4250
M&R Luncheonette 630 9Av ....CIrcl 6-1909
MRM CO INC machy
191Bery Bklyn EVrgrn 7-3936
M&R Prntng Co 37W20 ....ALgnqn 5-1344
MRS Operating Corp cgrs
1481Bway LOngacr 3-9096
M-R-S Svce Sta Inc 4076Bway ....WAdswth 3-9645
M&R Tomato Distributrs 289Wash ....REctr 2-9432
M&R Transptn CoInc
1200Adams HobokenNJ COrtlnd 7-0728
MR Twenty Sixth of July Club
206AmstrdmAv SUsqhna 7-9718
M-R TYPWRTR SVCE 2025Bway ....TRaflgr 3-4252
MRW Assocs Inc 200 5Av ....WAtkns 9-4687
M&S Agncy sales 147W42 ....WIscnsn 7-1180
M&S Auto Sales 4920Bway ....LOrain 9-0921
Branch 4470Bway ....LOrain 9-0490

MS Braid&Trimming Co 173Wostr ....GRmrcy 3-3562
M&S Cigar Co 3191A Bway ....RIvrsde 9-9789
MS Clothing&Uniforms Inc 51Bayrd ....WOrth 2-5697
M&S Coat Co 253W26 ....CHelsa 2-9200
M&S Const Co 112E19 ....SPrng 7-4354
M&S Dairy&Grocry 2822Bway ....MOnumnt 3-8261
M&S Dental Co 219E23 ....MUryhil 4-2983
219E23 ....LExngtn 2-9229
M&S Doll Co 50E11 ....GRmrcy 3-0382
Showroom 200 5Av ....ORegn 5-3597
M&S Exprt Co 506Bway ....WOrth 6-3196
M S Fashn Knit 350 4Av ....MUryhil 3-9525
M&S Flower 224W35 ....CHikrng 4-2090
M&S Folding&Book Svce Inc 509W56 ....CIrcl 7-1664
M&S Fruit Mkt 4049Bway ....WAdswth 3-1144
M&S Grocry&Delcatesn 3625Bway ....WAdswth 6-5130
M&S Halegua mts ParkAv&114 ....ATwatr 9-5192
M&S HrdwrInc 186ColmbusAv ....TRaflgr 4-5608
MS Haulage Corp 32E1 ....ORegn 4-3750
MSI COMMUNICATIONS CONSULTING ENGINEERS 1475Bway ....BRynt 9-8517
M & S INDUSTRL SPRAY SVCE whtwshg
131W118 UNvrsty 4-1603
MSJ Trucking Co 59E9 ....GRmrcy 7-8461
M&S Knitwr Co 487Bway ....CA nal 6-0765
M S L Fur Co 21W35 ....WIscnsn 7-4578
M&S Leathercraft Mfg Corp
85Lenard WOrth 6-2573
MS Levy&Sons Inc hats 350 5Av ....CHikrng 4-3710
M&S Lingerie Inc 4GtJones ....GRmrcy 7-2692
M&S Luncheonette 232W30 ....LAkwna 4-9872
M&S Luncheonette Inc 273W38 ....WIscnsn 7-5555
MSM Luncheonette Inc 275 7Av ....WAtkns 9-9797
MSM Luncheonette Inc 160W26 ....CHelsa 2-2232
MS Mfg Co 555 8Av ....BRynt 9-5560
M&S Mkt Inc mts 2028AmstrdmAv ....LOrain 8-8988
M&S Novelty Co 44W36 ....WIscnsn 7-7685
M & S PACKERS MOVERS & SHIPPERS
434E72 RHinlndr 4-5150
M&S Papr&Twine Co 55W22 ....CHikrng 4-7590
M&S Plating Co 307W38 ....BRynt 9-8378
M&S Plumbing Contrctrs ....See Federman Saml
M&S Polishers 74W46 ....JUdsn 2-5177
MS Prntng 161Grand ....CAnl 6-7630
M&S PrntngCo 193E7 ....CAnl 8-5660
MS Prodctns Inc 130W56 ....JUdsn 2-6116
M&S Prods Co 799Grnwch ....CHelsa 3-6257
M&S Prods CoInc 33UnionSqW ....WAtkns 4-2523
MS&S Const CoInc
180 SBway WhiPlns WHitePls 8-1300
M&S Sales 32E18 ....CHelsa 2-1747
M&S Sandwich Shop 255W35 ....LAkwna 4-5766
M&S Svce Sta 625 11Av ....JUdsn 6-9606
MS Shoe Store 1598PkAv ....SAcrmnto 2-0580
M&S Smoke Shop 1100LexAv ....REgnt 4-9540
M&S Stamp Svce 38PkRw ....CO rtlnd 7-2732
M&S Stationers 75MadAv ....MUryhil 5-3230
M&S Super Mkt 652AmstrdmAv ....TRaflgr 3-9094
M&S Truckg Co 552 8Av ....PEnna 6-0998
M&S Trucking Svce 130W26 ....ALgnqn 5-0908
M Streichler Trucking Co 512W19 ....CHelsa 3-1438
M&T Bar&Grill 1471 1Av ....REgnt 4-9804
MTC AIR CONDITIONING & REFRIGRATN SVCE INC 239E149 ....MOtHvn 5-1100
M&T Co of NY Inc The 801 2Av ....MUryhil 6-7077
M&T Discount Corp 61Bway ....WHitehl 3-4635
M&T Display Svce 40-03Bway Ast ....RAvnswd 1-5190
M & T INDUSTRL PLUMBING & HEATING CO INC 255Lafyet ....WAlkr 5-0860
M T Jwlry Prods 36W47 ....JUdson 2-2637
M&T Labs Inc 100ParkAv ....LExngtn 2-6300
M & T LIQUORS INC 500W149 ....AUdbn 1-4444
MT Mathews Publishng Co 418Broom ....BArcly 7-8981
MTP Inc 3E48 ....PLaza 8-2272
MTR Sales Corp 200 5Av ....ORegn 5-0570
M&T Tire&Batry Svce 127W128 ....MOnumnt 6-2437
M&T Welding Prods Corp
100ParkAv LExngtn 2-6300
M Truckg Svce 72Walkr ....WAlkr 5-3032
MV Backdate Magazines 108W49 ....COlmbs 5-8777
MVM Inc expt impt 48-50 34 LICity ....STilwl 6-8913
M&W Delcatesn 567 9Av ....MUryhil 7-8868
MW Dress Co 483 7Av ....LA ckwana 4-1546
MWG Dress Co 2393Bway ....SC huylr 4-4890
M&W Hat Co 571 8Av ....CH ickrng 4-0495
MWK Co 122E42 ....OXfrd 7-8550
M&W Mkts Inc mts 140 8Av ....CHelsa 3-0104
M&W Martin Inc womns wr
307W36 CHikrng 4-7866
M&W Parking Co 309W46 ....COlmbs 5-9157
M W Prince Hall Grand Lodge
454W155 AUdbn 6-9232
M&W Svce Sta 124 8Av ....CHelsa 2-9592
MW Sound Systms 273BenetAv ....LOrain 9-7645
M W Textile Corp 115W30 ....OXfrd 5-6190
M&W Thomas Co fabrcs 50W40 ....BRynt 9-6910
M W TOOL CO INC 138Bxtr ....WAlkr 5-0255
M&W Trucking Svce 113E29 ....MUryhil 5-5715
MW Underwear Corp 440Lafyet ....ALgnqn 4-5220
M&W Upholsterers Inc 192Hstr ....CAnl 6-4325
M&W Window&House Cleaning Co
50E11 GRmrcy 3-6457
M&Z Decorators 490Clntn ....GRmrcy 5-5134
M&Z Headwr Co 31Allen ....WAlkr 5-4856
MZL Factors Inc 125W29 ....WIscnsn 7-9558
MZ Undrgrmnt Co 627Bway ....GRmrcy 7-4025
Ma Cheong 11Essex ....GRmrcy 3-5335
Ma John T 417W121 ....MOnumnt 6-5782
Ma L 335WdswrthAv ....LOrain 8-3050
Ma Mere Inc matrnts 1400Bway ....PEnna 6-7341
MA-RO—See also MARO
Ma-Ro Hosry CoInc 112W34 ....LOngacr 4-8840
Ma Sharren Estates Inc 261W125 ....MOnumnt 6-9174
Ma-sun Press Inc 270Lafayette ....CA nal 6-7357
Ma T S 90LaSal ....ACdmy 2-5348
Maack Alexndr 416E9 ....ORegn 3-4170
Maack Christine Mrs 423W118 ....MO numnt 2-8223
Maack Hans 321E92 ....ATwtr 9-7076
Maack Hugo 448E20 ....ORegn 7-4297
Maag Joan L 509MadAv ....PLaza 5-0233
Maag Louis 400E59 ....ELdrdo 5-4650

Maak Zinowia Mrs 22E58 ....PLaza 8-1891
Maar Eleanor T Mrs 421W118 ....MOnumnt 6-7128
Maar Gabriella Mrs 424E82 ....REgnt 4-2034
Maar Hedda cosmtics 1472Bway ....BRynt 9-9642
Maarsen Press 119W23 ....CHelsa 2-0329
Maarsen S L 80BenetAv ....WAdswth 8-5875
Maartens Matilda J Mrs 2085LexAv ....LEhigh 4-2266
MAAS—See also MAASS, MASS
Maas A Mrs 345W55 ....CIrcl 6-9469
Maas Alfred E 330HavnAv ....TOmpkns 7-4752
Maas Alfred N CPA 11W42 ....LA ckwana 4-8855
Maas Bernard 247W109 ....UNivrsty 5-7112
Maas Bros of Flint Michigan
1440Bway LOngacr 4-5200
Maas Carl 5GramrcyPkW ....GRmrcy 3-2209
Maas Else J 310E74 ....REgnt 4-4135
Maas Esther 425CentPkW ....ACdmy 2-2056
Maas Geo artst 53E51 ....PLaza 3-6446
Maas Gerald 509W110 ....MO numnt 2-8341
Maas Gertrude 711WEndAv ....MOnumnt 2-0032
Maas&Ginsberg CPA 11W42 ....LA ckwana 4-8855
Maas Henry 425W205 ....LOrain 9-5373
Maas Herbert N 165PinehrstAv ....WAdswth 7-8880
Maas I&Sons 76 IrvngPl ....ORegn 4-9526
Maas I&Sons bldrs 201E20 ....GRmrcy 5-4064
Maas Irma 370W58 ....CIrcl 6-9883
Maas Jan A 1680YorkAv ....BUtrfld 8-4036
Maas Jos b 160Bway ....REctr 2-5970
Maas Julian 123W93 ....RIversde 9-1831
Maas Kenneth J
90MapleDr GrtNkEsts HUntr 2-4742
Maas L bus machs 119Lafyet ....WOrth 6-2440
Maas Leopold 317W93 ....RIvrsde 9-7510
Maas Ludwig Jr 204E53 ....PLaza 5-1148
Maas Margaret K Mrs 18E84 ....BUtrfld 8-8958
Maas Martha H 337E82 ....REgnt 7-1054
Maas Max 894RivDr ....LOrain 8-0654
Maas Michl 114E91 ....TRaflgr 6-1853
Maas Natalie R 145CentPkW ....TRaflgr 7-3180
Maas Natalie R atty 111Bway ....WOrth 4-2232
Residence 162E80 ....TRaflgr 9-1949
Maas Nathan R b 146CentPkW ....ENdicot 2-4520
Residence 145CentPkW ....TRafalgr 7-3180
Maas Peter 31W11 ....ALgnqn 5-3955
Maas Richd I 412W22 ....WAtkns 9-0899
Maas&Steffen Co furs 249W29 ....LAkwna 4-3674
Maas&Waldstein Co laqrs
2121McCarterHighway NewarkNJ DIgby 4-8983
Maas&Waldstein Co laqrs 2121McCarterHwy
AskOperFor NewarkNJ Humbolt 4-1600
Maas Walter 300W109 ....MOnumnt 3-1425
Maas Walter R 510E88 ....REgnt 7-1638
Maas Werner S 150RivDr ....TRaflgr 3-2347
Maas Wm H Mrs 462AmstrdmAv ....TRaflgr 7-7389
Maasbrock Robt J 207E89 ....FIlmor 8-8112
MAASS—See also MAAS, MASS
Maass A A jwlr 1W47 ....CIrcl 7-1061
Maass Arthur L 9E96 ....AT watr 9-2175
bus 11W57 ....ELdrdo 5-4981
Maass Bertha A 111W12 ....CHelsa 2-1413
Maass Charlotte 82Jane ....CHelsa 2-1983
Maass Davidson Levy Friedman&Weston attys
100ParkAv MUryhil 6-2676
Maass E J 1578 3Av ....AT watr 9-7026
Maass Elsa 838WEndAv ....RIvrsd 9-9477
Maass Ernest 52W87 ....TRaflgr 4-1508
Maass Grace Mrs 30Elwd ....LO rrain 7-6108
Maass Herbert H 781 5Av ....ELdrdo 5-2800
Maass Herbert H Mrs 111E56 ....MUryhil 8-3189
Maass John H atty 477MadAv ....PLaza 9-7733
Maass Lotte Mrs 52W87 ....TRaflgr 4-1508
Maass Richd b 285MadAv ....MUryhil 5-8448
Maass Robt G lwyr 40Wall ....BOwlGrn 9-5150
Maatta Anna Mrs 79W94 ....ACdmy 2-4291
Maatta Martha Mrs 1405 3Av ....TRaflgr 9-4865
Maattanen Lempi A Mrs 109E126 ....FIlmor 8-9356
Mab Svce Co 215W29 ....LOngacr 5-7360
Mab Svce Corp 39W60 ....JUdson 6-0058
Mabanaft Inc petrol prods 80Broad ....DIgby 4-5980
Mabarak Bros Inc hndkrchfs
321 5Av MUryhil 4-7419
Mabarak Jos J b 321 5Av ....MUryhil 4-7419
Mabardi Claire 39W55 ....COlmbs 5-5743
Mabardi Geo b 2E56 ....PLaza 5-7838
Mabbett Geo&Sons Co 40E34 ....MUryhil 3-6922
Mabbott Thos O Prof 1435LexAv ....TEmpltn 1-2338
Mabbs E G 20GarfldAv GlenHd ....GLenCov 4-0929
Mabe Jay BH 411E81 ....REgnt 7-4061
Mabeau Michel 565W139 ....AUdbn 3-2533
Mabeau T Mrs 60W76 ....EN dicot 2-6265
Mabee Eleanor M 409E58 ....MUryhil 8-4849
Mabee Grace Widney Mrs 11E87 ....FIlmor 8-5502
Mabel&Carrie Beauty Salon
300W140 AU dubn 3-8017
Mabel Dean Bacon Vocational High Schl
129E22 GRmrcy 5-6875
Mabel Edw R&Co CPA's 67W44 ....MUryhil 7-2404
Mabel Harry lwyr 67W44 ....MUryhil 7-2404
Maben Co 210E23 ....LExngtn 2-4487
Maben Enterprises Inc 165E64 ....REgnt 7-0777
Maben John J 285W150 ....ADrndak 4-6723
Maber Inc 295MadAv ....LExngtn 2-1700
Mabery R L 145W117 ....MOnumnt 6-6432
Mabie Anita Mrs 90PkTerE ....LOrain 9-3831
Mabie Janet 55EEndAv ....REgnt 4-3846
Mabie Laurence 425W23 ....ALgnqn 5-2097
Mabie Esther N Mrs 222W144 ....ADrndak 4-2846
Mabie Catherine Mrs 210N W153 ....SWinbrn 4-5598
Mabie Jean E 104W90 ....ENdict 2-2894
Mabob Realty CoInc 139E30 ....MUryhil 3-0969
Mabon&Co brkrs 115Bway ....REctr 2-2820
Mabon J B Jr 167E82 ....RHinlndr 4-0674
Mabon Jas B Mrs 870PkAv ....TEmpltn 8-0474
Mabon John Scott StarRdgRd Brewster
AskOperFor Brewstr 9-2449
Mabon K 340E72 ....RE gent 7-0213
Mabon Prescott C b 195Bway ....EXetr 3-1000
Res 36ComodrRd Chappaqua
AskOperFor Chapaqua 1-1101
Mabon Susan 126E83 ....UNvrsty 1-0954
Mabra Nannie Mae 335E100 ....FIlmor 8-1039
Mabra Reba 109W60 ....CIrcl 6-6755
Mabra Tena 107W78 ....ENdict 2-2680

prepare for a future nuclear attack. While the rest of the nation hid in their official bunkers, thirty-one friends from the Catholic Worker, FOR, and the WRL remained above ground, highlighting the futility of the bunker defense. The dissenters were arrested and charged with violating the New York State Defense Emergency Act of 1951. Among those arrested were the thespians Judith Malina and Julian Beck. The *New York Times* reported that Malina was sent to Bellevue Hospital for "observation" after she argued with the magistrate, and her husband was ejected from court for objecting to the magistrate's decision.[66] The staged nature of these protests and the disruption of court proceedings were ways in which the political and the personal were explored through the medium of Malina and Beck's performative tactics. The confrontation with the disciplinary institutions—police, justice, and feds—was a recurring theme within Malina and Beck's performance work as well as their real lives.

ARTISTS ESTATES

THEATRICAL ESTATES (1947–1963)

Judith Malina, along with partner, Julian Beck, founded the Living Theater in 1947. This experimental theater company explored the critical link between performance and political dissent. The deliberate act of getting arrested during the civil defense drills and spending jail time with veteran activists such as Dorothy Day activated the political imagination of the younger Judith Malina.[67] In her diaries, Malina describes her interactions with the Catholic Worker's Ammon Hennessey and deep admiration for Dorothy Day, in whom she saw "fire and poetry."[68] The anarchist pacifism of Day, with its focus on showing by example and public action, had resonance for Malina. The theatrical aspect of the protests found their way into the performance repertoire as Malina and Beck challenged the political and formal expectations of theater audiences. A pioneering experiment on many fronts, the Living Theater was influenced by the avant-garde theories of the French director Antonin Artaud and the radical pacifism of activists like Day in equal parts. From Artaud, the Living Theater developed its distaste of commercial Broadway productions and explored, instead, a stark, aggressive realism that sought to jolt the audience from passivity to awareness. From Day came the commitment to a revolutionary pacifism by bringing attention to violence and injustice as a way to live peaceably.[69]

These two subversive positions against the romantic, passive model of theater engagement symbolized by Broadway and their participation in the actions of the emergent new left in the '50s made the existence of the Living Theater group very precarious. Looking for a stable venue, the group performed in various makeshift storefronts, basements, and lofts all over the city that were serially shut down by the fire department or the police on the pretext of safety and security. In 1951, after having been ousted from a small basement space on Wooster Street on the allegation that the space was being deployed as cover for a brothel, the couple decided to move the venue to their apartment in the Upper West Side. The "Theater in the Room" was the performance that emerged in this intimate and unlikely environment. They hosted an audience composed mainly of their bohemian friends— painters, writers, and musicians.

Over the years, the Living Theater staged performances that invited composers such as John Cage and Lou Harrison, dancers such as Merce Cunningham, and the beat poets Allen Ginsberg and Lawrence Ferlinghetti to collaborate with them on projects that challenged the formal boundaries of performance art in general. Beck, who designed all the sets and costumes for the productions, shared an interest in the formal interdisciplinary innovation that was a part of the culture of music, painting, and performance in the '50s. However, the increasingly political content of the Living Theater performances set them apart from some of their friends and contemporaries who remained, at the time, more centrist in their political views.[70]

The Living Theater subsequently moved their productions from the apartment to the Cherry Lane Theater in Greenwich Village, and then further north to the Playhouse on Fourteenth Street and Sixth Avenue. In this location, the company repurposed an old department store and converted the second floor into a 150-seat theater. It was here that they produced Jack Gelber's *The Connection* (1959), a play about drug addiction, and Kenneth Brown's *The Brig* (1963), a brutal portrayal of life in a U.S. Marine Corps prison in Japan (**Figure 1.14**). Artaud's concept of a "Theater of Cruelty" was used in these stagings to depict the violence and dehumanization within society. The

1.14
Frames from a film by Jonas Mekas that documents the performance of the play, *The Brig*, by the Living Theatre, 1964.

unflinching representations of heroin addicts shooting up onstage and the in-character verbal abuse of the actors on- and offstage in rehearsal were meant to reveal the stark realities of addiction, war, and incarceration. These two productions approached pacifism in a para-doxical way by making the violence palpable to a point that made the audience uncomfortable.[71]

As part of the mission to make the work accessible, the Living Theater charged low admission fees and survived financially with grants from foundations and personal loans. The productions, run on a shoestring budget with a small following in the downtown theater scene, allowed the Living Theater to barely break even after fifteen years of challeng-ing existence. In 1963, toward the end of a five-year lease, the Four-teenth Street Playhouse was padlocked by the IRS for the nonpay-ment of taxes.[72] On October 19, the cast and crew of the Living The-ater, along with a few hardy audience members, broke into confiscated property and even as federal police prevented a hundred-plus crowd of agitating supporters from entering the premises, the Living Theater staged its final performance of *The Brig*. Twenty-five people were arrested and carried out of the building by the police and charged with obstruction of federal rulings. In the court proceedings that followed this arrest and the trials for tax evasion, Judith Malina and Julian Beck proceeded to turn the courtroom into a theater—using dramatic lan-guage and disruptive tactics to plead their case.[73]

The aspect of performance and dramatic reenactments was also an integral part of civil rights activism in 1960s America. The year 1963 was filled with civil rights demonstrations and nonviolent direct actions protesting racial segregation. Sit-ins, marches, and boycotts in Birmingham, Alabama, among other places, fired the imagination and desire for participation in the supportive east and west coast activist communities. The focus on everyday life and the staging of public pro-test against segregation in schools, parks, restaurants, and schools cap-tured the attention of the nation. The images of the stoic nonviolent resistance of the civil rights activists in the face of police brutality was transmitted through newspapers, radio, and television. The demon-strations of collective strength and street actions reverberated across the country and gave momentum to the new left. Collectivity, a phe-nomenon that was previously associated with organized labor party politics, was interpreted by anti-institutional activists and artists in its anarchic communitarian dimension. These enactments of dissent and the effective use of public space in its potential to generate theater were a precedent to the many civil disobedience actions during the Vietnam War years.

VANGUARD ESTATES

The Living Theater's underlying critique of war, prison, and the capitalist state on stage was fortified by the involvement of the founders in the anti-authoritarian, pacifist, and artistic movements mobilizing in Greenwich Village in the early '60s. With a focus on antinuclear proliferation, a coalition of peace activists and artists began the Greenwich Village Peace Center in 1961, in a rented storefront at 133 West Third Street. At this point in time, Vietnam was a small country on the other side of the globe, one that few Americans had heard of. With the active engagement of the United States Army, first in an advisory role, and then with the deployment of ground troops in the mid-'60s in a directly offensive role, the Greenwich Village Peace Center became a hub of anti-war organization. Educating themselves about Vietnam and forms of nonviolent resistance, the Peace Center showed films and engaged audiences through theater and teach-ins to prepare for the most contentious period in the war history of the country. The novelist Grace Paley, a founder of the center, in an interview with the *Nonviolent Activist*, described how theater, music, and art played a vital role in supporting and shaping the anti-war movement in Lower Manhattan.[74]

In this same milieu, Peter Schumann, a friend and co-conspirator of the Becks, began building puppets in a loft on Delancey Street, on the Lower East Side. Reviving a European folk tradition, Schumann, along with his wife, Elka, hosted puppet shows that examined urgent political issues using archaic, larger-than-life puppet characters. The Bread and Puppet Theater grew from these shows to become a part of the radical artistic and political scene unfolding around Washington Square Park. The doleful puppets, often as tall as fifteen feet, became a staple of the many anti-war demonstrations and parades in New York for the next few decades (**Figure1.15**). The reciprocal relationship between art and anti-war activism is clearest in the direct relationships between theater and public protest fostered through the relationships between the artists and activists around Washington Square.

As the demographics of what had been an immigrant Italian neighborhood around Washington Square changed, artists, writers, and musicians moved into the neighborhood and transformed the Italian cafés, churches, squares, and narrow streets into a bohemian haven for countercultural experimentation.[75] Judson Memorial Church, designed by McKim, Mead and White, with its distinctive campanile and spacious interior on the southern edge of Washington Square, an institution that had provided support for the Italian immigrants in the late nineteenth and early twentieth century, once more broadened its

1.15
Bread and Puppet Theater at an anti–Vietnam War parade, Greenwich Village, 1965.

Photograph courtesy of Robert Joyce papers,1952–1973, Historical Collections and Labor Archives, Special Collections Library, University Libraries, Pennsylvania State University.

mission as the constitution of the neighborhood changed (**Figure 1.16**). Under the leadership of the activist pastor Howard Moody, the church advocated for civil rights, abortion rights, treatment of drug addiction, and later, patients with HIV. Alongside these social campaigns, the church also opened its spaces to the growing colony of artists who were active in the area. The Judson Gallery (1959), Judson Poets Theater (1961), and Judson Dance Theater (1962), coordinated by young avant-garde painters, performers, musicians, and dancers, respectively, transformed the church into a place of experimentation with little constraint and no censorship.

Young artists looking for opportunities outside mainstream museum and performance venues found room to explore and collaborate within the sanctuary. The question of authorship and authenticity examined by artists such as Claes Oldenburg and Alan Kaprow at Judson resulted in "happenings" and multimedia events where the artwork was part of an environment that the audience experienced as a whole rather than a singular commodity object.[76] Influenced by these happenings, George Maciunas, a Lithuanian émigré with pro-Soviet affinities, formed the art collective Fluxus. Fluxus was a loose conglo-

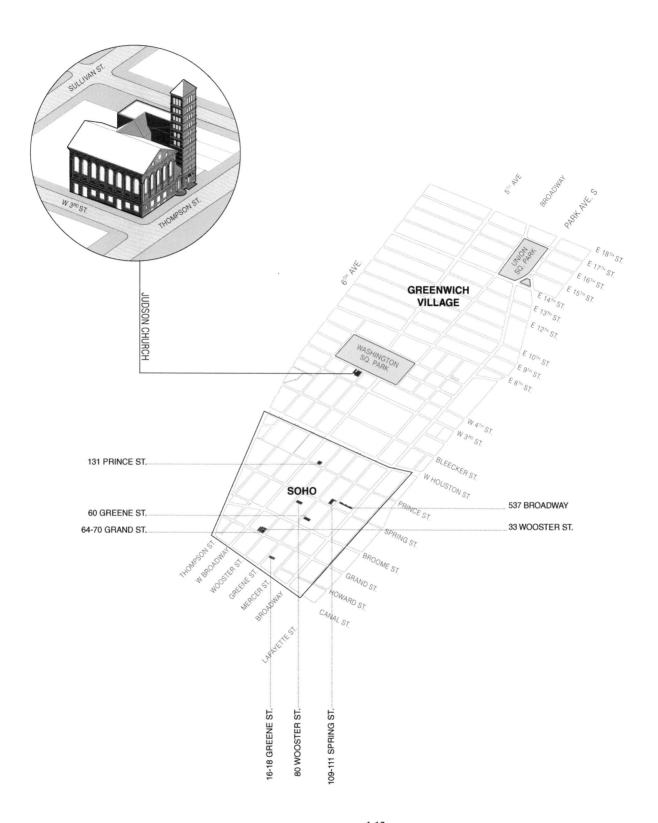

SULLIVAN ST.

W 3RD ST.

THOMPSON ST.

JUDSON CHURCH

5TH AVE

BROADWAY

PARK AVE. S

6TH AVE.

GREENWICH VILLAGE

UNION SQ. PARK

E 18TH ST.
E 17TH ST.
E 16TH ST.
E 15TH ST.
E 14TH ST.
E 13TH ST.
E 12TH ST.
E 10TH ST.
E 9TH ST.
E 8TH ST.

WASHINGTON SQ. PARK

W 4TH ST.
W 3RD ST.

BLEECKER ST.

W HOUSTON ST.

131 PRINCE ST.

SOHO

537 BROADWAY

PRINCE ST.

60 GREENE ST.
64-70 GRAND ST.

33 WOOSTER ST.

SPRING ST.

BROOME ST.

THOMPSON ST.
W BROADWAY
WOOSTER ST.
GREENE ST.
MERCER ST.
BROADWAY
LAFAYETTE ST.

GRAND ST.

HOWARD ST.

CANAL ST.

16-18 GREENE ST.

80 WOOSTER ST.

109-111 SPRING ST.

1.16
Judson Memorial Church in Greenwich Village and SoHo
buildings converted to Flux Houses by George Maciunas,
1967–1977.
Illustration by Nandini Bagchee.

merate of participating artists, including Yoko Ono, Nam June Paik, George Brecht, and La Monte Young. They were influenced by, and sometimes collaborated with, John Cage, Allan Kaprow, and Alison Knowles. The exact membership was unclear, as they collaborated with each other and with outsiders as well. Maciunas likened the group to a "fluid discharge," and in a manifesto he described the project as an effort to "purge the world of bourgeois sickness, 'intellectual,' professional & commercialized culture," and in its stead to "PROMOTE A REVOLUTIONARY FLOOD AND TIDE IN ART, Promote living art, anti-art, promote NON ART REALITY to be grasped by all peoples, not only critics, dilettantes and professionals."[77] This aspiration of Fluxus to make art a part of the everyday led Maciunas to engage in a series of experiments that pushed the limits of art by extending into the living space of the artists.

LIVE-WORK ESTATES (1967–1971)

In 1967 Maciunas advertised his plan to develop an artists' co-op in the neighborhood south of Houston Street (SoHo) to the well-connected Greenwich Village art community.[78] Maciunas's project, called the Flux House, involved creating a cooperative of affordable housing for artists on a large multi-building scale. To achieve this goal, Maciunas purchased sixteen loft buildings over a period of ten years and converted them into live-work spaces for invested artists. He began purchasing existing buildings by cobbling together small sums of money from fellow artists who were willing to enter into a precarious investment, as future co-op owners, within manufacturing lofts.[79] Maciunas renovated these spacious, commercially zoned work spaces with the help of an otherwise under-employed workforce of artists and carpenters and created an internal real estate/construction economy. Flux House II at 80 Wooster Street, a pilot project with two or three artist-owners, was the first to be established. In its first rendition the co-op housing included a cinematheque on the ground floor, which was run by fellow Lithuanian-born filmmaker Jonas Mekas.[80] Some version of this arrangement, which combined work spaces with residences, was owned and run by an artist's cooperative. Maciunas conceived this as a model of a collectivized estate designed for and by the Fluxus community.

The task of handling construction and making the buildings available while keeping the fire and building department at bay was the kind of challenge that Maciunas enjoyed. The ad hoc management of the properties and a series of run-ins with the workmen and city agencies ultimately frayed the patience of the loft dwellers. However, the

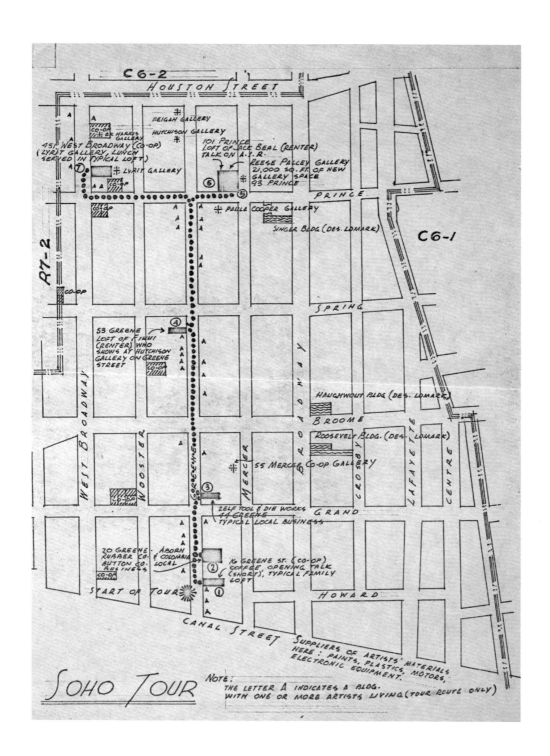

1.17

Map of SoHo tour, SoHo Artists Association 1968–1978.

Map courtesy of the Archives of American Art, Smithsonian Institution.

collective spirit that Maciunas and other artists had hoped to cultivate did materialize in some measure, despite the tensions that arose from the wheeler-dealer methods of purchase and the setting up of the mostly illegal cooperative. The artist/investors of the Flux Houses and others that followed in their footsteps managed to gain a foothold in the loft-scape of SoHo. They did so, perhaps not as radically opposed to the bureaucracy as Maciunas envisioned, but rather more pragmatically like other communities in New York by forming the SoHo Artists Association in 1968 and by lobbying for political support. Maciunas, having instigated the co-op and injected the artists into the industrial neighborhood, left the city dissatisfied with the outcome.[81]

In 1971 the New York Board of Estimate finally passed a zoning resolution that legalized the use of SoHo lofts as living quarters for bona fide artists. This victory for the artists marked the beginning of what many urbanists would subsequently regard as a city policy that used the artist community to further their agenda of gentrification and urban renewal without the trauma of destruction and dislocation.[82] In 1973 SoHo artists opened their lofts to the outside world to see how they lived. This event showcased their work, and a map outlined a "tour" along Greene Street (**Figure 1.17**). The lives of the artists living in SoHo, in this case, became more interesting than their work. In a reversal of the Living Theater project to make life a part of art, personal lives and the living conditions of artists had, here, become a part of life. The bare-bones loft aesthetic that emerged as a result of the scarcity of materials and means, later became attractive to investors and symbolic of the escalation in value of these same live-work estates in the '80s.

ACTIVIST ESTATES: A SWARM OF POINTS

> *Where there is power there is resistance, and yet, or rather consequently, this resistance is never in a position of exteriority in relation to power.*
>
> *Just as the network of power relations ends by forming a dense web that passes through apparatuses and institutions, without being exactly localized in them, so too the swarm of points of resistance traverses social stratifications and individual unities.*
> —Michel Foucault, *The History of Sexuality*

The activist estates described herein are, as Foucault suggests, embedded in the larger matrix of power relationships in a place through time (**Figure 1.18**). Their forces are distributed within a geographic terrain but their institutional goals are multi-centric, and hence, there is a dynamic of overlapping resistances. They operate in many ways like the larger institutions they seek to challenge and dismantle, creating their own networks that pass through the many different locations and spaces described here.

From the purpose-built settlement houses, public housing, churches, and social clubs to the appropriated theaters, churches, and live-work lofts, the spirit of activism found a place to challenge and mesh. The landscape of resistance as established through the *Progressive, Radical,* and *Artistic* imperatives of a wide-ranging but well-connected network of dissidents paradoxically intertwined with the fungibility of real estate. The existing infrastructure of properties (a swarm of points) and the meanings inscribed by the practices of generations of activists described in this chapter provide a background for the three types of counter-institutions that emerged in response to the militarism of the nation, the urban crisis of the city, and the commodification of culture within the fluid geography of the Lower East Side. Examining the ideas and ideals of the progressives, radicals, and artists in the late nineteenth and first part of the twentieth century makes it possible to understand why this small part of a large city has been a cauldron of progressive action for more than a century.

In the '70s, as the fiscal crisis affected New York's municipal structure, the existing network of people and the practices provided the foundation for different types of space-based resistance. The three case studies presented in the main body of this book represent three different but overlapping political constituencies that emerged in the Lower East Side in the '70s. Bolstered by widespread civil rights and anti-war movements nationwide, the first of these buildings, nicknamed the Peace Pentagon, was bought by the War Resisters League in 1969 and set up as offices for groups advocating for peace and social justice. The second building, El Bohio Community Center, set up by the Puerto Rican collective CHARAS in 1977, was a place to celebrate the culture of Loisaida (the Latinized pronunciation for the Lower East Side). The third building, ABC No Rio, was developed in 1979 as a storefront gallery by members of an artist's collective to pursue "non-commercial, community-oriented, experimental art practices." Despite profound changes in the neighborhood, in many respects the concerns and achievements of the earlier years continued to inform the next round of developments in the area.

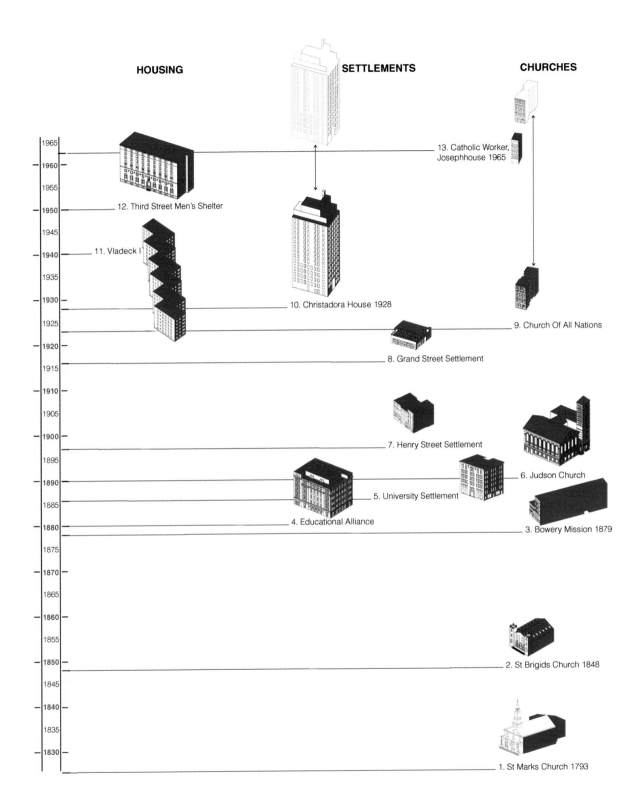

HOUSING

SETTLEMENTS

CHURCHES

13. Catholic Worker, Josephhouse 1965

12. Third Street Men's Shelter

11. Vladeck I

10. Christadora House 1928

9. Church Of All Nations

8. Grand Street Settlement

7. Henry Street Settlement

6. Judson Church

5. University Settlement

4. Educational Alliance

3. Bowery Mission 1879

2. St Brigids Church 1848

1. St Marks Church 1793

1965
1960
1955
1950
1945
1940
1935
1930
1925
1920
1915
1910
1905
1900
1895
1890
1885
1880
1875
1870
1865
1860
1855
1850
1845
1840
1835
1830

1.18
Selected "Activist Estates" of the Lower East Side,
1880–1968.
Illustration by Nandini Bagchee.

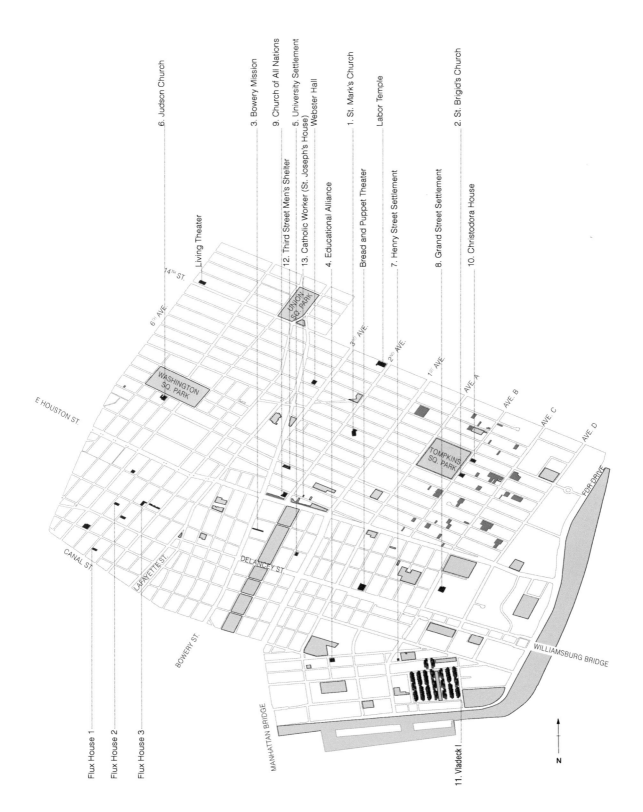

6. Judson Church

3. Bowery Mission

9. Church of All Nations

5. University Settlement

Webster Hall

1. St. Mark's Church

Labor Temple

2. St. Brigid's Church

Living Theater

12. Third Street Men's Shelter

13. Catholic Worker (St. Joseph's House)

4. Educational Alliance

Bread and Puppet Theater

7. Henry Street Settlement

8. Grand Street Settlement

10. Christodora House

14TH ST.

6TH AVE.

UNION SQ. PARK

3RD AVE.

2ND AVE.

1ST AVE.

AVE. A

AVE. B

AVE. C

AVE. D

WASHINGTON SQ. PARK

E HOUSTON ST.

TOMPKINS SQ. PARK

FDR DRIVE

CANAL ST.

LAFAYETTE ST.

DELANCEY ST.

BOWERY ST.

WILLIAMSBURG BRIDGE

MANHATTAN BRIDGE

Flux House 1

Flux House 2

Flux House 3

11. Vladeck I.

N

2

RADICAL PACIFISM AT THE PEACE PENTAGON

(1969-2016)

CHAPTER 2: RADICAL PACIFISM AT THE PEACE PENTAGON (1969–2016)

For the past forty-five years, anti-war rallies in New York City have begun and ended at significant urban sites. Demonstrators repeatedly target symbolic institutions and locations such as the United Nations Headquarters, the Main Branch Library on Forty-Second Street, City Hall, Wall Street, and the Armed Forces Recruiting Station in Times Square (**Figure 2.1**). Marches move up and down Broadway, the city's oldest north-south thoroughfare, passing some of the large public spaces in Manhattan, such as Washington and Union Squares, each with its own history of popular mobilization. Familiar landmarks and well-worn pathways, visited by countless citizens over the decades, are ritualized and reclaimed through these repeated occupations. The chant "Whose streets? Our streets!" is offered as a provocation to municipal authorities as well as a call to passersby and fellow citizens to join the action. The buildings and sites targeted by the rallies and marches are the symbolic embodiment of a government that is held accountable by the people. The commandeering of streets and side-walks and the areas in front of civic institutions becomes a means of asserting power by reclaiming public space. The temporary presence of bodies in protest both challenges and briefly dismantles the status of a site of state control to one of collective opportunity.

This participatory tactic of protest and demonstration effectively draws attention to a shared political will that goes beyond the immediate event to make a statement and to educate and form a resisting public body. "The end of rebellion is liberation," the political theorist Hannah Arendt wrote in her 1963 book *On Revolution*, "while the end of revolution is the foundation of freedom."[1] For Arendt, the larger purpose of revolutionary action, such as temporarily occupying a sidewalk or a square outside a public institution, is not merely liberation from tyranny and oppression. Rather, it is the potential beginning of a body politic—a new constellation of people with a shared political awareness and civic agency.[2] The open public square or street and the enclosed Town Hall are the spatial corollary to the two-part agenda of revolution: first to break the monopoly of power and then to construct a new political imperative.[3] The external, open domain, Arendt's "space of appearance," responds to the needs of a larger, more visible sphere of resistance, whereas the Town Hall responds to the foundation of a permanently engaged political community.[4] Today, the strength of

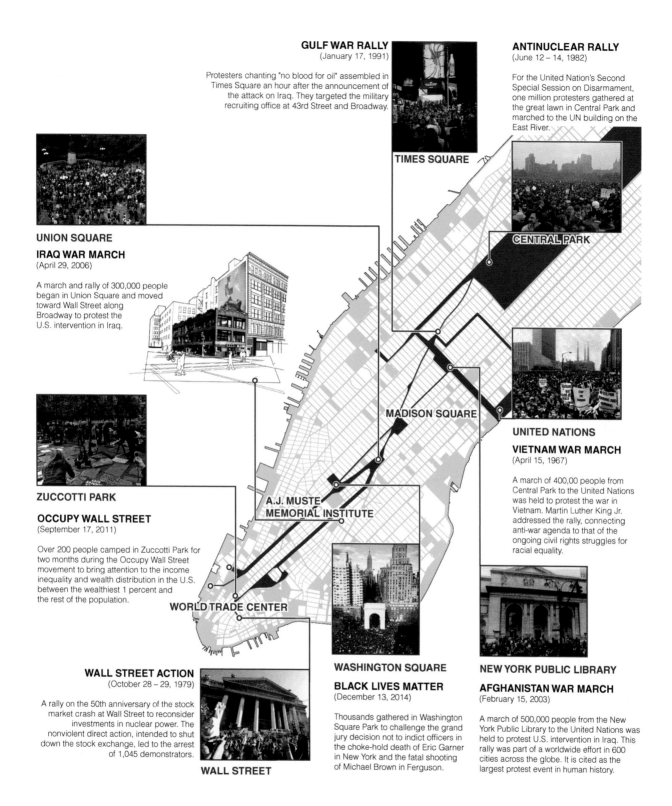

GULF WAR RALLY
(January 17, 1991)

Protesters chanting "no blood for oil" assembled in Times Square an hour after the announcement of the attack on Iraq. They targeted the military recruiting office at 43rd Street and Broadway.

TIMES SQUARE

ANTINUCLEAR RALLY
(June 12 – 14, 1982)

For the United Nation's Second Special Session on Disarmament, one million protesters gathered at the great lawn in Central Park and marched to the UN building on the East River.

CENTRAL PARK

UNION SQUARE

IRAQ WAR MARCH
(April 29, 2006)

A march and rally of 300,000 people began in Union Square and moved toward Wall Street along Broadway to protest the U.S. intervention in Iraq.

MADISON SQUARE

UNITED NATIONS

VIETNAM WAR MARCH
(April 15, 1967)

A march of 400,00 people from Central Park to the United Nations was held to protest the war in Vietnam. Martin Luther King Jr. addressed the rally, connecting anti-war agenda to that of the ongoing civil rights struggles for racial equality.

ZUCCOTTI PARK

OCCUPY WALL STREET
(September 17, 2011)

Over 200 people camped in Zuccotti Park for two months during the Occupy Wall Street movement to bring attention to the income inequality and wealth distribution in the U.S. between the wealthiest 1 percent and the rest of the population.

A.J. MUSTE MEMORIAL INSTITUTE

WORLD TRADE CENTER

WALL STREET ACTION
(October 28 – 29, 1979)

A rally on the 50th anniversary of the stock market crash at Wall Street to reconsider investments in nuclear power. The nonviolent direct action, intended to shut down the stock exchange, led to the arrest of 1,045 demonstrators.

WALL STREET

WASHINGTON SQUARE

BLACK LIVES MATTER
(December 13, 2014)

Thousands gathered in Washington Square Park to challenge the grand jury decision not to indict officers in the choke-hold death of Eric Garner in New York and the fatal shooting of Michael Brown in Ferguson.

NEW YORK PUBLIC LIBRARY

AFGHANISTAN WAR MARCH
(February 15, 2003)

A march of 500,000 people from the New York Public Library to the United Nations was held to protest U.S. intervention in Iraq. This rally was part of a worldwide effort in 600 cities across the globe. It is cited as the largest protest event in human history.

2.1

Seminal marches and demonstrations in New York City, 1967–2014.

Illustration by Nandini Bagchee.

2.2
The "Peace Pentagon" at the
corner of Lafayette and Bleecker
Streets, 1978.
Photograph by David McReynolds.

both of these types of spaces is greatly diminished through various forms of surveillance and legal stipulation. The street and square are policed both physically and electronically, while the Town Hall's role as a place for spontaneous discussion and debate has been co-opted by top-down politicking. What, then, are possible places for organizing and staging political dissent? What are the alternative forums for public participation?

One such place in New York City, an architectural eyesore and an unlikely candidate for urban glory, was a three-story office building situated at the northwest corner of Lafayette and Bleecker Streets— just north of Houston Street (**Figure 2.2**). This nine-thousand-square-foot building, suffering from many physical ailments and owned by the anti-war organization—the A. J. Muste Memorial Institute[5]— provided low-rent office space for activists and advocates of social justice in New York City from 1969 to 2016. In imagining a place capable of nurturing radicals, one seldom thinks of a privately owned office building, replete with desks, computers, phones, filing cabinets, and general clutter. A far cry from Arendt's notion of a public sphere, neatly separated from the private realm,[6] this well-worn space nonetheless served as a forum to antinuclear activists, artist collectives, housing advocates, open-information media collectives, international solidarity groups, and many other politically motivated organizations. Well known amongst a multigenerational activist community, the building provided a place to meet and stuff envelopes, plan marches, and attend nonviolence training sessions in a central New York City location. The range of activist and social justice groups under a single roof over the years created a synergetic and supportive environment for the myriad of individuals and collectives working to effect political, economic, and social change. Over the course of a four-decade-long occupancy, the building's fluctuating tenant base carved out a space for civic participation, reinforcing a democratic vision of citizenship in a continuing process of political engagement. The use of multiple tactics of spatial occupation and civil disobedience to expose and critique state policies outside the electoral process earned this building the nickname "Peace Pentagon."

The formation, endurance, or dissolution of different groups within the Peace Pentagon reflected the political currents that roiled the nation over the last half century. By examining the projects undertaken by what A.J. Muste Institute refers to as the "movement tenants," one can see how the physical space within the building was connected to a political space outside its walls. The trajectory of actions by the building's resident groups working to create an awareness of armament, environment degradation, and social justice generated a multifaceted network of connections both nationally and globally. The building, the city, the country, and the world were connected via the mobilizations centered within this building. The various actions, marches, rallies, sit-ins, and creative forms of nonviolent civil disobedience engaged participants at different geographic scales to construct a more inclusive and variegated public sphere. Lefebvre's proposition that space is a social product and not simply a neutral container capable of producing dynamic power relations informs this reading of a small building, in effect, shaped by a larger revolutionary project.[7] The necessity of physical space to plan, exchange ideas, and pool resources made the mission of the Muste Institute as the steward of this obscure building a challenging but important contribution to the sustenance of the pacifist movement in New York City.[8] In the '90s, as activists reached out to larger audiences through mass media, the spatial boundaries of social and political engagement expanded into the global realm. Despite this shift toward a more "virtual" means of organization, the benefits of proximity and conviviality achieved in physical space continued to keep this building relevant.

2.3
War Resisters League office at 5
Beekman Street in New York City
after a raid, 1969.
Photograph by Ricky Schneider. Courtesy
of Swarthmore College Peace Collection.

RADICALS AND REAL ESTATE (1969–1974)

For several years the War Resisters League (WRL), a long-standing, anti-war organization, had occupied an office on the tenth floor of a grand building at 5 Beekman Street, near City Hall.[9] One morning in 1969 the staff of the WRL arrived to find their office had been burgled. File cabinets had been ransacked, papers lay strewn everywhere, and phone lists of contacts and affiliates were conspicuously missing from the scene (**Figure 2.3**). The disinterest of the police to investigate the crime led WRL members to surmise that the FBI was involved and that the alleged burglary that turned their work space upside down was in fact a covert raid.[10]

Being under government surveillance was par for the course for the WRL membership. The founder of the movement, Jessie Wallace Hughan, was on a list of radicals being investigated by the Overton Commission as early as 1919 for her role in organizing anti-war activities during World War I. This official antipathy toward war resisters increased as many members of the WRL refused to participate in World War II and continued to actively condemn the United States armament in the postwar period. "Being a pacifist in the 1950s was a lonely business," recalled WRL member David McReynolds.[11] The radical pacifism of the WRL and the affiliations of its members with various anarchist, socialist, and civil rights organizations were viewed by most Americans as unpatriotic at that time. This perception changed by the late '60s as opposition to the Vietnam War mounted, and the veterans from the so-called popular World War II resistance were joined by a younger anti-war, mainly student lobby. The WRL's prominent role in draft-card burning and anti-war rallies made the organization a continued target of government investigation.[12] The ongoing threat of surveillance and the potential eviction from future rented office space led the organization to seek out a more permanent safe haven.

They found their new home in a building at 339 Lafayette Street in downtown Manhattan. Built in 1922, the utilitarian three-story steel-framed structure with a yellow brick exterior was designed for "factory" use.[13] Located on a hundred-by-thirty-foot corner lot at the intersection of Bleecker and Lafayette Streets, the modest building appeared small in contrast to the surrounding neighborhood of robust six-story masonry buildings. The generous window bays on the second and third floors, facing south and west, were intended to provide ample light for workshops. The continuous glass storefronts at street level once accommodated window displays and engaged shoppers on the busy thoroughfare of Lafayette Street (**Figure 2.4**). By the end of the '60s

2.4
339 Lafayette Street, 1934.
Photograph courtesy of the New York
Public Library Digital Archives.

garages and auto parts shops had replaced the thriving streetscape at Lafayette Street. The struggling remains of manufacturing activity in the form of garment-industry sweatshops, cigar factories, and storage facilities gradually moved out of the city, and property owners sought more profitable uses for buildings in a postindustrial metropolis. This exodus by industry left the large stock of small-scale manufacturing buildings in the heart of downtown Manhattan open to new uses. These buildings, with their well-lit open spaces and inexpensive rents, attracted artists and poets as well as political dissidents who saw the raw and ill-kempt buildings as an appropriate place to experiment with new modes of living, working, and organizing.[14]

In 1969, after being evicted from their old offices, the WRL rented the top two floors of the building at 339 Lafayette Street. Two years later, during a rare moment in New York City, with the real estate market in decline and the anti-war movement in ascendance, the WRL negotiated with the owner of this same building and bought the property for a sum of sixty thousand dollars.[15] WRL staff members and volunteers removed the vestiges of a dentist's office from the second floor and celebrated their new acquisition with a party and invited their allies—the Catholic Peace Fellowship (CPF), the Liberation Magazine, the Fifth Avenue Vietnam Peace Parade Committee, and the Committee for Nonviolent Action (CNVA)—to join them as tenants within the new building.[16] The WRL, with a few full-time staff members and many part-time volunteers, occupied a majority of the second floor for the next forty-six years.[17] The Catholic Peace Fellowship, a close associate that was active within the building until 1983, occupied a portion of the third floor. Over time, the building's top two floors were partitioned along the divisions of the existing window bays into smaller offices and workrooms of different sizes to accommodate the various projects generated by the WRL, as well as to accommodate new tenants. The luncheonette and locksmith shop at street level, inherited from the previous owners, continued paying market-rate rent and provided the fledgling real estate investment of the WRL with an additional source of income.

Shortly after the move into the building, members of the WRL established the A. J. Muste Memorial Institute as a legal, nonprofit entity to accept tax deductible funding and to act as a financial conduit for the larger activist community. Named after the recently deceased and well-regarded stalwart of the pacifist movement, Abraham Johannes Muste (1885–1967), this institute had an official board which initially comprised mainly WRL members. The Muste Institute was viewed by the WRL as a "front" for the many subversive projects generated within the building.[18] In 1978 the WRL found it prudent to officially transfer the 339 Lafayette Street building over to the stewardship of the Muste Institute. The institute assumed the remaining loan on the property and paid the WRL an additional sum for the interest already accrued on the first mortgage of the property. Moving forward, the Muste Institute was tasked with managing the building, collecting rents, acting as a fiscal sponsor, and providing grants to individuals aligned with their pacifist mission. Inviting like-minded political activists to share the building established a precedent and an organizational strategy that seemed both ideologically and economically sound. The first generation of activists in the building worked somewhat interchangeably on the various peace and social justice projects generated by the leadership of the WRL. The subsidized rent offered by the Muste Institute to the "movement tenants" kept many a left-wing effort afloat. In later years—with the emergence of new perspectives—antinuclear, anti-apartheid, feminist, and environmental collectives sought out the congenial work space. New groups brought with them different and sometimes conflicting strategic and ideological convictions. Yet the activism at 339 Lafayette Street, fundamentally bound by a shared belief in social change through nonviolent action, created a solidarity within the building. In finding a new home for their own organization, the WRL had de facto established a headquarters for the radical peace and justice movement in New York City.

2.5

Continental Walk for Disarmament
and Social Justice desk on the
third floor at 339 Lafayette Street,
1976.

Photograph by Ed Hedemann.

ENGAGING THE NATION: THE CONTINENTAL WALK FOR DISARMAMENT AND SOCIAL JUSTICE (1974–1976)

> *What the map cuts up, the story cuts across.*
> —Michel de Certeau, *The Practice of Everyday Life* (1984)

The move into the building at 339 Lafayette Street coincided with the winding down of the Vietnam War—an event that galvanized strong resistance to American imperialism abroad and a lack of social and civic accountability at home. Emerging from the struggle against this war in the early '70s, WRL acted quickly to channel the energy of the movement into postwar actions. The idea that war was a symptom of broader socioeconomic problems had long been a part of the WRL's stance. The trajectory of the civil rights movement and the initial gains through nonviolent civil disobedience and the devastating violent aftermath led the WRL to not simply oppose war but rather "to strive nonviolently for the removal of all causes of war, including racism, sexism, and all forms of exploitation."[19]

With this broader goal in mind, the Continental Walk for Disarmament and Social Justice was initiated in 1974 at 339 Lafayette Street.[20] The main goal of the walk was to create public awareness of the fact that the increased militarism of the American government detracted from meeting the needs of the average citizen at home. The undertaking indicated a turn toward a national/domestic concern within a movement that had previously focused on international affairs.

To facilitate this project, a dedicated desk and phone line were set up on the building's third floor, in Room 302, directly above the WRL offices (**Figure 2.5**). A call for participation, sent to various organizations nationwide, yielded hundreds of responses from participants and volunteers. A large map of the country tacked onto the bulletin board used pins, lines, and notes to chart a complex itinerary through thirty-four states. The nine-month-long trek launched after a year and a half of intense planning and coordination began on January 23, 1976, and ended on October 18 that same year. The main route for the walk ran from the West Coast town of Ukiah in California and ended in Washington, D.C. Two independent routes, one from Boston and another from New Orleans, brought the northeastern contingent and a crucial arm of the civil rights movement—the Southern Christian Leadership Conference—into the fold (**Figure 2.6**). A core group of walkers traveled across the country along the primary route, while local participants joined the walk from their respective locations, carrying banners, props, and signs. Local churches, charities, and individuals played host to visiting activists by coordinating meetings, actions, and lectures.

Along the route, the walkers targeted crucial nuclear weapon manufacture sites to warn residents of the potential hazards of nuclear contamination. At a facility in Colorado, they released balloons tagged with the message, "This balloon was released from the Rocky Flats on April 5, 1976. If you found this balloon, you live downwind from the nuclear weapons plant at Rocky Flats where radioactive plutonium is manufactured into atom bombs parts. Plutonium has accidentally been released into our atmosphere several times in the 20 year history of the plant. To help us gather data on the radiation pollution in our area, please send this tag back to us c/o Rocky Flats Action Group."[21] Similar balloons were released from nuclear plants in Wisconsin, Massachusetts, Connecticut, and New York. The ideal of building a national community of pacifists spearheaded by the WRL linked concerns about nuclear weapons to the emerging antinuclear environmental movement.

The cross-country walk, with its multiple participants, connected the vast demography of the United States and consolidated the disparate resistance groups into a unified whole. The movement's outreach to a wider audience was an important step in promoting and disseminating

The following text appears within the balloon illustration on the map:

This balloon was released from the Rocky Flats on April 5, 1976. If you found this balloon, you live down wind from the nuclear weapons plant at Rocky Flats where radio-active plutonium is manufactured into atom bombs parts. Plutonium has accidently been released into our atmosphere several times in the 20 year history of the plant. To help us gather data on the radiation pollution in our area, please send this tag back to us c/o Rocky Flats Action Group.

2.6

Map charting the route of the Continental Walk for Disarmament and Social Justice, 1976.

Illustration by Nandini Bagchee.

Based on data and photographs published in Vickie Leonard and Tom MacLean, eds., *The Continental Walk for Disarmament and Social Justice*, 1977.

Nuclear Plants Visited
Weapon Stations Visited
Nuclear Plant Locations

WISCONSIN
Rochester
Toronto
Niagara
Madison
Wisconsin Dells
Milwaukee
Waukegan
Davenport Chicago
Gary
South Bend
Bloomington
Springfield
INDIANA
Muncie
ILLINOIS
Bloomington
St. Louis
Evansville
MISSOURI

NEW YORK
Saratoga
Worcester
Boston
Syracuse
Plymouth
Buffalo
Erie
Providence
CT
New Haven
Cleveland
New York City
Youngstown
PENNSYLVANIA
Bethlehem
Stony Brook
Toledo
Doylestown
Fort Wayne
Harrisburg
Pittsburgh
York
Philadelphia
OHIO
Hagerstown
NJ
MD
Baltimore
Washington, D.C.
Fredericksburg
Charlottesville
Richmond
VIRGINIA
Roanoke
Bristol
Winston-Salem
Rocky Mt.
Ahoskie
Oak Ridge
NORTH CAROLINA
Greenville
Knoxville
New Bern
Asheville
Charlotte
TENNESSEE
Columbia
SOUTH CAROLINA
Atlanta
Augusta
Birmingham
MISSISSIPPI
ALABAMA
GEORGIA
LOUISIANA
Jackson
Meridian
Laurel
Hattiesburg
Baton Rouge
New Orleans

the idea that the accelerating arms race had co-opted large tracts of public land and put communities across the country at risk. This social awareness of the larger landscape of the country imperiled by the nuclear-military complex produced a new spatial dimension for the anti-war movement. In contrast to the marches within the city, this longer walk, which involved considerable behind-the-scenes coordination from 339 Lafayette Street, synchronized the participation of labor unions, civil rights activists, women's rights advocates, and other groups fighting for social justice. The crooked path of the Continental Walk superimposed on the rigid outlines of state boundaries created a new story of space. By challenging the infrastructure of the nuclear arms industry, the walk yielded a new knowledge of geography and generated a support network of grassroots activism.

COALITION BUILDING AT THE PEACE PENTAGON (1979–1985)

In addition to the major cities along the east and west coasts that were already hubs of anti-war activism, the longer walk across the American continent targeted a larger and more dispersed suburban and rural constituency. In its aftermath, many local chapters of the War Resisters League emerged across the country, and the model of cooperative demonstration was seen as an effective tool in consolidating the fragmented sphere of grassroots social organization. Back in New York, new issues-based groups proliferated in adjacent desks and offices within 339 Lafayette Street. With its effective model of alliance building and its focus on nuclear disarmament, the walk triggered initiatives such as Sound-Hudson against Atomic Development (SHAD). This organization—a coalition of more than twenty groups in southern New York State concerned with nuclear proliferation—facilitated a series of large rallies and sit-ins at nuclear plants along the Long Island Sound and the Hudson River. Many of those participating in these actions were briefed in nonviolence training workshops at 339 Lafayette Street. In 1979 eighteen thousand people rallied against the construction of the Shoreham Nuclear Power Plant in Suffolk County on Long Island. More than five hundred people were arrested as they climbed over the chain-link fence to occupy the power plant in an act of civil disobedience. The resistance to Shoreham dragged on for several years, and the arduous process of litigation turned many a citizen into activists and created a groundswell of public support. After a long and contentious battle, the Shoreham plant was finally decommissioned in 1994.[22]

During the early years SHAD organized their rallies and direct actions at the Shoreham and Indian Point Nuclear Power Plants out of Room 204. Banners and flyers used in antinuclear street demonstrations carried the address 339 Lafayette Street, thus advertising the headquarters of the resistance effort (**Figure 2.7**). The group briefly shared their small office with an organization called the Solar Energy Workshop, which researched alternative energy sources. Through their proximity within the building and by collaborating on undertakings like pamphleting at rallies, these two groups linked the problems of nuclear arms production and nuclear power to broader ecological and environmental concerns.[23] In a separate but related project, WRL chairperson Norma Becker initiated the project Mobilization for Survival directly above the SHAD office. Five years later, Mobilization for Survival facilitated a coalition of antinuclear groups to organize the largest demonstration in the history of the United States. An estimated one million people gathered in Central Park and paraded down Fifth Avenue on June 12, 1982, on the eve of a special session of the

2.7
An anti–nuclear rally in New York City in 1979, with Jim Peck (WRL) holding "No Nuclear" banner. The War Resisters League banner bears the address 339 Lafayette Street.
Photograph by Dorothy Marder. Courtesy of Swarthmore College Peace Collection.

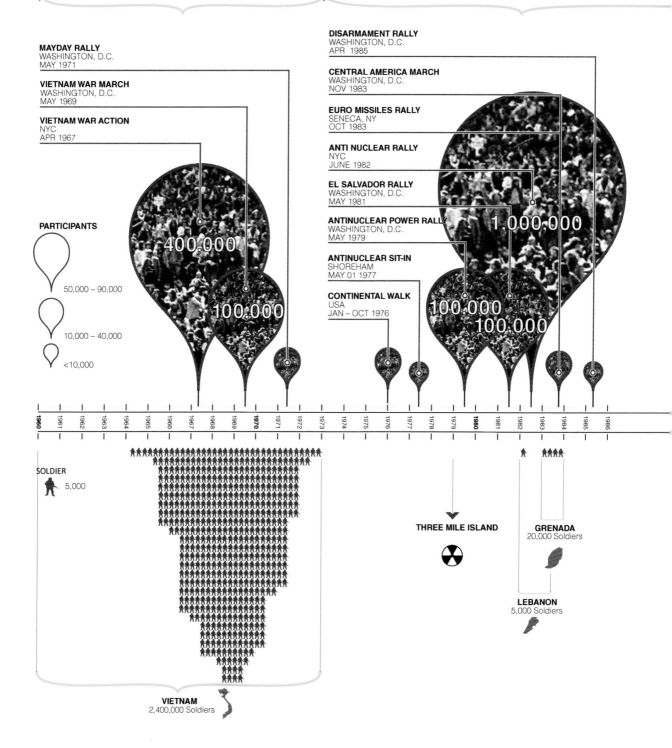

VIETNAM

ANTINUCLEAR / CENTRAL AMERICA

DISARMAMENT RALLY
WASHINGTON, D.C.
APR 1985

CENTRAL AMERICA MARCH
WASHINGTON, D.C.
NOV 1983

EURO MISSILES RALLY
SENECA, NY
OCT 1983

ANTI NUCLEAR RALLY
NYC
JUNE 1982

EL SALVADOR RALLY
WASHINGTON, D.C.
MAY 1981

ANTINUCLEAR POWER RALLY
WASHINGTON, D.C.
MAY 1979

ANTINUCLEAR SIT-IN
SHOREHAM
MAY 01 1977

CONTINENTAL WALK
USA
JAN – OCT 1976

MAYDAY RALLY
WASHINGTON, D.C.
MAY 1971

VIETNAM WAR MARCH
WASHINGTON, D.C.
MAY 1969

VIETNAM WAR ACTION
NYC
APR 1967

PARTICIPANTS

50,000 – 90,000

10,000 – 40,000

<10,000

400,000

100,000

1,000,000

100,000

100,000

1960 1961 1962 1963 1964 1965 1966 1967 1968 1969 **1970** 1971 1972 1973 1974 1975 1976 1977 1978 1979 **1980** 1981 1982 1983 1984 1985 1986

SOLDIER

5,000

THREE MILE ISLAND

GRENADA
20,000 Soldiers

LEBANON
5,000 Soldiers

VIETNAM
2,400,000 Soldiers

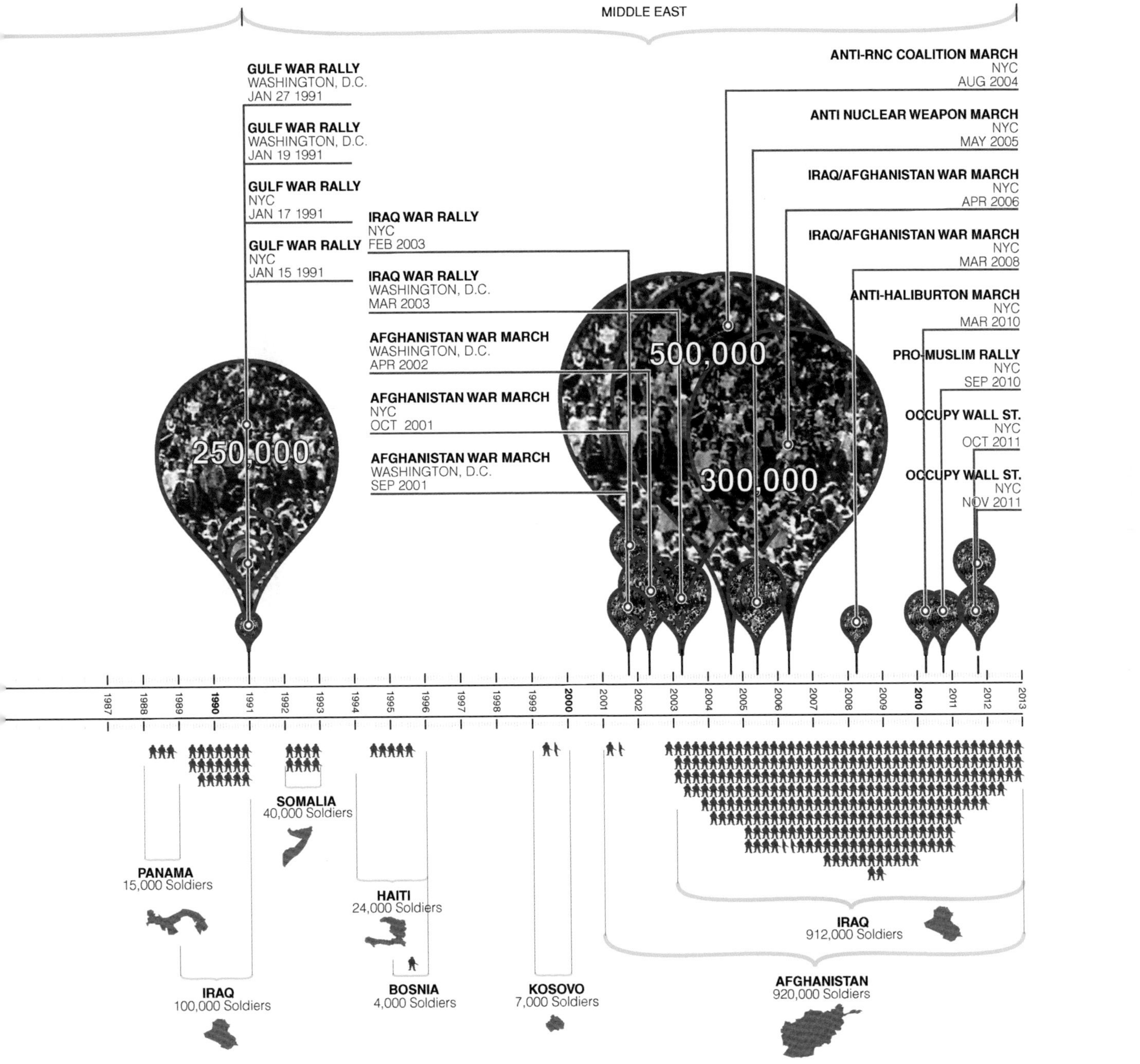

MIDDLE EAST

GULF WAR RALLY
WASHINGTON, D.C.
JAN 27 1991

GULF WAR RALLY
WASHINGTON, D.C.
JAN 19 1991

GULF WAR RALLY
NYC
JAN 17 1991

GULF WAR RALLY
NYC
JAN 15 1991

IRAQ WAR RALLY
NYC
FEB 2003

IRAQ WAR RALLY
WASHINGTON, D.C.
MAR 2003

AFGHANISTAN WAR MARCH
WASHINGTON, D.C.
APR 2002

AFGHANISTAN WAR MARCH
NYC
OCT 2001

AFGHANISTAN WAR MARCH
WASHINGTON, D.C.
SEP 2001

ANTI-RNC COALITION MARCH
NYC
AUG 2004

ANTI NUCLEAR WEAPON MARCH
NYC
MAY 2005

IRAQ/AFGHANISTAN WAR MARCH
NYC
APR 2006

IRAQ/AFGHANISTAN WAR MARCH
NYC
MAR 2008

ANTI-HALIBURTON MARCH
NYC
MAR 2010

PRO-MUSLIM RALLY
NYC
SEP 2010

OCCUPY WALL ST.
NYC
OCT 2011

OCCUPY WALL ST.
NYC
NOV 2011

250,000

500,000

300,000

1987 1988 1989 **1990** 1991 1992 1993 1994 1995 1996 1997 1998 1999 **2000** 2001 2002 2003 2004 2005 2006 2007 2008 2009 **2010** 2011 2012 2013

SOMALIA
40,000 Soldiers

PANAMA
15,000 Soldiers

HAITI
24,000 Soldiers

IRAQ
100,000 Soldiers

BOSNIA
4,000 Soldiers

KOSOVO
7,000 Soldiers

IRAQ
912,000 Soldiers

AFGHANISTAN
920,000 Soldiers

2.8

Time line of demonstrations and rallies (top) and nuclear
threats and wars (bottom) measured in terms of participants and "boots on the ground," 1960–2013.

Illustration by Nandini Bagchee.

Data for anti-war rallies from multiple news sources compiled with
assistance from Ed Hedemann. Data for wars from Military Records,
National Archives.

United Nations devoted to disarmament.[24] These numbers far exceeded those of the anti-war rallies during the Vietnam War, and the demonstration remains the single largest disarmament rally in the history of the nation. Festive protests in the park were fueled by musical events, appearances by celebrities, leafleting, and creatively designed floats and banners. Two days later, a smaller group intent on civil disobedience organized blockades and sit-ins at the United Nations Missions of five nations with nuclear capabilities (Great Britain, France, India, the Soviet Union, and the United States). These actions led to sixteen hundred arrests and made front-page news in the *New York Times*.[25]

This rally marked a watershed moment in the history of New York City, where a public park designed for recreation and an institution established to arbitrate world peace were aligned through celebration and mass demonstration. The faith-based roots of the anti-war movement, born out of conscientious objection to war, merged in post–Vietnam War America with the antinuclear and nascent environmental movement. In tandem with other antinuclear efforts in the previous decades, this event symbolized a victory for the pacifist left. In the aftermath of what grew to be a nationwide movement, the scheduled construction of several nuclear power plants was terminated in the '80s, and the Nuclear Regulatory Commission did not authorize the construction of any new plants for the next thirty years.[26]

These three main actions—the Continental Walk, the SHAD occupations of nuclear power plants, and the Mobilization for Survival rally at Central Park—demonstrate the ways that 339 Lafayette Street, with its warren of office spaces, functioned as a synergetic hub of activism connecting the city to the nation where movements formed and evolved. A time line of American involvement in wars since Vietnam, mapped against the major demonstrations[27] organized by the WRL in collaboration with other groups, in the period extending from 1969 to 2013, shows the ways in which the building helped counter the institutional history of the United States by providing a home base for individuals and organizations participating in myriad forms of nonviolent protest (**Figure 2.8**). Coalitions built around specific issues occupied offices and rented desks but then dissolved and realigned as new social and political concerns appeared within the building.

A NON-NEIGHBORHOOD AND THE BELOVED COMMUNITY (1970–1980)

> *The nonviolent resister must often express his protest through non-cooperation or boycotts, but noncooperation and boycotts are not ends themselves; they are merely means to awaken a sense of moral shame in the opponent. The end is redemption and reconciliation. The aftermath of nonviolence is the creation of the beloved community, while the aftermath of violence is tragic bitterness.*
> —Martin Luther King, Jr.

While marches, demonstrations, and spectacular acts of civil disobedience energized and invigorated the activists and members of the public, the organizing work that took place in the background, at 339 Lafayette Street, proved taxing. Describing the office during the Continental Walk in 1976, one of the event's organizers wrote, "There were times peering out the grey windows of 339 Lafayette Street to the muddy assemblage of factory buildings, local alcoholics, Jesus freaks, and streaking traffic, the Walk seemed a phantom thing."[28]

The building, located in a triangular wedge of no-man's-land to the north of Houston Street and sandwiched between Broadway and the Bowery in the '70s, was a desolate postindustrial cityscape. David McReynolds, a full-time staff member of the WRL and a longtime resident of the Lower East Side, described this stretch of land as a "non-neighborhood." By day, the auto body shops, plumbing parts, and hardware supply stores provided some semblance of business along Lafayette Street. By night, homeless people—many struggling with drug and alcohol addiction and mental illness—flocked to the Bowery looking for food and shelter. The Bowery, known for its homeless shelters, soup kitchens, and other charitable institutions for most of the twentieth century, became the visible epicenter of an emerging homelessness crisis in 1970s New York. This non-neighborhood, once the vibrant center of labor movements and an empowered working class, gradually became a catchment area of the disenfranchised and destitute population of the city.

The Peace Pentagon bore witness to the changes in its surroundings. Visible from the second-floor corner office of the Muste Institute was the elegant brick and terra-cotta office building at the corner of Lafayette and Bond Streets. This building was converted in 1970 by the Department of Social Services into a welfare center that treated mentally ill patients.[29] A block and a half away, on Third Street between the Bowery and Second Avenue, was the infamous city-run men's "intake" shelter. This large building was a center through which all the

2.9
Members of a church group handing bread to homeless men on Lafayette, across the street from the Peace Pentagon, 1977. Photograph by Ed Hedemann.

homeless male population had to pass in order to be directed to other locations in the city where they could stay for the night. As a result, this shelter alone drew thousands of homeless people to the neighborhood, many suffering from mental illness and/or substance abuse problems.[30] Unless they were confronted with extreme weather conditions, most of the homeless folk preferred the streets where they could pick their friends and associates rather than be forced into the company of the unpredictable cast of characters that were herded into a large reception lobby at the Third Street Men's Shelter.[31]

Across the street from the Peace Pentagon, a liquor store sold alcohol from behind sheets of security glass, and men and women looking for a drink and company often gathered outside to share a bottle with paper cups. The small alleyways and quiet streets around the building were a comfortable place for those in need of shelter and a place to settle in for the night. Ed Hedemann, a veteran of many sit-ins, remembers arriving at work in the offices at 339 Lafayette and having to wake up a person that had blocked the entry door.[32] His photograph captures members of a church group distributing bread to homeless men across the street from the building (**Figure 2.9**).

2.10
Igal Roodenko in the WRL office at
339 Lafayette Street, 1981.
Photograph by David McReynolds.

While the core missions of WRL and many other groups located at
339 Lafayette Street focused on international and national politics, a
few of the building's occupants were also involved more locally in volunteer work within the neighborhood. A few blocks to the east of the
Third Street Men's Shelter, the Mary House, which was set up by the
Catholic convert and social activist Dorothy Day in an old music
school, provided lodging and food to homeless women.[33] Two blocks
south on East First Street, St. Joseph's House, a similar facility with a
large soup kitchen, catered to the men. These two Catholic Worker
houses were a spiritual center for the Catholic Peace Fellowship
(CPF), headquartered at 339 Lafayette Avenue. The Catholic Worker
houses encouraged CPF staff members and other volunteers to live
communally with the homeless and help them without trying to pros-
elytize.[34] The informal housing arrangements modeled in the Mary
and St. Joseph's Houses, in which volunteers committed themselves to
communal living and spiritual sharing, formed a counterpart to the
political organizing taking place at 339 Lafayette Street.

At the other end of the spectrum of this faith-based engagement was
the secular, communitarian approach of WRL member Igal Roodenko
(**Figure 2.10**), who lived at nearby Mott Street since his release from
prison as a World War II conscientious objector. Roodenko, an

optimist despite his many arrests and incarcerations, defined a pacifist as "someone who can see a silver lining before normal people even know there are clouds around."[35] He was responsible for housing many of the extended families of anti-war activists in a carriage house which was entered through a long corridor at 217 Mott Street. Brad Lyttle, a colleague and member of the Committee for Nonviolent Action, described Roodenko's shared accommodation as a dingy building with "bad heat, bad plumbing, and bad everything."[36] The good thing was that the monthly rent of twenty-five dollars for two spacious apartments provided shelter to many an impoverished activist.[37] Lyttle lived in an adjoining tenement building and remembered the block as one known for housing people involved in the anti-war and antinuclear movements. Lyttle was also one of the early tenants who rented storefront space at the Peace Pentagon. He used this space to build props and provide sound systems for demonstrations. A 1971 photograph by Lyttle shows the storefront setup of his "Lafayette Service Company." A typist works amidst a cluttered space with a band saw, an extractor fan, a set of metal file drawers, a placard from a celebrated march to Moscow, and portraits of the revered trinity of radical pacifists—M. K. Gandhi, A. J. Muste, and M. L. King (**Figure 2.11**). The philosophic, the revolutionary, and the quotidian aspects of the pacifist movement thus converged within the interior of this "light manufacturing" building. Cheap rents and fellowship allowed the activists to remain politically engaged, even as the substandard living and working conditions in the run-down tenements and ill-maintained former factories were not comfortable to their everyday existence.

The camaraderie and tolerance, long cultivated by a beleaguered left, carried over to the Vietnam Era newcomers like Joanne Sheehan, who moved to New York in 1970 to work on the defense for the draft-board raids. Sheehan worked with the CPF in Room 304 at the Peace Pentagon, and along with other young pacifists involved in the anti-war movement, she lived in what she referred to as a "communal house" on Avenue C and Seventh Street.[38] Sheehan was impressed with the multigenerational community within the building and the diverse skill sets—of artists, typesetters, writers, and builders—that contributed to the creative resistance actions fomenting within the building.[39] This mixture of civic purpose, collective responsibility, and conviviality per-meated the lives of the staff members and volunteers at the Peace Pentagon.

The tenants working out of 339 Lafayette Street, or sometimes simply using the convenient downtown location as a meeting place, over the years built a network of activist connections that expanded through a system of personal relationships and lifelong commitments. This structure was fluid, as individuals engaged in more than one project and could, in fact, belong to a variety of affinity groups, thus bringing different associates and resources into the building. The WRL has been referred to as a "halfway house of social movements," and this characteristic of the organization was transferred to the building itself. Throughout the '70s, the early round of tenants worked in adjacent offices, lived within walking distance of the Peace Pentagon, and knew one another. As issues surfaced and interests unfolded, an office or desk was created in support of a new undertaking. This ad hoc method of accumulating tenants and forging new alliances with the WRL at the center helped to form a "beloved community" within a city and a neighborhood that appeared outwardly inhospitable.

ARTISTS AT THE PEACE PENTAGON (1980–1982)

This loose organizing structure began to change in the '80s as the run-down area along the Bowery and Lafayette Street, full of large com-mercial spaces, became attractive to artists, theaters, art galleries, and eventually posh boutiques and restaurants. The influx of artists and art institutions, experienced at first as a countercultural development in the Greenwich Village, SoHo, and Tribeca areas, ultimately brought the attention of the city and developers to these areas. Large-scale abandonment and speculation due to city policy caused real estate values to escalate, ultimately pushing the younger wave of artists drawn to these neighborhoods further east in search of affordable living and work space.[40] Despite its central location and proximity to desirable SoHo, the neighborhood around the Bowery and the non-neighborhood north of Houston Street, later re-named NoHo, continued to elude investors well into the '90s. The presence of single residency hotels, shelters, and missions that catered to the homeless population of the city kept property values relatively low in this sliver of a city between the East and West Villages. Taking advantage of the relatively low commercial rents along the Bowery and Lafayette Street, many bulk restaurant supply stores cropped up in the neighborhood, creating a dystopian streetscape where the homeless hustled to eke out an existence amidst stainless steel appliances, pots, pans, and china. These changes outside the building coincided with several of the older tenants moving out of the city or simply closing shop as long-standing projects came to an end. With the responsibility of a mortgage and a building with deferred maintenance on their hands, the Muste Institute struggled to find new tenants and evict some that, despite many concessions, failed to pay their rent.

Amidst this slowly shifting commercial terrain and in synch with the growing art scene, Karen DiGia, an activist and collector of protest art, initiated a project she called "Gallery 345 Art for Social Change" in a vacant ground-floor space at the Peace Pentagon. Karen DiGia's curation of exhibitions, such as the "Radical Theater in America" and "Children in Crisis," focused on works that had explicitly political content or highlighted social problems.[41] These temporary shows were intended to educate the public and provoke discussion about issues involving social justice and to highlight the often-invisible mission of the building to a larger, more local audience. By locating the gallery at street level, DiGia provided a downtown venue to explore the breadth of artists' contributions to the broader peace and justice movements by linking to prescient issues and changes taking place in the city at that time. In an interview, Karen DiGia emphasized the educational intention of this enterprise, and the events and gatherings in the gallery attracted the attention of artists in the neighborhood seeking more meaningful ways to engage with politics in their work.[42]

In the '80s, with the rise of conservative politics in the city and the cutbacks in federal funding on social services, a more critical, self-aware generation of countercultural artists found fertile ground in which to produce a new type of politicized art. The art critic Lucy

Lippard, at the vanguard of activist practices, invited artists to discuss the need to document and support the production of various politically engaged artists across the country. In 1980 the group Political Art Documentation/Distribution (PAD/D) grew out of this discussion "to provide artists with an organized relationship to society."[43] The mission of PAD/D was to archive political artworks and to invest in the production of new work around emerging social issues.[44] In May 1981 PAD/D organized a project called "Death and Taxes" and held an opening of this show at Gallery 345 on Lafayette Street. A year later in 1982 they rented Room 301, a space facing Bleecker Street at the Peace Pentagon. This move into the building was partially motivated by the logistics of a central location and low rent. However, as the editorial in the PAD/D newsletter *Upfront* titled "Fanning the Spark" states, the collective aspired to "create a new audience for the new forms developing from collaboration between social groups and artists—an audience combining both constituencies."[45] By moving into the Peace Pentagon, this collective of artists had the possibility of engaging more directly with the movement groups with a longer history of political mobilization.

Artists and performance collectives, such as the Bread and Puppet Theater, have traditionally contributed to political movements by producing protest props, signs, posters, and banners.[46] This type of participation, visualizing the movement message, is a time-honored tradition of artists' activism. Initially, PAD/D artists followed this familiar trope and created posters and joined demonstrations in the '80s, protesting the urban policies of Mayor Koch locally and the Reagan administration on the national front.[47] Some members of PAD/D sought a different means to use their specific skills as image-makers— one that went beyond the format of a march or propaganda poster—to create a subversive intervention that used space more tactically and spontaneously. To this end, they invited artists to participate in a project titled "Death and Taxes" in the spring of 1981.[48] For this action, PAD/D solicited artists' proposals to create unsanctioned public works to draw attention to the fact that vast sums of federal tax dollars were being allocated to military spending in lieu of social programs.

The opposition to tax revenues being spent on war and the refusal of individuals to pay a large portion of the taxes that fund war have a long history within the larger anti-war movement within the United States.[49] What better way to get the attention of a government than to stop paying your taxes? Each fiscal year the WRL publishes a "Tax Pie Chart," showing the large chunk of tax money assigned to war and war-related undertakings. The aim of this exercise is to convince citizens to refuse to pay taxes which, through the many presidencies, have

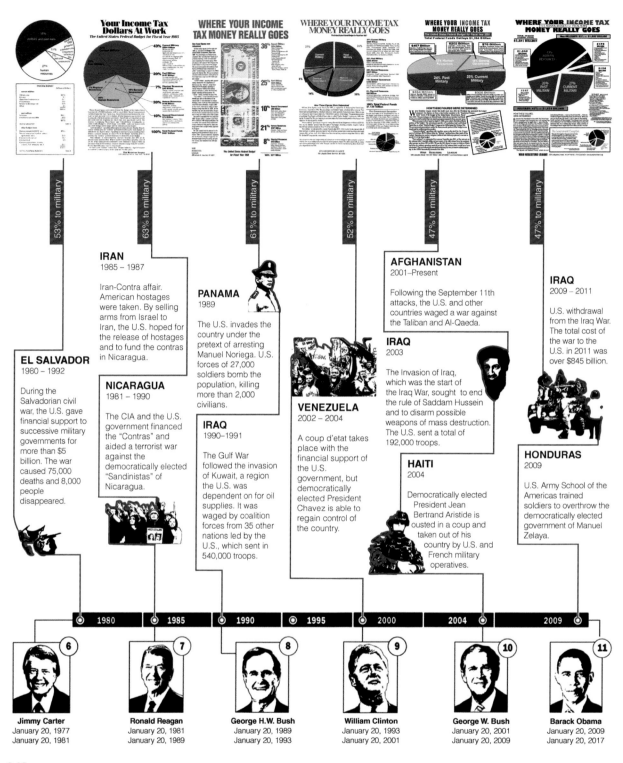

53% to military

63% to military

61% to military

52% to military

47% to military

47% to military

IRAN
1985 – 1987

Iran-Contra affair. American hostages were taken. By selling arms from Israel to Iran, the U.S. hoped for the release of hostages and to fund the contras in Nicaragua.

PANAMA
1989

The U.S. invades the country under the pretext of arresting Manuel Noriega. U.S. forces of 27,000 soldiers bomb the population, killing more than 2,000 civilians.

AFGHANISTAN
2001–Present

Following the September 11th attacks, the U.S. and other countries waged a war against the Taliban and Al-Qaeda.

IRAQ
2009 – 2011

U.S. withdrawal from the Iraq War. The total cost of the war to the U.S. in 2011 was over $845 billion.

EL SALVADOR
1980 – 1992

During the Salvadorian civil war, the U.S. gave financial support to successive military governments for more than $5 billion. The war caused 75,000 deaths and 8,000 people disappeared.

NICARAGUA
1981 – 1990

The CIA and the U.S. government financed the "Contras" and aided a terrorist war against the democratically elected "Sandinistas" of Nicaragua.

IRAQ
1990–1991

The Gulf War followed the invasion of Kuwait, a region the U.S. was dependent on for oil supplies. It was waged by coalition forces from 35 other nations led by the U.S., which sent in 540,000 troops.

VENEZUELA
2002 – 2004

A coup d'etat takes place with the financial support of the U.S. government, but democratically elected President Chavez is able to regain control of the country.

IRAQ
2003

The Invasion of Iraq, which was the start of the Iraq War, sought to end the rule of Saddam Hussein and to disarm possible weapons of mass destruction. The U.S. sent a total of 192,000 troops.

HAITI
2004

Democratically elected President Jean Bertrand Aristide is ousted in a coup and taken out of his country by U.S. and French military operatives.

HONDURAS
2009

U.S. Army School of the Americas trained soldiers to overthrow the democratically elected government of Manuel Zelaya.

| 1980 | 1985 | 1990 | 1995 | 2000 | 2004 | 2009 |

6 **Jimmy Carter**
January 20, 1977
January 20, 1981

7 **Ronald Reagan**
January 20, 1981
January 20, 1989

8 **George H.W. Bush**
January 20, 1989
January 20, 1993

9 **William Clinton**
January 20, 1993
January 20, 2001

10 **George W. Bush**
January 20, 2001
January 20, 2009

11 **Barack Obama**
January 20, 2009
January 20, 2017

2.12
Time line of the United States presidents, their support of wars, and tax pie charts published by the War Resisters League, 1980–2013.

Illustration by Nandini Bagchee.
Pie chart from War Resisters League. Time line of conflicts from multiple news sources.

been funneled toward unjust wars. Ed Hedemann and Ruth Benn, makers of this pie chart, explain how the U.S. government assigns a fictitiously low percentage to the military budget by excluding debts from past wars, money spent on defense contractors, veterans' benefits, and other items directly related to military spending (**Figure 2.12**).[50]

Drawing inspiration from this age-old form of anti-war activism, twenty artists responded to the call to participate in "Death and Taxes." They placed their works in publicly accessible spaces, such as subways, restaurant toilets, post offices, and banks, with the express purpose of confronting people where they least expected to find political messages (**Figure 2.13**).[51] A particularly subversive project by the artist Micki McGee altered standard IRS 1099 forms and then mixed them in with official forms provided to the public at H & R Block, banks, and post offices in downtown Manhattan. In the columns meant to report income were silhouettes of tankers, fighter jets, bombs, and marching soldiers, and at the bottom of the form the words "Can you afford a war?" were typewritten in by the artist. On the second page, another line of type asked, "How would your life be different if your taxes went to . . . ," and then listed a series of choices that included "public transportation instead of aircraft carriers, daycare instead of the draft, and alternative energy research instead of strategic nuclear arms." Unsuspecting New Yorkers picked up these forms only to discover that they were being asked to reconsider the use of their income taxes.

In the weeks approaching April 15, the war tax resisters are conspicuously visible with anti-tax/anti-war signs on large sandwich boards, leafleting and distributing the tax pie chart on the steps of the post office, City Hall, and IRS offices around the city. The PAD/D artwork, by contrast, exposed this same issue more surreptitiously by locating their work in the unexpected junctures of daily life. By altering the tax forms in an ad hoc way and by placing them in banks and post offices, the artists laid claim to the public through the co-option of space within these institutions. An installation in an abandoned lot, stickers in restaurant toilets, and a projection on an armory building turned the everyday space of urban experience into a forum for spontaneous dissent. In a slide presentation held at Gallery 345 on April 18, 1981, the artists shared the reactions of the passersby to the various works. These early collaborations brought PAD/D into 339 Lafayette Street and introduced a new generation of conceptually oriented artists to the established movement groups within it. Unlike the early period of political movements discussed in Chapter 1, there was no organic cohesion and collaboration between activists and artists. In New York, the idea of political art as a separate entity rather than an embedded

2.13
PAD/D Project Death and Taxes, 1981.
Image from PAD/D: First Issue, May–June 1981, no 2.

Tito's Incubator, "The Tax Shelter" was constructed in an abandoned city lot next to Anne's house on 13th Street and Avenue A. It consisted of army tank camouflage nets over which was sewn a hand-painted 2-D Tyrannosaurus Rex skeleton in fluorescent pink vinyl. The finished canopy was approximately 30 x 50 feet and stretched from the top of the adjacent building to poles that we erected in the lot. A hand painted "construction site" sign on the fence (in English and Spanish) explained the imaginary shelter, which was called "Skeletal Estates—the very best in underground living." People were encouraged to invest their money in underground condos that looked very much like bomb shelters or coffins. Many people thought we were actually building them. Others didn't understand the piece. But most people loved the dinosaur, and thought it made the block beautiful and famous.

Anne Pitrone and Thomas Masaryk

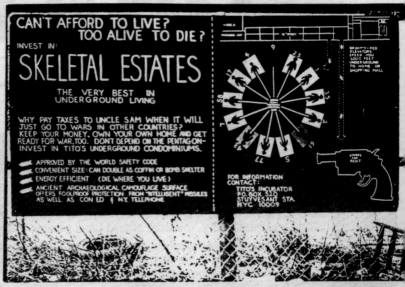

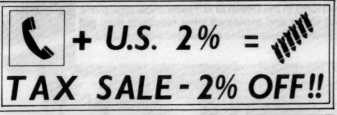

Tax Sale—2% Off, This piece was constructed to be installed on 250 public telephone units within New York City. The purpose was to inform people that a 2% tax is issued and collected by the telephone company for the IRS for the government's use specifically for the military.

Lyn Hughes

Other participants: Stan Baker **"The Human Television"**, Washington Square Park; Rudolf Baranick, **"Death"** (poster); Patrick Brennan, **"Defensive Discourses"**, Union Square East; Edward Eisenberg, **"The 1040 Bomber"** (poster); D.A.R. **"In God We Trust"**, (poster) South and John Streets; Roberta Handler, **"Unfare Subway Tax"**; Donna Henes **"Chants/Chance for Peace"**, performance at the IRS building (Church and Murray Streets" at noon on April 15 to coincide with rally by the War Resisters League at noon; Ellen Levine, **"Children, Animals, Guns and Money"**, (poster); **Women's Pentagon Action Street Theatre,** April 12 starting at noon in front of 339 Lafayette Street and touring the village, Lower East Side and Lower Manhattan.

War on the Armory: A 30 x 20 foot image projected from my bedroom window onto the 167th regiment armory at 26 Street and Lexington Avenue in New York City. This projected image alternated with the image of the work "Remember...". Slides went on approximately three hours every evening, and are still going on every night. Reactions range from sidewalk cheers to rotten fruit thrown at the window.
Tim Rollins

One thousand altered 1040 and 1040A forms informing taxpayers that over 50% of their tax dollar goes to military/defense spending were intermixed with unaltered tax forms and left at eight banks and savings and loan offices in downtown Manhattan from April 5-15, 1981 for taxpayers to inadvertently carry home. **Micki McGee**

53¢ of every U.S. tax dollar goes to military and defense budgets...
...over half your tax dollar...

Can you afford another war?

How would your life be different if your taxes went to...

public transportation instead of aircraft carriers

daycare instead of the draft

national health insurance instead of military surveillance

alternative energy research instead of strategic nuclear arms

housing and food subsidies instead of past war debts

the arts and humanities instead of artillery

Half this note could be used to improve your cities. . .it will be used instead, to improve the military

The idea of putting the stickers in bathrooms was, frankly, to get a captive audience; they were put at eye level on the backs of doors of toilet stalls (for women; men's were on the wall above the toilet) in Manhattan, The Bronx, and Brooklyn, I only saw one response-a woman in a restaurant who came out chuckling.
Lucy Lippard

DON'T PISS AWAY YOUR TAXES ON MILITARY SHIT WITHHOLD A SYMBOLIC DOLLAR. BETTER WELFARE THAN WARFARE

Blood Money; I wanted to do a chain letter, but what better way for mass communication than money. It passes through everyone's hands. (50 dollar bills were written on, with the same statement.)
Liliana Dones

presence within the movement staking its own tactical ground was, in effect, one that was fomented as an alternative to museum- and market-controlled institutionalized art practices.[52] The particular attempt of PAD/D to engage directly with the activist agendas and tactics while maintaining an interest in an autonomous art practice distinguished this collective.

While the Peace Pentagon often created synergistic relationships between old and new radical organizations, these relationships were not without conflict and requisite negotiation. Even as Karen DiGia brought interested artists from the outside, the support for Gallery 345 Art for Social Change was lukewarm within the building. Beset by financial difficulties, at the time, some within the Muste Institute board argued that the lower storefronts should be reserved exclusively for market-rate commercial tenants to generate income for the building.[53] Perhaps the commodification of art, the galleries, and the heterogeneous art scene unfolding in the Lower East Side was viewed by 339 Lafayette's old guard with skepticism. They welcomed the artists' participation in marches and the display of creative artwork and design input into the production of calendars, posters, and graphic magazine art. They also welcomed the generous support of established artists, such as Donald Judd, who occasionally raised money through art benefits for the movement.[54] However, the board members of the Muste Institute were not certain how the novel tactics deployed by the '80s artists were an asset to the overall agenda of the movement.

WHISTLE-BLOWING ON CABLE TV (1982–1991)

By 1983, four years after its initiation, Gallery 345 Art for Social Change made way for an old furniture shop that remained in place at street level for the next twenty-five years. Despite the closure of the Gallery, the PAD/D artists' collective became a part of the building and remained active until 1988. They initiated a "No Nukes" window display at the Peace Pentagon on the eve of the Nuclear Disarmament UN Session in 1982 and got acquainted with the movement tenants. The tenures within the building it seems were, as always, a reflection and response to the socioeconomic culture in the surrounding neighborhood as well as the national and global events that engaged the movement tenants.

2.14
Video frames from Paper Tiger TV, "Ann Marie Buitrago Reads Agents' Names Censored by the U.S. Congress, 1982."

In the '80s, with Ronald Reagan as president, covert proxy wars and a divide-and-conquer policy allowed the United States to intervene in the Middle East and to aid repressive regimes and militias in South America. Officially not at war, the U.S. government funded death squads in El Salvador, and when the news of the funding surfaced, it caused a national outcry among human rights activists. New U.S.-based organizations formed in solidarity with the popular uprisings in El Salvador and Nicaragua. Within the building, the Nicaraguan Solidarity Network of Greater New York supported the Sandinista Revolution and opposed U.S. aid to the counterrevolutionary military movement—the Contras. As hundreds of activists in the United States and Central America went missing, Ann Marie Buitrago, chairperson of the Fund for Open Information and Accountability, housed in Room 302 of the Peace Pentagon, worked for the release of the pertinent documents using the federal Freedom of Information Act.[55] Her whistle-blowing and dogged drafting of appeals in 1982 revealed that the U.S. government had surveilled more than two hundred groups that were critical of the government's involvement in Central America.[56] As Buitrago completed her project and prepared her report, she also participated in a public-access television project, "Ann Marie Buitrago Reads Agents' Names Censored by the U.S. Congress, 1981"[57] (**Figure 2.14**). This video project was produced by the video collective Paper Tiger TV (PTTV), at the time a sub-tenant of the Fund for Open Information and Accountability. Along with office space, the two groups shared the common agenda of making critical information available to the larger public. Public-access cable channels became available in the '60s, when private companies brokered deals with the government to lay their underground cables alongside other public utilities. In exchange for this private use of public land, the cable companies provided public-access television channels. It took another decade for artists and activists, such as PTTV, to exploit this medium to its full political potential. Using low-budget video footage shot with readily available VHS technology, the collective members sought to create a greater consumer awareness and to provide critical commentary on the news.

PTTV's early collaborations grew out of the "Communications Update," a weekly cable television show initiated by the video artist Liza Béar. In one segment of this show, Herbert Schiller, a renowned media critic, read articles from popular news sources, commenting on the form and content of the reportage and pointing out the underlying political biases and assumptions of the writers as he went along[58] (**Figure 2.15**). This quick and easy format for dissecting corporately controlled print media expanded as other known artists, judges, and intellectuals were invited to "read" such publications as *Vogue*, *Newsday*, *Artforum*, and *USA Today*. The series was taped in a rented studio, with hand-drawn backdrops that evoked familiar urban settings. The subway car, the view out of an apartment window, and an old apartment boiler room were rendered in a populist cartoon style by the

artists of PTTV. The clownish antics of the participants and the hand-made aesthetic of the productions that included a roaring paper tiger rendered the serious content quirky and accessible.[59]

In 1983, with Buitrago's project finished, PTTV took over the entire corner office on the third floor above the WRL. Here the video collective met, generated ideas for new projects, and did postproduction work. The working groups were small, dynamic, and effective. They worked on a voluntary basis and produced alternative newscasts every day. Soon, their office space was piled high with tapes to process and mail to public-access networks nationwide. To keep up with the furious pace of production and dissemination, they formed a separate distribution arm called Deep Dish TV (DDTV). Their catchphrase "Don't Just Watch TV, Make It" spurred both ordinary citizens and media activists to participate in collective video productions by sending footage of their work to Room 302 at 339 Lafayette Street.[60] In addition to distributing the works of PTTV and other emerging media collectives, DDTV began collaging clips from multiple sources to reflect different perspectives on issues ranging from war to health care. Over time, using the more flexible emerging technologies, DDTV began uploading content via satellite to local public-access networks.

COUNTERING MEDIA DISINFORMATION
(1990–2001)

With the fall of the Berlin Wall in 1989 and the dissolution of the Soviet Union in 1991, the anti-communist propaganda that had long been the pretext for U.S. military vigilance appeared outmoded. With this shift, the activism that had contextualized the activities of the WRL since their move to the Peace Pentagon during the Vietnam War also shifted course. With the arms buildup that defined the U.S. military-industrial complex firmly in place, and the Soviet Union no longer acting as a buffer to its global ambitions, the United States boldly asserted a militaristic agenda in the Middle East. The quest for control over the world's largest energy reserves made this region the focus of a new geopolitical warfare.

In 1991, a pivotal moment in the global history of conflict, the U.S.-led coalition forces authorized by the United Nations launched a series of airstrikes against former ally Iraq in retaliation to its invasion and annexation of Kuwait. The broadcasts leading up to this war and the war itself, transmitted via global satellite, presented a highly mediated image of U.S. intervention in the Middle East. Dramatically billed as "Operation Desert Storm," and broadcast live on mainstream news and media outlets, this war purportedly allowed viewers access to the frontlines as Iraqi cities were bombed, and U.S. troops moved swiftly across the desert, followed by journalists armed with videos and cameras.

In response to this first-of-its-kind reportage of a war, with live coverage provided by embedded official reporters, PTTV embarked on a series of programs to counter what DeeDee Halleck, founding member of PTTV, describes as "media disinformation."[61] The result, a ten-part video series entitled the "Gulf Crisis TV Project," was created through a collaboration of local and international video activists. This informative documentary project began by examining the history of the Gulf region, went on to document the dissent on the home front, and finally, recorded the losses, grief, and anger of the Iraqi people as the armed assault ended.[62] The network of television activists nurtured by PTTV and its distributing arm, DDTV, participated in this undertaking. The videos sent to the group's offices on Lafayette Street and spliced together by the volunteer videographers in Room 302 formed a collective record of the deep opposition to this short but devastating war.

Within the building, this project allowed a rare degree of collaboration between PTTV and the WRL, and a fifty-foot-long banner bearing

2.16
"Talks, Not Troops!," Peace
Pentagon during the Gulf War,
1991.
Photograph by Ed Hedemann.

the words "Talks, Not Troops!" was strung from the parapet of the
building (**Figure 2.16**). The words echoed the long-cherished goal of
the WRL and the raison d'être of the Muste Institute to use words and
persuasion rather than force to dissipate conflict. The Gulf War programming aired by PTTV promoted the war-resistance activities
taking place in the building, such as the nonviolence training, the GI
hotline in support of soldiers refusing to fight, and war tax resistance.
DeeDee Halleck observed that "WRL, while a cordial neighbor for
over five years, had scarcely taken notice of our media work, as it did
not fall within the standard Left classifications of "organizing." However, with the coming of the war, we began collaborating on many
aspects of the anti-war activities, exchanging information and
resources on a daily basis."[63] The realization that a collective of video
producers could be active organizers and that television could be a
vehicle of mobilization helped PTTV gain respect in the eyes of its
old-school neighbors on the left.

Equally important, the dedication to a common cause of many participants outside the building once again created a unity of purpose
within the building, reaffirming the status of the Peace Pentagon as a
headquarter of the peace and justice movement. The documentation of
diverse voices and opinions via the medium of video, followed by the
dispersion of these voices and opinions through satellite networks,

helped usher in a new era of DIY media. Through its coverage of the war, PTTV created an alternate communications network that challenged the singular narrative of the war being broadcast on mainstream media outlets. The repercussions of this brief but potent war, as captured in the "Gulf Crisis TV Project," continue to serve as a powerful account of public dissent.

Throughout the decade of the '90s the national psyche was lulled into complacency as the economy picked up. In this period New York City emerged as a prime global city centered on its insurance and real estate economy. The price of oil dropped down to a historic low by the end of the decade, and everyone seemed to outwardly benefit from this state of affairs. Even as the fast-paced globalization and emerging communications brought everything closer, the gap between the rich and poor increased exponentially. The 1993 truck bomb detonation in the basement of the World Trade Center in New York City, seen as a one-off act of terrorism, was a signal of more to come. The Gulf War, after all, had lasted a mere hundred days with minimum casualties for the allied western forces. The memory of this invasion was brought

2.17
Response to September 11th World Trade Center bombing, 2001.
Photograph by Ed Hedemann.

home afresh as two hijacked American Airline planes full of passengers were deliberately flown into the World Trade Center in New York's financial district on September 11th, 2001.

Murray Rosenblith, executive director of the Muste Institute (1985–2008), along with colleagues, stood on the roof of the Peace Pentagon that morning and watched with sadness as the second tower of the World Trade Center collapsed before their eyes. Two days later a sign painted by volunteers at the *Catholic Worker* and fastened to the metal railing by members of the Nicaraguan Solidarity Network appeared on the roof bearing the words, "An eye for an eye makes the whole world blind"[64] (**Figure 2.17**). The banner, hung toward the Bleecker Street side of the building, confronting the iconic New York skyline, minus the fallen towers, was cautionary rather than didactic. It steered passersby away from President Bush's declaration of the "War on Terror" toward the Gandhian notion that violence begets more violence.

The national mood following the attacks of September 11th was initially somber, as vigils and marches paid tribute to those affected by the tragic loss of life. But within two months, the deployment of troops in Afghanistan presaged the beginning of what became the longest war in United States history. Despite strong and continuous opposition to this war, the actions of protestors failed to attract the kind of front-page attention that the activism of the '60s had garnered. With the passage of the Patriot Act in October, a few weeks after the attacks, a new and increasingly intrusive means of government surveillance of citizens and foreigners was put into effect. The role of local police expanded in the name of public safety and resulted in greater restrictions in the streets and homes across the country. Despite large turnouts to oppose the retaliatory wars in Afghanistan and Iraq, the occupation of public space to express opposition to war appears to have receded in the public imagination. State and local police became adept at managing crowds and mainstream media at ignoring them.

LIVE-STREAMING ONLINE (2011–2015)

There are, however, moments when a certain energy and momentum coalesce at a particular time and place, and the movements that have maintained themselves in the city through the patience and fortitude of a few are suddenly rekindled in the many. Such was the case on September 17, 2011, a whole decade after the World Trade Center bombing, when a younger generation of activists camped out in Zuccotti Park in downtown Manhattan to bring public attention to the crises within the global financial community. Their grievance was that the majority (99 percent) remained locked with debt and financial insecurity while corporate finance flourished. This action, known as Occupy Wall Street, was part of a worldwide movement, as multiple sites across the globe were occupied to launch a call for economic justice. Social media was instrumental in building up this new type of collective opposition, as real-time footage and actions on the ground were shared electronically to produce solidarity among a dispersed political community. The newly formed media collective Global Revolution TV documented these activities in New York City by collecting and uploading a continuous stream of videos from the events unfolding at Zuccotti Park and making them accessible to viewers globally. For the most part, this two-month-long occupation progressed in an orderly fashion with the mechanism of impromptu General Assemblies fashioned to make collective decisions for what was consciously billed as a leaderless movement. David Graeber, one of many voices for this movement, viewed the "kitchens, libraries, clinics, media centers and a host of other institutions, all operating on anarchist principles of mutual aid and self-organization—a genuine attempt to create the institutions of a new society in the shell of the old."[65]

During the occupation, Global Revolution TV worked on battery-powered laptops within the park, using "hotspots" to connect to the wireless network. However, rain, police harassment, and the constant loss of equipment eventually required them to find a more stable indoor option. A contact through DDTV led to a small office on the second floor of 339 Lafayette Street.[66] Global Revolution TV was grateful for the proximity of the office to the encampment site but also maintained a more extensive setup at a collective loft space in Bushwick, Brooklyn. In 2012, in a familiar case of history repeating itself, Global Revolution TV's live-work quarters in Bushwick were raided by the police, thereby making Room 204 at 339 Lafayette Street a semi-permanent home for an itinerant population of live streamers.

Four years after its formation, Global Revolution TV had more than a hundred contributing members with an avowed commitment to be a leaderless movement.[67] These members, known by the quality of their tweets and short videos, were dispersed in Syria, Turkey, Yemen, Spain, and the United States, with followers around the globe. The collective comes alive when political crisis necessitates political action and broadcast. Such was the case on November 24, 2014, when a grand jury in St. Louis County declined to indict the police officer responsible for the fatal shooting of Michael Brown in Ferguson, Missouri. The small office at Lafayette Street, chock-full of cables, servers, monitors, keyboards, and sleeping bags, was a hive of activity as sleep-deprived collective members made sure that events related to #BlackLivesMatter were fed to their Twitter and Facebook followers.

Global Revolution TV saw itself as organizationally different from the other, more traditional leftist organizations that shared the building on Lafayette Street. It was run entirely by volunteers, and there was no active fund-raising or community building, although donations for items such as equipment were gratefully accepted. Spinning out of the Occupy movement, Global Revolution TV sought to create a process, a new way to use their dispersed base of volunteers to work on multiple platforms through virtual communication.[68] In this regard, they differed from the issue-based whistle-blowing associated with the earlier generation of activists.

Despite the growing importance of the Internet and social media to organizing and movement building, the emergent electronic commons still relied on a centrally located physical office in New York City. Urban sociologist Saskia Sassen's hypothesis that space within the globally networked city becomes even more important as it affords the opportunity to create privileged nodes to control the global economy applies to both global corporations and the groups that criticize them.[69] Observers of recent technological changes have pointed to the continuing importance of physical place as a location in which to express dissent. Given the wider geographies of resistance and the cultural heterogeneity of organizing, some argue that this space needs to be reimagined creatively through insurgent occupations.[70] Despite this call for temporality, a strength of many grassroots movements within the real estate–driven economy of New York is that they have always counted on the more stable left-leaning institutions such as the Muste Institute to help them survive. At the best of times, these new and sometimes short-lived initiatives challenged and brought more vitality to the building in a continual process of making and remaking the space.

WAGING PEACE FROM WORK DESKS: 1969–2016

> *There is no way to peace. Peace is the way.*
> —A. J. Muste

This often-quoted saying by A. J. Muste summarizes the aspirations of the early generation of activists at the Peace Pentagon, whose commitments to the movement were lifelong and integrated into their daily lives. They hoped to convince by personal example, and they sought to build a small but potent social movement in opposition to the prevailing values of a democracy driven purely by economic imperatives. Muste's call for "peace" is therefore an ultimate form of resistance, critical to the implementation of a grassroots democracy. To this end, grants, communal housing, and side jobs that did not compromise one's personal ethics subsidized the work of the first generation of organizers that headquartered at 339 Lafayette Street. For the radical pacifists constituting what was seen as the "new left" in the '60s, the ideal of peace was not simply a tactical alternative to war but a way to create a new and, thus, revolutionary society. This type of nonviolent revolution has long been influenced philosophically by the Gandhian concept of Satyagraha, but it has been shaped more specifically by the experience of the civil rights and anti-war movements in the United States in the '60s and the personalist politics emerging from countercultural movements at the same time.[71]

With the end of the Vietnam War in 1974, new suborganizations such as the Continental Walk sprouted within 339 Lafayette Street to bring attention to emerging issues and to voice different perspectives. After that walk, as WRL grew, one of the core concerns was to eradicate racism and sexism, beginning with the male-dominated, mainly white leadership within the pacifist organizations that emerged after the Vietnam War.[72] At the Peace Pentagon, feminist perspectives against patriarchy combined with the antinuclear movement to form the ecofeminist movement in the '80s.

Four decades later, in a bright yellow cubicle (**Figure 2.18**) within the WRL office, Ali Issa, WRL's national field organizer, spoke of a renewed push toward inclusivity and the need to expand and sustain a movement whose anti-war message is pertinent in an era in which the nation is engaged in a seemingly endless war with an elusive enemy: global terrorism.[73] In this brave new world, the concept of the community is ever more fragmented. Issa seems to support the nonhierarchical structure of the Occupy movement. He describes his job as an organizer to get himself out of the task of "organizing" by empowering others to take over the projects.[74] He sits in the cubicle formerly occupied by Ralph DiGia, who was a member of the WRL staff for fifty-two years and ran the organization's office at Lafayette Street until his retirement in 1996. DiGia was the embodiment of the dedicated pacifist, appearing at the office every morning and rarely missing a march, a rally, or a demonstration well into his nineties. His commitment to the movement dated back to 1941, when he refused induction into the military and spent three years in prison for refusing to participate in World War II as a secular conscientious objector.[75]

2.18
Ali Issa's (National Field Organizer, WRL) work desk— formerly Ralph DiGia's desk, 2014.

Photograph © Jade Doskow.

With its profusion of anti-war posters, pamphlets, buttons, and other political paraphernalia, the WRL office seemed to be a visual archive of four decades of activism rather than a functioning office. Lined up against a wall were shallow shelves displaying books, pamphlets, and other literature. *The Handbook for Nonviolent Action* and *War Tax Resistance,* two best-selling political how-to books, shared space with collections of polemical essays by renowned pacifists like Jeannette Rankin, A. J. Muste, Barbara Deming, and Dr. Martin Luther King, Jr. Above these shelves hung posters that highlighted the various WRL campaigns against war, poverty, and the penal system. Literature, WRL calendars, posters, buttons, and stickers were all for sale. The promotional volunteer work at the office involved processing orders for merchandise. These sales, membership dues, and endowments constituted the bulk of the organization's income over the years. In February 2015, the group had a full-time staff of four people—an office manager, a bookkeeper, and two field organizers. In addition, a

2.19
Rusty the office cat, War Resisters
League office, 2014.
Photograph by Nandini Bagchee.

small team of interns and a staff of volunteers worked out of the
second floor office.

The eight workstations set up along the windowed walls of the office
were partitioned off from the main space by banks of metal file cabinets. Rusty, the beloved office cat, named after onetime WRL member
and famous civil rights leader Bayard Rustin, sauntered around an area
plastered with stickers that describe various causes and pithy responses to crises: "Free Chelsea," "Goin' Broke Paying for War," "Boycott
Israel: Free Palestine" (**Figure 2.19**). In the center of this room, a large
conference desk faced a whiteboard scribbled with to-do lists. This is
where staff meetings, planning, and group discussions took place and
ongoing projects were fleshed out (**Figure 2.20**).

2.20
War Resisters League Office 2014.
Photograph © Jade Doskow.

Linda Thurston, the organization's office manager, sat at the corner desk overlooking the intersection of Bleecker and Lafayette Streets, where she had a dramatic view of downtown Manhattan to her right and the office's red front door to her left. Thurston, who was responsible for the upkeep of the office, was hired for the post in 2000. She had worked in other nonprofits before and discussed her job and her role in transforming the WRL from a paper-based operation to a digitally oriented one. In 2015 she viewed the size and setup of the office as a holdover from the past, when there were many more projects, people, mailings, and meetings being held in the space.

As the original owner/occupant of the building, the WRL commandeered the largest office within the building. Its central location, up the first flight of stairs from the main entrance, made it a touch point within the building. Other groups with little or no paid staff tended to use space at 339 Lafayette more sporadically and after hours—in the evening or on weekends. Gregory Sholette, a former member of the artists' collectives PAD/D and REPOHistory, recalls that their small three hundred-square-foot space was convenient to the participating artists since, at the time, most of them lived or worked in the neighborhood.[76] They used the office to meet, plan, and store materials. The affordable office in the downtown location provided an intimate space for critical exchange and strategic planning. Run by a mainly volunteer workforce, the accessible downtown location was a big attractor. The structure of the artist collectives such as PAD/D shared similarities with that of the older leftist organizations. In inviting like-minded artists to document and distribute political art, the founder, Lucy Lippard, wanted to archive their projects and create a network of support and visibility for a scattered left.[77] Like the WRL, PAD/D collected dues, generated projects through consensus, and published a newsletter to announce events and provide critical commentaries. Their office, like that of WRL, was a center for organization and communication and, in this sense, not a place of labor but rather a place for planned action.

OFFICE SPACE AS PUBLIC REALM

The projects and activities at the Peace Pentagon represented a larger scope and practice of resistance—one in which the public realm can be seen in terms of three different scales of engagement: between the internal community of groups within the building; between the local coalitions demonstrating and occupying sites within the city; and between national and global networks working to connect online and off. These scales of collaboration demarcated the geographies of participation where the unlikely spaces of the offices at the Peace Pentagon became the synergetic center of an interconnected resistance.

A time line tracing the movement groups that occupied the Peace Pentagon over the years serves as a reflection of this interconnected political landscape (**Figure 2.21**). War, violence, and economic inequality within in the United States and beyond from 1969 to 2016 shaped the counter-institutional history of the organizations within the building. Long-established anti-war groups such as the War Resisters League and their partners, the Women's International League for Peace and Freedom and the Granny Peace Brigade, maintained a steady presence on the building's second floor with a focused anti-war agenda. Other groups that burst into prominence in the '70s and '80s, such as the anti-nuke SHAD alliance, the Mobilization for Survival, and the artists' collectives PAD/D and REPOHistory, endured for a short but productive spell and then disbanded, leaving a legacy of subversive intervention and issue-based organization. The focus on bottom-up communications media by PTTV and DDTV was prophetic of the Internet-era organizing, as it provided a precedent to collaborate with others separated by distance and paved the way for the creation of a real-time global commons. In 2016 most groups, both old and new, relied on social media to connect to larger populations and navigate an increasingly complex globalized political terrain. The small office building at 339 Lafayette Street absorbed these changes and remained a place where the utopian ambitions and the concrete realities of building a political community were expressed.

The A. J. Muste Memorial Institute, with its sheltering mission for its movement tenants, provided a critical service in a downtown area where unaffordable commercial rents pushed many other nonprofit and activist organizations out of the city or into extinction. Over four decades, this privately owned building operated as a public forum for many thousands of participants interested in the "town hall" style of community action that Arendt idealized as the traditional and radical basis for a uniquely American revolutionary participation.[78] Critical reevaluations of Arendt's work, such as that by gender theorist Judith Butler, point to the weakness in Arendt's definition of a public sphere as a place where appearance matters and action is important. Butler evokes "other spaces" that allow those excluded from the visible public sphere to participate.[79] Along these same lines of thought, other advocates of public space have pointed out that the space is not an end in itself but rather that it is vital for the creation of new "publics" in a fragmented, post-national, global world.[80] The public realm, by extension, is a concept that lies beyond the confines of ownership; it is formed wherever people seek to encounter one another, argue, debate,

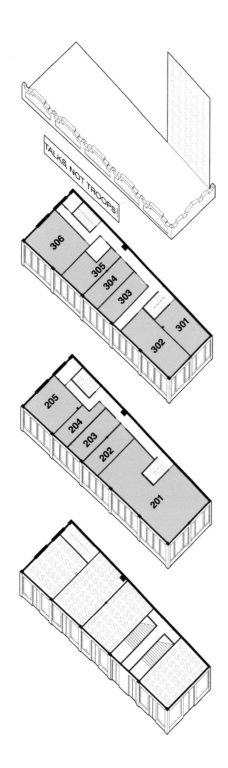

ROOM 306
A.J. Muste Memorial Institute ··

ROOM 305
Catholic Peace Fellowship (CPF) ······································
Deep Dish TV (DDTV) ··

ROOM 304
New York State Youth Leadership Council
Nicaragua Brigades
Coalition for the Human Rights of Immigrants (CHRI)
Mobilization for Survival ···
Nicaragua Solidarity Network of Greater New York ····················

ROOM 303
Episcopal Peace Fellowship (EPF)
Free Assata Shakur
Episcopal Church People for a Free Southern Africa (ECFSA) ············
Free Space Alternative University
Socialist Party (USA) ··

ROOM 302
Gay Activist Alliance
Middle East Peace Project (MEEP)
WIN Magazine ···
Continental Walk for Disarmament and Social Justice (CWDSJ)
Fund for Open Information and Accountability (FOIA) ···················
Middle East Peace Project (MEPP)
Nicaragua Solidarity Network of Greater New York ····················

ROOM 301
Appleseed
Turkish Students Association
National War Tax Resistance
Iran House
Political Art Documentation/Distribution (PAD/D) & REPO History ·········
BAILOUT!
Asian American Arts Alliance
Metropolitan Council on Housing ·····································

ROOM 205
Workroom (WRL)

ROOM 204
Sound-Hudson Alliance Against Atomic Development ···················
Alternative Resource Center
Solar Energy Workshop ···
Options for the Future
Global Revolution TV (GRTV) ··

ROOM 203
National Committee to Reopen Rosenberg Case
Women's Pentagon Action
Healthcare Now
Women's International League for Peace and Freedom Metro NY ··········
Granny Peace Brigade (GPB)

ROOM 202
Libertarian Book Club
Good Old Lower East Side
New York City Organizing of NYC United Teachers ····················
Worker Solidarity Alliance
Anarchist Black Cross (ABC)

ROOM 201
War Resisters League (WRL) ···
Liberation Magazine
Enola Gay Action Coalition (EGAC)
One Big Union

STOREFRONT
345 Art Gallery
Lafayette Service Company

2.21
Time line of occupants, their rooms, and their actions at
the Peace Pentagon, 1969–2016.
Illustration by Nandini Bagchee.
Tenant list compiled with the assistance of Ed Hedemann, past tenants,
correspondence, newsletters, and meeting notes from A. J. Muste
Memorial Institute.

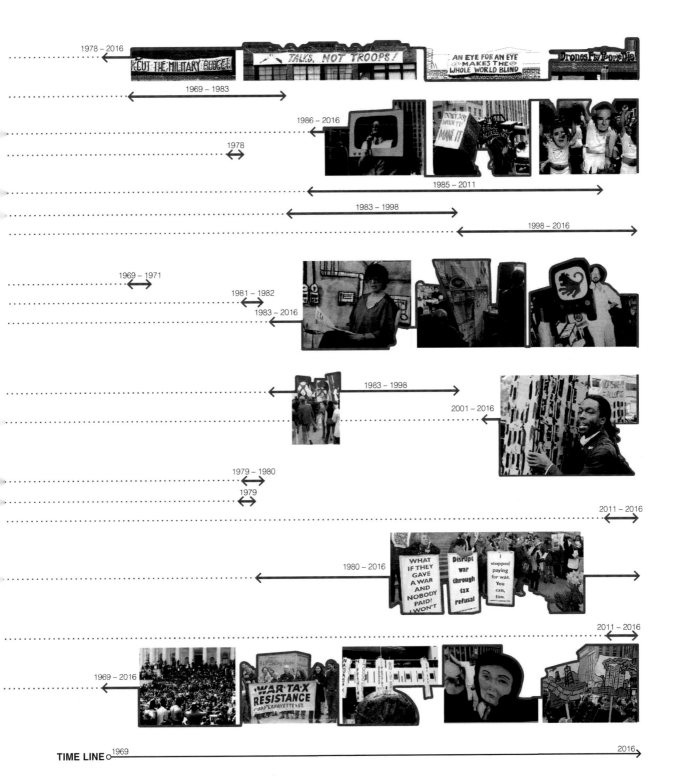

1978 – 2016

1969 – 1983

1986 – 2016

1978

1985 – 2011

1983 – 1998

1998 – 2016

1969 – 1971

1981 – 1982

1983 – 2016

1983 – 1998

2001 – 2016

1979 – 1980

1979

2011 – 2016

1980 – 2016

2011 – 2016

1969 – 2016

TIME LINE 1969   2016

2.22
Paper Tiger TV Office, 2014.
Photograph by Jade Doskow.

and negotiate. The existence of the building and the access to space were incidental and not central to the expectations and aspirations of the movement tenants. Unlike some of the other "right to city" grass-roots organizing that was unfolding in different parts of the city, this building was a by-product rather than a focus of the activism.

Despite its physical decrepitude, or perhaps because of its generally undesirable appearance, the building at 339 Lafayette Street served as a vital node that permitted and, in fact, encouraged the formation of new political perspectives. In a city driven by an escalating real estate market and policies that emphasize privatization based on maximized profit, the existence of the Peace Pentagon and its collective mission allowed groups and individuals to remain involved in various plat-forms where normally they might not have found a foothold. The presence of connected affinity groups in this small building facilitated the flow and exchange of ideas and created a much needed literal and figurative forum in a city where the voice of the political left could express itself. Having a space to meet, plan, and work allowed and encouraged continuing dialogue, resulting in cross-pollinations across social groups that contributed to a broader production and evolution of political action.

With its potential to empower individuals and facilitate social, political, and economic conversations, the space allowed multiple groups to confront issues involving energy sources, climate change, housing, income inequality, and war. The building, along with its larger history, points to the hybridity of urban space and architecture not only in its symbolic dimension as a signifier but also in its practical function as a place to enact and live public life. Without the subsidized rents and available work area, the spaces tagged with broken guns, raised fists, and roaring paper tigers would not have endured as long as they did (Figure 2.22).

3

THE COMMUNITARIAN ESTATES OF LOISAIDA

(1967–2001)

CHAPTER 3: THE COMMUNITARIAN ESTATES OF LOISAIDA (1967–2001)

In 1978, after helping residents of the Lower East Side establish control over poorly managed and abandoned apartment buildings, the housing advocacy group Interfaith Adopt-a-Building (AAB) was looking to adopt a building of its own. They looked for a space large enough to accommodate its hundred-plus staff members and organizers. They set their sights on an abandoned schoolhouse, the former PS 64, on a block adjoining Tompkins Square Park. They leveraged their connections with the city to gain access to the property and invited CHARAS, a Puerto Rican collective dedicated to community organizing, to join them in occupying and running the large facility.[1] Working together, they formed a community center to pursue a three-part agenda to build "Housing, Community, and the Environment."[2] The center was named El Bohio—"the hut"—to signify the ideals of a movement that had emerged from the community activism of the Puerto Rican population of the Lower East Side. Through their combined efforts, a building designed to educate and nurture successive generations of low-income Lower East Side residents was thus restored to its intended function.

This large schoolhouse, built at the beginning of the twentieth century to serve the historically working-class immigrant neighborhood, represented an important connection to the Progressive Era history of the Lower East Side (**Figure 3.1**).[3] The school's closing in the '70s indicated a broader strategy of consolidation and shrinkage of public services adopted by the city in the wake of a fiscal crisis. There was a meteoric drop in the overall population in New York City that was particularly drastic in lower income neighborhoods, such as the Lower East Side. PS 64, which once served 2,500 children, was reduced to a population of 884 at the time of its closing in 1977.[4] The building, left unattended by the board of education, was vandalized and reduced to a state of shambles in a short period of time. Its large windows were broken, lighting and plumbing fixtures were stolen, and sections of copper from the roof had been ripped off to be sold in the black market. This pillaging by vandals and lack of management left the interior exposed to both natural and human elements. The large classrooms and wide hallways became a haven for all manner of people seeking shelter. Drug dealers purportedly conducted a brisk trade within the building, and the stately schoolhouse, once an asset to the

neighborhood, quickly became a menace to residents of the surrounding blocks.[5]

Establishing a community center on city-owned property was not an
impromptu act of occupation but rather the embodiment of an ongoing struggle for political and social autonomy by the neighborhood's
marginalized Puerto Rican community. Since the late '60s, AAB,
CHARAS, and their many collaborators had fought on multiple
fronts to halt the physical and social destruction of a broad swath of
the Lower East Side. This self-proclaimed jurisdiction, indicated on

3.1
Public School 64, view from East
Ninth Street, 1908.
Photograph courtesy of New York City
Municipal Archives.

the many maps prepared by AAB, extended from Fourteenth Street in the north to Houston Street in the south and from Avenue A in the west to the blocks of public housing lining the East River.[6] This area, with its commercial spine along Avenue C, had been home to a large community of Puerto Ricans since the '50s.[7] They followed in the footsteps of immigrant groups—the Germans, the Irish, the Jews, and the Ukrainians—for whom this neighborhood had served as a stepping-stone toward a more prosperous future in America. The Puerto Ricans, however, came at a time when the post-industrializing city offered fewer opportunities to a blue-collar workforce. The gradual disappearance of manufacturing jobs from the city left the new arrivals with few employment options to face the grim reality of the postwar economy.

They settled in neighborhoods such as the South Bronx, East Harlem, the Lower East Side, and Williamsburg and Bushwick (**Figure 3.2**), following the trail of available tenement and public housing in New York City. It was in these neighborhoods, or "barrios," as they came to be called, that they saw their living conditions worsen in the '70s as federal subsidies for housing and social services dwindled, schools and hospitals closed, and a city on the brink of bankruptcy began cutting back on police protection, garbage collection, street cleaning, and municipal services. Diminishing support from the public sector was followed by a depreciation of the value of private real estate. Absentee landlords stopped maintaining their properties, squeezed out poorer tenants, evaded taxes, and sometimes even burned down buildings to collect the insurance on structures whose value had precipitously declined. Charred buildings, boarded-up windows, and garbage-strewn lots characterized the urban landscape. And the lack of heat, electricity, and hot water was a domestic constant that plagued the many families trying to survive in the barrios within New York City.

The multiple crises of employment, housing, and education unfolding in these neighborhoods transformed many residents into activists and generated new forms of political agency among the city's Puerto Ricans. On the Lower East Side, deteriorating buildings and public spaces became the staging ground for experiments in alternative community organization. Residents converted rubble-strewn vacant lots into gardens, rundown tenements into cooperative housing, and storefronts into community centers. These actions created new uses and meanings for neglected urban spaces and generated a network of support through community-organized resistance to urban disintegration.

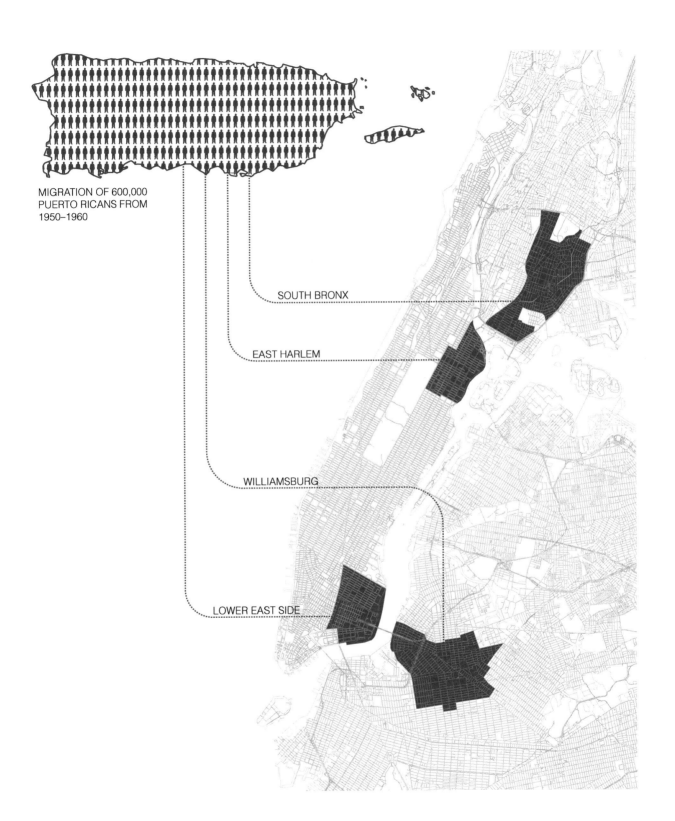

MIGRATION OF 600,000
PUERTO RICANS FROM
1950–1960

SOUTH BRONX

EAST HARLEM

WILLIAMSBURG

LOWER EAST SIDE

3.2
Map of Puerto Rico and New York City showing enclaves of Puerto Rican settlement.
By 1960, over 600,000 people of Puerto Rican birth or parentage lived in New York City.
Illustration by Nandini Bagchee.
Map based on data from the U.S. Census Bureau.

3.3

Loisaida: View from above.
Looking north from East Fourth
Street are the tenement at 309 East
Fourth Street and the bare-bones
playground, El Jardin del Paraiso,
in the foreground, 1979.

Photograph by Marlis Momber.

In 1974, when the Puerto Rican poet-playwright-plumber Bimbo
Rivas memorialized this blighted territory in his poem "Loisaida," he
took a significant step in claiming the neighborhood as a spiritual as
well as a physical home for the struggling Puerto Rican community
(**Figure 3.3**).[8] Once the neighborhood was claimed as "Loisaida," it
generated a new narrative of hope for the community of Puerto
Ricans in the postindustrial city.[9] The name "Loisaida," derived from a
Spanish-inflected pronunciation of "Lower East Side," helped galvanize support for a series of actions involving the idea of a place that
was variously reimagined as a "movement, an ideology, and a state of
mind" and, later, as a "fight-back mentality" and a "philosophy of
responsibility, cooperation, and determination by the people."[10] These
sentiments were transmitted by word of mouth, poetry, and performances, and they were reinforced by the work of activists and ordinary
citizens who transformed the neighborhood through work and play.

Temporary occupation of streets and parks through performance,
combined with the reclamation of buildings and green spaces through
reconstruction and ecological stewardship, constituted the ethos of
this grassroots Puerto Rican movement (**Figure 3.4**). Harnessing the
skills and energy of many engaged participants, the Loisaida movement was rooted in claiming a variety of urban sites through embodied actions. These sites, acquired through negotiation with multiple
constituencies—citizens, police, negligent landlords, and the city— were

brought to life by ephemeral acts of performance and more permanent acts of construction and occupation. The reclamation and transformation of urban spaces was indicative of a broader neighborhood movement to piece together a fragmented cityscape by multiple big and small acts of public participation.

3.4
Loisaida: View at street level. Fourth Street block party, with Baile Boricua performing, 1979. Tenement at 309 East Fourth Street is in the background.
Photograph by Marlis Momber.

EDUCATION IN THE STREET (1967)

> *There is nothing more exciting to me now than the fact that within the community on these streets I find leaders emerging who don't just want to take the law into their own hands, who don't want to protest, but who, with a deep and intuitive earnestness and dawning awareness, want to make things work.*
> —Buckminster Fuller, *CHARAS: The Improbable Domebuilders*

> *Man, these streets are a whole life experience. I'm now using techniques I learned when I was a gang leader. You know, it's a simple decision to make. You destroy things or you make them.*
> —Chino Garcia, *CHARAS: The Improbable Domebuilders*

In 1968 the renegade architect/environmental provocateur Buckminster Fuller stopped briefly on his travels around Spaceship Earth to lecture a youthful audience in a small building on the corner of

Tompkins Square Park in the heart of the Lower East Side. In his talk, Fuller encouraged his audience to join a global grassroots movement to eliminate poverty and design a sustainable future. His call to join in a new world order—one that existed outside the official political system—fired the imagination of a group of young men whose own experiences of poverty and the criminal justice system made them mistrustful of the government. These young men were members of the Real Great Society (RGS), a newly formed Puerto Rican youth collective based in the barrios of the Lower East Side and East Harlem.

The Real Great Society, named audaciously in response to President Johnson's Great Society, sought to achieve bottom-up self-sufficiency within the poverty-stricken neighborhoods of New York City.[11] Introduced to community organization through their involvement in street gangs, the leaders of this new constellation were eager to use their leadership skills more productively to help create a robust future for their community. The news media celebrated the mythical aspect of this transformation of gang members into agents of positive neighborhood change.[12] The charismatic young leaders of the Real Great Society were invited to talk to young people in poor urban neighborhoods around the country and to educate their more well-to-do counterparts on college campuses about their initiatives in the inner-city neighborhoods of New York. With a growing concern about urban crime, there was a pressing interest by both private foundations and government agencies to fund programs targeting juvenile delinquency in cities like New York, Chicago, and Los Angeles. The Real Great Society, while fundamentally opposed to the paternalism embedded in such charity, leveraged their visibility to apply for grants, and organize for self-sufficiency in New York City.

In 1967 a seed grant from the Astor Foundation allowed the Real Great Society to set up small, locally controlled businesses: a leather goods store, a day care center, and a nightclub.[13] A second grant of twenty-five thousand dollars from the same foundation allowed the group to begin one of its most enduring projects, the University of the Street, the place where Buckminster Fuller delivered his lecture. Begun in a rented storefront at the southwest corner of Tompkins Square Park, this university sought to remedy the shortcomings of the official education system by providing a free supplemental education with the help of a volunteer teaching staff.

Because of the positive press coverage and its location in the Lower East Side, the University of the Street attracted not only local low-income residents from the neighborhood but also a number of curious middle-class white students from the outside.[14] The student body, at any given time, generated the course list, which ranged from the remedial to the intellectual. The curriculum included classes in English, Spanish, math, karate, music, dance, and philosophy. It also included job training courses in areas such as television and radio repair. This curriculum, which combined the liberal arts with much needed job training courses, was partly driven by its two primary sources of funding: private foundations and the federal government. The federal government was more interested in the job training, whereas the private institutions were more interested in the arts and cultural programming.

In 1968, after four years of building networks both inside and outside the neighborhood, the Real Great Society got its first substantial federal grant of $258,447.[15] The money enabled the university to expand its operations and lease five floors within the same building on East Seventh Street with the intention of establishing a similar program in East Harlem. The grant brought with it both possibilities and new responsibilities that ultimately strained the Real Great Society's informal working structure. The original group split up, but the members continued to expand their community-focused work along different fronts.[16] The East Harlem branch of the Real Great Society went on to create an Urban Planning Studio that began as a collaboration with Columbia University but went on to become a one-of-a-kind community-controlled planning organization.[17] The University of the Street continued to operate independently, eventually buying the building and becoming a privately funded nonprofit institute.

DOMES IN VACANT LOTS (1968–1972)

Lower East Side–based Real Great Society members Chino Garcia and Angelo Gonzalez enlarged their community agendas, forming a new collective in 1968 with four other people whom they had met and connected with while on an Outward Bound trip to Mexico. Upon their return to the city, they named the new collective CHARAS, an acronym based on the first names of the founding members—Chino, Humberto, Angelo, Roy, Anthony, and Sal (**Figure 3.5**). Over the next decade, this six-person group quickly expanded into a fluctuating collective of more than two hundred participants that included Puerto Ricans from the island and locals who wanted to implement change and rebuild an inclusive city through self-organization. Some of the group's founders used the philosophy of self-reliance under extreme conditions, cultivated in Outward Bound's outdoor leadership training program, to understand and address urban abandonment on the Lower East Side.[18]

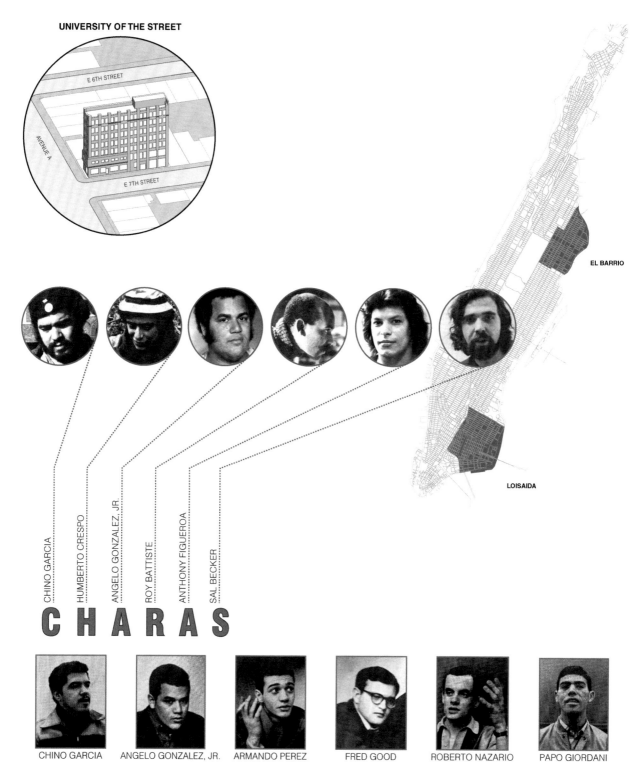

UNIVERSITY OF THE STREET

E 6TH STREET

AVENUE A

E 7TH STREET

EL BARRIO

LOISAIDA

CHINO GARCIA

HUMBERTO CRESPO

ANGELO GONZALEZ, JR.

ROY BATTISTE

ANTHONY FIGUEROA

SAL BECKER

CHARAS

CHINO GARCIA   ANGELO GONZALEZ, JR.   ARMANDO PEREZ   FRED GOOD   ROBERTO NAZARIO   PAPO GIORDANI

3.5
Real Great Society (RGS) members (lower row), as featured in *Life Magazine* article,1967 and later,
CHARAS founding members (upper row), as featured in *CHARAS: The Improbable Dome Builders*, 1973.
Above, the University of the Street, an alternative educational institution founded by the Real Great
Society on Avenue A in Loisaida.
Illustration by Nandini Bagchee.

In its early period, CHARAS focused on educating the community while addressing the lack of quality housing, health care, and employment opportunities in the neighborhood. In 1970 they reestablished contact with Buckminster Fuller in an effort to tackle the prescient question of housing in their neighborhood. Fuller, age 75, and always on the lookout for fresh collaborations, responded with enthusiasm to this request. Together, they decided to build a prototype geodesic shelter as a first step toward addressing the affordable housing crisis in New York City.

The modular geodesic-dome house, originally designed by Fuller to address a postwar housing need in the United States, was adopted in the '60s by an unexpected constituency—a mainly white, middle-class, countercultural youth movement in rural settings.[19] However, these build-it-yourself domes also appealed to a young welfare-weary Lower East Side audience that saw in its unique design a novel appeal—a low-cost, collectively built alternative to government-subsidized housing. In a landscape full of vacant lots and ill-functioning residential buildings, Fuller's dome residence seemed like a hopeful step forward. Providing an alternative to the prevailing rhetoric and financial support of the existing anti-poverty programs in the neighborhood, they desired to follow a different course of action. The domes required a certain level of involvement in direct problem-solving that appealed to the DIY sensibility of the CHARAS collective. For CHARAS and their growing youth corps, the urban dome project symbolized a way out of the deadlock between poverty and a dependence on welfare. Syeus Mottel's book, aptly titled, *CHARAS: The Improbable Dome Builders*, provides a vivid first-person account of the project. His interviews with the main participants, photographs, and observations provide a start-to-finish account of this project.

Roy Battiste, the "R" in CHARAS, the most mathematically inclined of the founding members, took a leading role in the project. In 1970, he leased the third floor of a condemned, city-owned warehouse at 303 Cherry Street in the southern end of the Lower East Side and skillfully converted it into a workshop and living quarters for the working collective. The first of the geodesic structures was built to fit inside this open loft space with a triangulated wood frame skinned with canvas panels. This intervention in the loft demarcated space for different activities and provided privacy for the residents. The expansive live-work quarters were gradually filled with tools, models, drawings, and mock-ups. This active design-build studio generated interest among the children living nearby, and the teenagers recruited by CHARAS for this project became a part of the growing collective (**Figure 3.6**). Volunteers from neighborhood art programs, along with what Mottel

3.6
Kids with wireframe dome model in Cherry Street loft, 1972.

Photograph by Syeus Mottel. Courtesy of Matthew Mottel.

described as "uptown people and dome freaks," were drawn to this makeshift dome laboratory.[20] Within this soon-to-be-demolished warehouse, serious learning formed the basis for a "continuous low-ebb party."[21]

Fuller's assistant, the architectural student Michael Ben-Eli, intermittently visited New York from London and provided instruction on geodesic science to the collective. In consultation with Ben-Eli, CHARAS members planned a version of the dome constructed with bent cardboard triangles, reinforced with metal mesh, and plastered with ferro-cement. This structure was a prototype designed to provide temporary housing for a family of four. With Fuller's support and growing interest around the work, CHARAS secured a New York Foundation for the Arts grant to help fund the actual installation.[22] By late fall of 1972, the collective installed two dome structures in a vacant lot at Jefferson and South Street, with the permission of the Department of Housing and Urban Development. Assembly took much longer than anticipated, as heavy rains, blackouts, and flailing morale took their toll on the volunteers that had rallied behind the project. The first of the domes met a tragic end at the hands of the fire department when, ironically, a homeless man seeking shelter lit a fire inside the structure. The second one, completed in January of 1973, enjoyed some publicity and prompted a visit by Fuller on his way to a lecture at Carnegie Hall.[23] This test dome enjoyed a brief sojourn in the shadow of the LaGuardia and Rutgers public housing develop-

3.7
CHARAS dome cardboard sub-
structure in vacant lot on South
and Jefferson Streets, with
Manhattan Bridge in the back-
ground, 1972.
Photograph by Syeus Mottel. Courtesy of
Matthew Mottel.

ments, close to the piers of the Manhattan Bridge, before being dismantled by the city to make way for a housing development (**Figure
3.7**).[24]

Although the prefab dome urban housing proved untenable in New
York City, CHARAS's dome-building activities and the group's outreach to neighborhood youth continued to expand over the next two
decades. The Cherry Street loft, a transitional communal space, provided a blueprint for the live-work, collectively run spaces that became
central to CHARAS's organizational structure. They branched out
from the Lower East Side to the other barrios of New York, forming
networks and creating participatory projects focused on youth education.[25] The domes, manufactured on rooftops, in lofts, and in storefronts, appeared regularly in New York's public spaces. These skeletal
triangulated structures, clad with different materials, were deployed in
street festivals as band shelters, in community gardens as greenhouses,
and on rooftops as temporary shelters.

A tubular frame structure assembled inside a communal loft space
on Avenue B appears in German photographer and CHARAS

collaborator Marlis Momber's 1978 German documentary "Viva Loisaida."[26] This loft, rented from a private owner, was one of many communal quarters and could sleep and support up to twenty-five people.[27] The beds were arranged dormitory style with drop-down curtains for privacy. At one end of the loft, along the street-facing side, was the CHARAS meeting and work area, demarcated with the tubular dome frame. In the '70s CHARAS began producing these domes through their port-a-dome initiative. For the next twenty years, these prefab domes cropped up in nuclear and housing protests within the city and were also adapted as more permanent enclosures further afield. The dome symbolized both the self-sufficiency of CHARAS and the group's autonomous participation in a larger global-environmental movement. This outward projection and promotion of a grassroots movement were important steps in educating and getting the support from a wider external audience while maintaining a strong foothold within the geographically inscribed territory of Loisaida.

YOUNG LORDS AND THE LOISAIDA MOVEMENT

In their quest for autonomy, RGS and CHARAS were part of a larger civil rights movement unfolding within a politicized Puerto Rican community in the United States. In Chicago the Young Lords, a radical Puerto Rican activist party, emerged in response to the race-based displacement and discrimination faced by their community. Their efforts and narratives galvanized other Latinos and Puerto Ricans in cities across the United States. In the summer of 1969 the New York City chapter of the Young Lords announced its formation in a ceremonious gathering in Tompkins Square Park. The group set up an office in the Christodora House, a vacant, city-owned building originally built as a settlement house on the eastern edge of the park. Although a larger proportion of the Puerto Rican youth population was located in East Harlem, the decision to stage the formation of the New York City chapter of the Young Lords on the Lower East Side was geopolitical. Tompkins Square Park was the historic locus of many radical political movements. The Young Lords' symbolic claiming of this park, with its long history as a locus of radical dissent, was strategic. It was a public expression of their interest in leading a citywide movement toward progressive reform.[28] The day after the chapter's formation, the members of this group mounted the "garbage offensive," demanding better sanitation services from the city by piling mounds of uncollected garbage in the middle of Third Avenue in East Harlem and setting fire to it.[29] This act of civil disobedience in the streets was followed by a well-publicized occupation of a church, where the Young Lords created a breakfast program, a clothing drive, a day care center, and cultural programs to demonstrate the potential of a marginalized community in action. Their performative acts of claiming space, backed up by providing social services, challenged the establishment and fueled the imagination of a younger generation of Puerto Ricans.[30] The control and repurposing of urban space fueled the resistance. In their demand for space and their right to self-determination, the Young Lords frequently evoked a longer history of spatial struggle against Spanish colonialism and American corporate interests in Puerto Rico.[31] The fifth point of a thirteen-point program publicized by the Young Lords through *Palante*, their bilingual newspaper, called for taking "Community Control Over Our Institutions and Land."[32] By occupying and repurposing institutionalized spaces, such as churches, streets, and hospitals, the Young Lords brought attention to issues involving housing, sanitation, health care, and education.

These visible public actions were a call to arms to the traditionally marginalized Puerto Ricans across the city. Within the Lower East Side Puerto Rican community, which was closely linked to the East Harlem organizers, these takeovers of space resonated positively. Their own practices of spatial appropriation were less militant and more pacifist. As RGS/CHARAS founding member Chino Garcia put it, "If the Young Lords' symbol was the rifle, ours was the hammer."[33] The Lower East Side's greater racial and ethnic diversity and the long history of social reform made the contours of the Puerto Rican organizing in Loisaida different from that in East Harlem. While asserting the primacy of the Puerto Rican experience in New York, the broader Loisaida movement was closely engaged with other Latinos, as well as African Americans and white activists who lived and worked in the neighborhood. The civil rights and anti-war movements discussed previously in this book had created an enclave of radical political resistance in Greenwich Village in the '60s. With the end of the Vietnam War in 1974, many of the activists and artists, in search of affordable living quarters and attracted to the social dynamics of the neighborhood, began migrating east to the Lower East Side. The returning Vietnam War veterans, as well as the new generation of draft resisters, found common cause with the grassroots factions organizing around "right to city" causes.

In June 1978 *WIN* magazine, which typically covered the topics of war, peace, and nonviolent action, dedicated an entire issue to Loisaida (**Figure 3.8**). In the editorial, the magazine noted that "the people of Loisaida have risked voicing their lives to an unknown audience, stepping beyond the boundaries of their neighborhood to speak to their sisters and brothers in the nonviolent left."[34] The articles in this issue of *WIN* described the concerns and accomplishments of the people of

December 20, 1979 75¢

win

PEACE & FREEDOM THROUGH NONVIOLENT ACTION

SPECIAL ISSUE

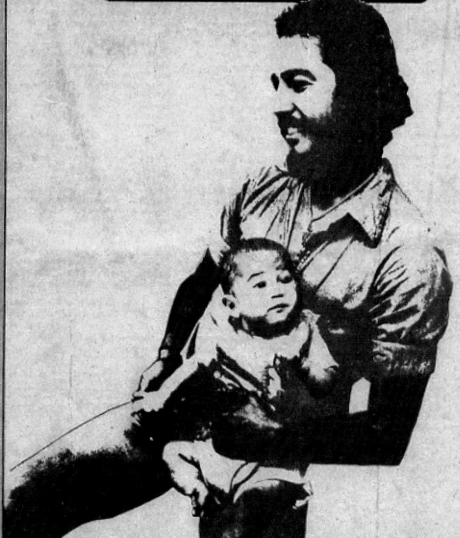

LOISAIDA
Portrait of a Community

Loisaida, in the areas of housing, environmental initiatives, poetry, music, and performance. The type of publicity helped connect people working on social justice in Loisaida with a larger network of politicized organizers. This, in turn, catapulted a relatively local group of organizers into a broadly recognized social movement.

NO HEAT, NO RENT: ADOPTING BUILDINGS (1970–1975)

Community organizing in 1970s New York City often centered on the lack of jobs and the scarcity of quality affordable housing. In a vicious cycle of cause and effect, the ongoing exodus of the middle class to the suburbs and the perception of the city as a dangerous place were major factors in the disinvestment of private real estate.[35] Property owners, a historically powerful constituency in the city's economic landscape, sought ways to make good on their troubled investments in a flailing economy. In low-income neighborhoods, many landlords stopped paying taxes and maintaining their properties. As the cost of fuel rose, property owners sought to recoup their losses and drive out rent-regulated tenants by cutting off heat, electricity, and water.[36] Forced evictions and warehousing—a strategy of keeping buildings vacant for extended periods of time—left people without homes while buildings sat abandoned and empty. Neglected properties were vandalized and sometimes deliberately set on fire by building owners in a last-ditch effort to collect insurance. Once vibrant and densely populated residential neighborhoods all over the city were abandoned and, in some instances, reduced to rubble by fires and preemptive demolitions.

In response to this escalating housing crisis, tenants across the city galvanized support from faith-based organizations, legal service agencies, and housing advocacy groups. "No Heat, No Rent" banners appeared on buildings as renters fed up with substandard living conditions took matters into their own hands and declared rent strikes.[37] Some advocates and tenants went beyond the traditional rent strike, taking collective control over the management of their buildings. In 1970 a radical Catholic clergyman, Monsignor Robert Fox, organized a group of residents in East Harlem and rehabilitated two fire-damaged buildings on East 102nd Street, facilitating their conversion into cooperatively owned apartments.[38] This process, dubbed sweat equity, allowed future residents of the co-ops to contribute construction labor as a form of down payment toward a future apartment.

As tenants organized rent strikes and took over the management of their buildings in many low-income neighborhoods, the city was on the brink of bankruptcy. To press delinquent property owners into paying their back taxes, the city took possession of many of these "in rem" properties through tax foreclosure with the intention of selling them at public auctions. Paradoxically, this pressure hastened the process of abandonment as owners simply walked away from their properties, leaving tens and thousands of run-down buildings filled with unhappy tenants in the hands of the city. The Housing and Development Administration (HDA),[39] an agency tasked with property development and management, saw in the sweat equity movement a reprieve in its role of unwilling landlord and property manager. By 1974 urban homesteading, as this process came to be known, was recognized by the federal government as a legitimate way to rehabilitate housing in several cities across the country facing similar housing crises.[40] The actual implementation of this seemingly simple idea—putting apartments back into the hands of the users—was a long and complex process. It began with assembling construction crews, negotiating construction loans, fixing the buildings using the labor of people that were potentially unskilled, and then ensuring that buildings were up to code and habitable. The agencies' goal went further to make sure that these buildings were financially and organizationally secure long-term and able to pay back their loans. The city and federal agencies looked to local housing advocacy groups to provide the infrastructure and community outreach to make these projects viable, and to provide the tenants with the technical assistance necessary to self-manage a building long-term. Once the homestead proved to be under a stable internal management structure, the apartments were transferred from the agency to the resident homesteaders as limited equity cooperatives.[41]

The housing advocacy group Interfaith Adopt-a-Building (AAB), introduced at the start of this chapter, was one of the many tenants' rights and housing advocacy groups operating in New York City in the early '70s.[42] They began by organizing rent strikes in East Harlem and relocated their offices to the Lower East Side in 1974—to an area that was most drastically affected by the disinvestment. This area, bounded by Fourteenth Street in the north, Houston Street in the south, Avenue D in the east, and Avenue A in the west, lost 40 percent of its population between 1970 and 1980 (**Figure 3.9**). Many residents left the area voluntarily or were forced out because of the worsening conditions of the neighborhood during this time period. Of those remaining, census data shows that a majority were of "Puerto Rican birth or parentage." The increase in the ratio of Puerto Ricans in this area was not a result of new influx but rather indicative of the overall departure of all but the poorest residents.[43] One out of every three buildings in this blighted territory, renamed "Loisaida" by the Puerto Rican poets/ activists, was city-owned and imperiled with demolition.

This high rate of disinvestment, vacancy, and public ownership gave AAB the opportunity to negotiate the outcome of these properties on behalf of the tenants, as well as those dislocated and homeless. The group maintained an inventory of all properties within the thirty blocks of Loisaida and used this data to plan for a more comprehensive development while providing aid to one building at a time. AAB put up signs around the neighborhood, offering help to tenants seeking to take control of buildings in various states of abandonment and decline. In the early years a mainly volunteer group of coordinators divided up the blocks among themselves and approached residents of their assigned blocks. The coordinators kept track of all the tenement buildings and helped residents become aware of their rights. They facilitated the formation of block associations, offered support to groups seeking to manage their buildings collectively, and were actively engaged in keeping up to date within this specific geography of Loisaida.[44]

AAB's work, however, did not stop at addressing housing needs. They frequently collaborated with other community organizations such as CHARAS and aspired to bring a more holistic vision of a neighborhood-wide development. In a report prepared for the U.S. Department of Housing and Urban Development, AAB described its mandate as looking at all scales of life in Loisaida—beginning at the level of the city and moving down to the scale of the block and the building.[45] The work of AAB intersected with that of several other locally based arts, education, and community outreach organizations, and its success depended on keeping everyday concerns of the residents connected to broader planning and property management goals. To this end, AAB brought together concerned citizens and organizers from community-based groups at "town meetings" to exchange information and ideas about housing and plan events designed to raise the morale of an economically depressed community. These town meetings had a double purpose: first, to help unify different groups within the neighborhood who were working toward a common goal, and second, to encourage residents to express their views within an open public forum. The meetings were conducted in English and Spanish, and "emceed" by Bimbo Rivas, who punctuated serious discussions of jobs and housing with spontaneous bursts of poetry.[46] Music, performance, and celebrations were a necessary part of this forum intended to solve problems with creative ingenuity.

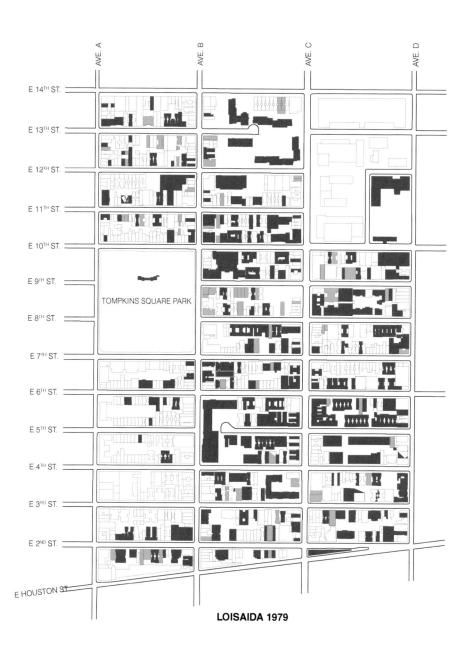

LOISAIDA 1979

■ City-Owned Properties
■ Properties in Remission

3.9
Visualization of city-owned property in 1979 with the blocks of "Loisaida" mapped
against corresponding demographic data of that same area. Drawing shows the
de-population of the blocks between 1970 and 1980. The green figures denote
Puerto Rican residents and the black figures indicate non–Puerto Rican residents.
Illustration by Nandini Bagchee.
Drawings based on U.S. Census Data as well as maps compiled by Interfaith Adopt-A-Building in
HUD report, "Loisaida: Strategies for Neighborhood Revitalization and Self-Determination," New York.
December 18, 1979.

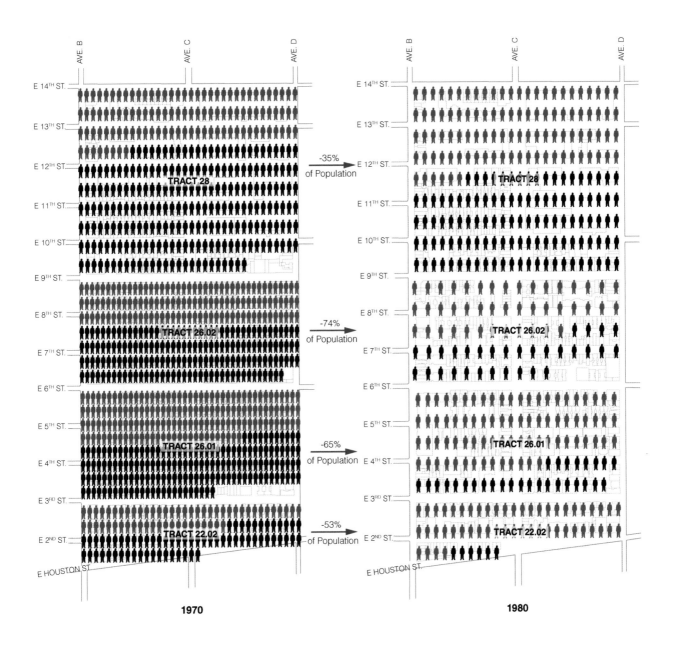

E 14TH ST.   E 13TH ST.   E 12TH ST.   E 11TH ST.   E 10TH ST.   E 9TH ST.   E 8TH ST.   E 7TH ST.   E 6TH ST.   E 5TH ST.   E 4TH ST.   E 3RD ST.   E 2ND ST.   E HOUSTON ST.

AVE. B   AVE. C   AVE. D

TRACT 28

TRACT 26.02

TRACT 26.01

TRACT 22.02

-35% of Population

-74% of Population

-65% of Population

-53% of Population

1970

1980

25 People of Puerto Rican Descent
25 People of Non-Puerto Rican Descent

3.10
"Loisaida Townhouse" at the corner of Avenue C and East Fourth Street, 1980.
Photograph by Marlis Momber.

The well-attended sessions were first convened in a building on the corner of Avenue C and Fourth Street, in a building that came to be known as the "Loisaida Townhouse" (**Figure 3.10**). This structure, a former yeshiva dormitory,[47] offered the right mix of big and small rooms for use as an ad hoc community center. The first floor was used for meetings, gatherings, and performances. A larger vestry on the second floor was converted into an open training gym with what was described as an "Olympic size boxing ring."[48] El Teatro Ambulante, a traveling performance troupe founded by Bimbo Rivas and his mentor, the renowned poet Jorge Brandon, rehearsed in the building, preparing for public performances on the streets of New York, Boston, Philadelphia, and Chicago. Nicknamed "El Coco que Habla" (the Talking Coconut), Brandon was a respected figure in the Loisaida community. Having recited poetry in the streets and squares of New York City since the '40s, he brought the rich oral traditions of Puerto Rican spoken word, infused with political activism, to Loisaida. Performances by El Teatro Ambulante explored the theme of territorial conflicts in Puerto Rico as well as the more contemporary struggle for survival in Loisaida. The narrative of dispossession articulated through these ambulatory performances acquired weight through the adopting of buildings in Loisaida.

NO HEAT, NO RENT: ALTERNATIVE TECHNOLOGY (1974–1978)

In 1974, AAB sponsored its first successful urban homesteading project at 519 East Eleventh Street. This badly damaged building, slated for demolition by the city was, instead, rehabilitated through sweat equity. In order to fund the renovation, AAB obtained financing through a municipal loan program and brokered a deal with the city's Department of Real Estate.[49] They advertised the project by word of mouth and, working in collaboration with CHARAS, quickly gathered a crew interested in the work. If AAB was involved with the legal and technical aspects of homesteading, CHARAS, operating out of their communal loft quarters on Avenue B, was the force that brought social cohesion. The critical mass of people needed for the implementation of the sweat equity projects was gathered from their flexible network of associates and DIY ethic. CHARAS member Luz Rodriguez, a second-generation Puerto Rican and a native Loisaidan, joined the homesteading effort at 519 East Eleventh Street as a "sweater" at the age of seventeen.[50] A year later she had an apartment of her own in the building and was the youngest equity owner within the building. For Rodriguez and other members of her generation, projects such as these provided the physical and conceptual challenge of doing something outside the framework of normative social expectations.

Besides the CHARAS contingent, the participants of the Eleventh Street homesteading project included a heterogeneous group of locals with little or no construction experience as well as an outside group. Brent Sharman, a volunteer coordinator for AAB visiting the site in its early phase, recalls a daunting, empty shell of a five-story brick tenement with a pile of rubble at the bottom.[51] Despite these odds, those deployed in the physical reconstruction secured ownership of eleven apartments within the building in a short period of two years. For AAB, the realization of this project was a watershed moment. It allowed them to expand the scope of the organization's work from tenant organizing to workforce development for the repair and renovation of vacant buildings. In the aftermath of this project, AAB qualified for a substantial federal grant that allowed them to expand their operation and create an infrastructure for job training in construction and building management.[52]

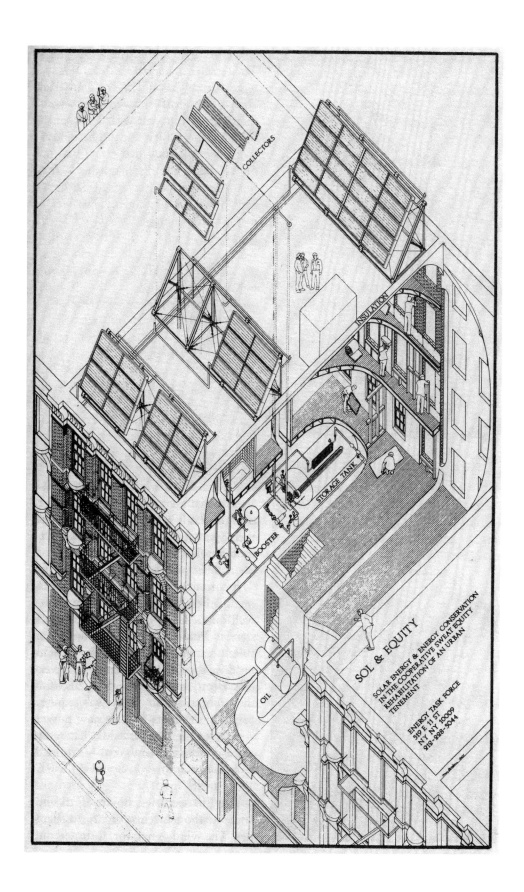

COLLECTORS

INSULATION

STORAGE TANK

BOOSTER

OIL

SOL & EQUITY

SOLAR ENERGY & ENERGY CONSERVATION
IN THE COOPERATIVE SWEAT EQUITY
REHABILITATION OF AN URBAN
TENEMENT

ENERGY TASK FORCE
349 E 11 ST
NY NY 10009
212-966-9044

The model homesteading project at 519 East Eleventh Street inspired two other homesteads and a wave of civic improvements on the same block. Residents cleaned out vacant lots and garden enthusiasts planted a fruit and vegetable garden. El Sol Brilliante, created on two adjoining city-owned lots, made use of discarded building materials from the renovation of the homesteads to create raised beds, planters, and benches. A multigenerational and multiethnic endeavor, the garden of the sun represented an early example of organic farming in the city and was among the first properties to become a part of a larger land trust in 1980.[53] This flurry of activity on a block best known for the sale of auto parts from stolen cars was collectively known as the "Movement on Eleventh Street."

The publicity garnered by this effort[54] attracted the attention of a group of sympathetic young architects and planners. This contingent, seeking to implement small-scale alternative energy–generation technologies into new models of affordable housing, found its way to Loisaida. The ever ambitious Loisaida community welcomed the new "Energy Task Force" as it set about making the building on East Eleventh Street more energy efficient (**Figure 3.11**). They began by adding improved insulation in the exposed surfaces of the building and then went on to install solar collectors on the roof as a way to reduce future operating costs. This group published its work in a manual entitled "No Heat, No Rent," turning a slogan for a rent strike into a do-it-yourself, long-term, energy-conservation goal.[55] A year later the same group, in collaboration with the homesteaders, upped the ante by installing a wind turbine on the building's roof to generate electricity. The turbine's dramatic forty-foot-high presence in the New York City skyline created a media sensation.[56] The *Washington Star* featured a photograph of the turbine with solar collectors in the foreground and the Empire State Building in the background. The write-up described the approach as "small-scale and innovative—providing a quiet contrast to the traditional energy empires and the bigger-is-better philosophy" (**Figure 3.12**).[57]

MIRACLES IN LOISAIDA (1978–1982)

The amount of energy generated by the turbine was not significant, but the symbolic impact of this "windmill" competing in a New York City skyline with the Empire State Building spire to the west, and the Con Edison chimney stacks to the east, provided a significant boost to what sociologist Daniel Chodorkoff described as the Alternative Technology (AT) movement in Loisaida.[58] He documented and studied both the social and the environmental aspects of this movement in Loisaida

3.11
Drawing of 519 East Eleventh Street showing solar collectors on the roof and energy generation cutaway section of the tenement building.
Image from Energy Task Force, *Windmill Power for City People: A Documentation of the First Urban Wind Energy System*, New York City, 1977.

3.12
Windmill write-up in the *Washington Star*, Saturday, October 7, 1978.

in his PhD thesis, *Un Milagro: Alternative Technology and Grassroots Efforts for Neighborhood Reconstruction on New York's Lower East Side.* In 1980 this movement aspired to explore the use of renewable energy as a means to achieve greater self-sufficiency. Recycling, gardening, and seeking alternatives to energy preoccupied CHARAS as well as other neighborhood youth groups such as C.U.A.N.D.O. One third of Chodorkoff's dissertation focuses on CHARAS and views their prioritization of a holistic social alternative to economy, culture, housing, and energy as the true goal of the AT movement. He describes CHARAS's use of simple technologies to apply environmentally sound practices as not an end in itself but rather a transformation of society inside out. The combination of homesteading, gardening, and forming consensus through local town hall meetings in Loisaida came close to what social theorist Murray Bookchin advocated as a way to create a "Libertarian Municipal society."[59] In this model of governance, small urban self-governed assemblies with specific social and ecological goals form the basis of a democratic confederation. The professionals and homesteaders involved with the Energy Task Force and some of the organic gardening advocates had met as students at a summer program at the Institute of Social Ecology, which was run by Bookchin and Chodorkoff in rural Vermont.[60] Bookchin was a product of an older, more radical anarchist tradition with roots in the Lower East Side. He reconnected with this geography through his young students and Chodorkoff, who found among the camaraderie of groups such as CHARAS the lived reality of Bookchin's socioecological utopia.[61]

In the summer of 1980, ten years into its port-a-dome enterprise, CHARAS was invited by the Institute for Social Ecology in Vermont to build a year-round aquaculture dome.[62] The communitarian vision of CHARAS, a decade after its foundation, continued to challenge the status quo on many levels and redefined the Nuyorican (New York–Puerto Rican) identity. Through their creative endeavors, they sought to dismantle not only the stereotype of the welfare-dependent Puerto Rican but also the stagnant alternative of the assimilated middle-class Puerto Rican moving out of Loisaida into what the poet Miguel Algarín refers to as the "dark void of the American dream."[63] In 1972 Algarín began informal poetry jams in his living room to give voice to the poets, playwrights, and musicians experimenting with language and the experience of life in New York City as Puerto Ricans. The Nuyorican Poets Café grew out of this soiree and, by 1980, established itself in a tenement building on East Third Street. This building and the many well-known poets that emerged from the institution brought visibility to the movement. In his introduction to *Nuyorican Poetry: An Anthology of Puerto Rican Words and Feelings*, Algarín captures the spirit embodied in the efforts of CHARAS and other community-based initiatives during this time: "The next day the Renegades continue their work, and the Dynamites initiate their construction. The work at first is slow and there is no existing language to express the feelings and work to be done. Language and action are simultaneous realities. Actions create the need for verbal expression."[64] The synchronicity of word and action represented by the theatrical and logistical interventions in Loisaida was about creating a culture of resistance, experiment, and change.

CHARAS, at the forefront of many of these actions, remained relatively flexible in terms of defining a specific mission. Chino Garcia described their role at the time as a catalyst in the neighborhood.[65] Within Loisaida, they organized on a project-by-project basis and partnered with a variety of people and organizations to launch urban space-based initiatives that brought visibility to their causes. A core collective of six to eight full-time members worked with many different teams of volunteers on a variety of reconstruction projects.[66] They made decisions collectively and were committed to the idea that youth empowerment and self-knowledge rooted in culture, ecology, and education were the key to breaking the cycle of poverty, violence, and demoralization. They gathered a large following of young volunteers from New York and Puerto Rico who lived communally and provided

3.13
Grupo Cemi performs in La Plaza Cultural. The audience in the background is seated in the open amphitheater, 1980.
Photograph by Marlis Momber.

3.14

Top: Entry detail of the recycling center from the *Quality of Life in Loisaida* (1979). The crew posing in front of the door are CHARAS members. The headline from the newspaper reads "Don't waste it."

Bottom: La Plaza Cultural in foreground with CHARAS recycling center to left in the middle ground, 1980.

Top photograph by Marlis Momber. Bottom photograph by Josie Rolon, published in the *Quality of Life in Loisaida* (1979).

the support to get projects off the ground.[67] They used this power base to consolidate public space, and they established three important alternative institutions in the blocks between Avenue C and Tompkins Square Park: La Plaza Cultural, a large open-air assembly space; CHARAS Recycling Center; and El Bohio Community Center.

The first of these, La Plaza Cultural, was an open gathering space fashioned from a ragged assortment of city-owned lots bordering the southwest corner of Avenue C and East Ninth Street. In 1978 the lots were filled with trash, construction debris, and the carcasses of old cars. CHARAS installed a chain-link fence around the perimeter of the fifty thousand–square-foot site to protect it and cleaned up the property using the energetic labor of its collective members. Liz Christy, the founder of the Green Guerillas, donated plants for the plaza. Other members of the organization set up a rain harvesting and composting facility within this park. However, La Plaza Cultural, named and planned in the grand tradition of public squares in Latin American cities, was far more than a garden. It was a space for everyday encounters and a forum for public events. To this end, volunteers piled up a large mound of dirt at its center and fashioned an amphitheater out of wooden railroad ties. The program for the space was fluid. In the summer, town meetings; informal gatherings of musicians; and celebrations with theater, poetry, and dance transformed this patchwork of vacant lots into a beloved and valued community resource. The revival of folkloric performances such as the *bomba* and *plena* from Puerto Rican sugar plantations transposed into this Loisaidan context made relevant the radical performance-based resistance of a distant place and time (**Figure 3.13**).[68] With its openness to street and avenue, La Plaza Cultural provided a perfect place at which political resistance and social life converged.

Environmental stewardship of the streets around the Plaza was the natural next step for CHARAS. In 1978 a grant from the National Center for Appropriate Technology (NCAT) allowed the group to convert a vacant five thousand–square-foot former oil depot into a community-run recycling center. The vast amount of trash littering the neighborhood became the instigation for this venture. A "cash for trash" incentive publicized by posters throughout the neighborhood brought mounds of recyclable glass, paper, and aluminum into the facility (**Figure 3.14**).[69] This for-profit venture created employment for the youth and turned waste into an asset. The conversion of the polluted single-story garage structure (also filled with garbage) into a place of environmental stewardship was indicative of the longer-term goals of a community planning for a sustainable future.

In March 1979 the *Quality of Life in Loisaida/Calidad de Vida en Loisaida,* a free bilingual quarterly, documented the successful ventures and positive changes taking place within the neighborhood and warned residents about the imminent threats to these gains. One article described the annual Three Kings Day parade in Loisaida, an event in which a costumed procession of kings, angels, and camels moved through the blocks around Avenue C, giving "Miracle Awards" to properties that had been "saved" in the previous year. These included several sweat equity buildings, a community center, a music studio, the Nuyorican Poets Café, and CHARAS's recycling center. The writer of the article characterized this last "miracle," the recycling center, as "a place where not only our garbage but our spirit is recycled."[70]

COMMUNITY AT EL BOHIO (1978–1998)

The rehabilitation of PS 64 and its transformation into a community center was the most ambitious undertaking, one that completed the "campus" of properties claimed, rescued, and eventually managed by CHARAS. The grand five-story brick and terracotta structure, straddling the block between East Ninth and East Tenth Streets, between Avenues B and C, was designed in 1906 by the architect C.B.J. Snyder, Superintendent of School Buildings, as a state-of-the-art public school for the then populous immigrant community of the Lower East Side.[71] Snyder's innovative H-shaped plan integrated two raised outdoor courts at the north and south ends of the building, facing East Tenth and East Ninth Streets respectively. These generous terraces served multiple functions: They allowed light into the classrooms, provided a buffer from the street, and allowed outdoor space for recreation and events. A 350-seat auditorium tucked under the Tenth Street terrace with a separate entrance was included in the original design of the school. This public hall provided a venue for evening lectures, performances, and political rallies for three generations of residents from the time of its construction to its closure in the '70s (**Figure 3.15**). In this manner, the school had always been an architecturally and socially significant community asset. Despite its deteriorated physical condition, the school—with its many classrooms and large public spaces—was well suited to become El Bohio Community Center.

CHARAS's move into the prominent schoolhouse, introduced at the start of this chapter, came at a time when the Loisaida movement was at its apogee. AAB officially leased the building from the city to manage its expansive job training program, which was funded by a federal Comprehensive Employment and Training Act (CETA)

3.15
Auditorium at PS 64, 1910.
Photograph courtesy of the New York City
Municipal Archive.

grant.[72] In 1978 this bootstrap organization, run for several years by a mainly volunteer staff, was able to hire a hundred employees consisting of program coordinators, planners, and paid trainees.[73] AAB capitalized on this trainee task force to initiate the repair and renovation of the fifty thousand–square-foot building. However, given the enormity of the task, the grudging support from the city, and the limited resources, they quickly realized that they would need the support of the larger Loisaida community. They invited CHARAS to share the building. Within a year, raising money from private and public sources and with the volunteer labor of friends and comrades, CHARAS and AAB managed to make the first two floors of the building reasonably habitable. The renovation was provisional, but CHARAS's motto "Doing more with less"—attributed to the group's mentor, Buckminster Fuller—kept the operation afloat and attracted tenants and programming to the building. The gym, the theater, the printing press, and the town meetings—activities first begun and housed in the Loisaida Townhouse—were gradually absorbed and expanded within the partially renovated community center.[74]

AAB set up their offices on the second floor in the southeast wing of the H-shaped schoolhouse building. They used the many classrooms on this floor to conduct workshops and run job training programs for construction and building management. The CETA grant came with tremendous responsibilities, and AAB, which had been so effective in their grassroots role, struggled to keep pace with their newfound affluence. So, although it was AAB that initially negotiated the occupancy in PS 64, it was CHARAS that eventually took over the role of building manager and program facilitator for El Bohio Community Center. They arranged a couple of desks, a bulletin board, and some filing cabinets on the first floor, below AAB, toward the Ninth Street side of the building. From this vantage point, they kept an eye on the main entrance and kept track of the activities within the building. Securing the schoolhouse in a neighborhood still rife with drugs, crime, and destitution was a challenge all by itself. CHARAS renovated the classrooms one room at a time and invited their colleagues and collaborators from the art, educational, and environmental organizations to join them in populating the expansive interior.

In exchange for space, various professionals and nonprofits joined the enterprise offering instruction in art, dance, photography, and martial arts. Among the early operatives within the building were Seven Loaves Inc., a nonprofit arts coalition, and the magazine *Quality of Life in Loisaida*. Seven Loaves provided administrative support to smaller arts collectives, including Children Arts Workshop, Printshop, Fourth Street I, Cityarts, Los Hispanos, and the Teatro Ambulante.[75] Some of these same arts organizations, in turn, worked out of the building, generating a synergy of exchange between housing, culture, and the environment that had emerged in the neighborhood. The *Quality of Life in Loisaida*, headquartered right next to Seven Loaves on the second floor, continued to report and inform on the economic, social, and political dimensions of life in Loisaida.

During the first few years, the cultural and educational programs promoted by CHARAS became the mainstay of El Bohio. Chino Garcia, in his role as chairperson of El Bohio board, recruited several different people and organizations to take charge of various aspects of the new community center (**Figure 3.16**). Describing the CHARAS approach to community organizing, Garcia explained in a recent interview, "If someone came to us and said they wanted to work on the project, we said, 'Sure, here is your desk, there is the phone, get started!'" He credits this method as having led to the launch of several successful grassroots efforts in this building—among them, Picture the Homeless, an organization that sought to put a human face on city residents who had no place to live, and Recycle-a-Bicycle, an organization that taught kids to build their own bicycles from old parts.[76] This laissez-faire approach allowed programs located in the community center to evolve organically out of the interests and concerns of old and new residents. This process of expanding incrementally, in step with the gradual renovation of the building, contributed to El Bohio's open-ended and egalitarian character. With the influence of Seven Loaves, artists of color and alternative art practices were nourished and lent weight to the creative endeavor of forming an institution based on the holistic approach championed by CHARAS.

One of the principal projects that absorbed CHARAS in El Bohio was the renovation of the 350-seat auditorium in the basement. The many successful performances produced by CHARAS in the parks and around the neighborhood found a more permanent indoor venue in the basement of El Bohio. In 1981 the New Assembly Theater reopened with *Winos*, a play written by Bimbo Rivas about the problems of alcoholism and drugs within the community. Rivas, an alumnus of PS 64 and author of the poem *Loisaida*, was one of the leading figures of the activist theater movement that was a means to disseminate the message but also a creative expression of a besieged people in the survivalist landscape of Loisaida. The importance of performance as a tool to examine social issues led to the creation of other radical theater groups such as Divaldo Theater, Big Bucket Theater Company, Ninth Street Theater, and Carnival Knowledge. All of these groups used the building to rehearse, offer workshops, and stage regular performances.

In 1981 a group of experimental film enthusiasts began screening movies in the building that highlighted politically themed films focused on housing, social movements, and community development. They invited young but relatively unknown directors such as Spike Lee to screen their films and engage in a dialogue with the audience. They built a projection booth in the old school cafeteria on the first floor at the rear of the building, and Matt Seig, along with Doris Kornish—a recent arrival from West Virginia—coordinated a regular film series in this makeshift cinema.[77] Doris had her own desk in the main office, where she spent hours poring through newspapers, film criticism, and movie catalogs to create a unique film program built around themes that were pertinent to the center (**Figure 3.17**).[78] Classic films were paired with the work of local and lesser-known filmmakers from Latin America, Africa, and Asia to explore common themes of struggles against capitalism, war, and poverty. This well-attended program was advertised through attractively designed posters that CHARAS pasted around the neighborhood. *Films CHARAS* became a neighborhood institution and included conversations with filmmakers to encourage audience participation.

As artists moved into the neighborhood and new commercial and non-profit art spaces opened in the Lower East Side, El Bohio also became a venue for visual arts exhibitions. The walls of the building's main

3.16
CHARAS office within the El Bohio Community Center with Emily Rubin, Doris Kornish, Cynthia, Chino Garcia, and Slima. On the desk are a set of blueprints of the building renovation, 1981.
Photograph by Marlis Momber.

entry lobby on Ninth Street were cleaned, painted, and fitted with lighting so the space could be used as a gallery. It was here that many local artists got an opportunity to present their work and participate in group shows. Openings were enlivened by performances of jazz and Latin music, and the presence of a makeshift bar made for a festive reception of new works. In 1980 El Bohio was one of several venues on the Lower East Side that presented a large group show on nuclear disarmament sponsored by the collective Artists for Survival.[79] A floor-to-ceiling mural by the artist Anton Van Dalen, executed on the southern wall inside the gallery, focused attention on local housing problems by depicting the neighborhood with a giant "real estate cockroach" at the center (**Figure 3.17**). The two small Puerto Rican flags within the mural, according to the artist, were a reference to the community's predominant ethnic makeup in the '80s.[80] This mural, entitled *Lower East Side: Portal to America*, made clear that despite the success of El Bohio and the many community initiatives, the neighborhood was still very much at the center of a continuing housing crisis.

While forging new relationships and widening its networks in its role as the moving force behind El Bohio, CHARAS also reconnected with its long-term associates in its continued pursuit of an ecological agenda. In June 1982 Daniel Chodorkoff organized an "Urban Alternatives" conference at El Bohio. The conference combined the center's three-part mission: housing, social ecology, and the role of the arts in building community. Over the course of two days, twenty panels convened to discuss topics ranging from food supply and auto-free zones in New York City to energy alternatives and housing.[81] The classrooms at El Bohio were used for multiple, simultaneous panels along with a range of workshops conducted by alternative technology advocates, housing activists, local politicians, anarchists, and artists. According to the *East Village Eye*, the forty-five-minute keynote address delivered by Murray Bookchin encompassed "1848 Marx to New Deal pragmatism, but settled somewhere on the steps of Loisaida." For Bookchin, the continuing efforts of groups like CHARAS represented a heartening example of a participatory, self-organized democracy in action.[82]

Other conference participants included a group of more established politicians who echoed this same call for self-determination. A panel on housing and gentrification focused on how small gains within Loisaida were threatened as the city, under Mayor Edward Koch, moved aggressively to create incentives for developers. Councilwoman Miriam Friedlander, a strong voice for community control and a vociferous critic of the mayor's policies, insisted that when it came to the housing market, the city should be held accountable in its role as "regulator" rather than "speculator."[83] This conference, simultaneously festive and thought-provoking, led to the possibility of exchange between those in office and their constituents, the citizens of Loisaida. It also made visible the tensions between the more utopian strands of the Loisaida movement and the shifting priorities of the city and the neighborhood as New York City slowly emerged from its fiscal crisis.

The acts of physical reclamation, accomplished through a creative process of inventing an integrated vision of self-governance, could not have been possible without often circumstantial and sometimes deliberate support from local and federal agents. In describing the work of AAB, the pragmatist-poet and founder of the Nuyorican Café, Miguel Algarin, wrote, "To stay free is not theoretical. It is to take your immediate environment. Who owns the building in which you live? Find them out, then deal directly. Who is willing to talk his way through the legalese that puts wrinkles on the tongue? Roberto Nazario is willing. He can chew a Municipal Housing Authority contract down to its bold deceits."[84] Algarin presents Roberto Nazario, the coordinator of AAB at the time of the move into PS 64, in a respectful fashion, as someone who is capable of dealing with the city and federal bureaucracy while remaining "free." This balancing act of depending on federal aid while organizing on behalf of tenants ultimately strained the organizational structure of AAB. The transition from tenant organizing to managing a federally subsidized CETA program created a rift within the tight-knit Loisaida community. Some of the tenants and block associations that had viewed AAB as an advocate and cohort began to view the organization as part of the establishment as it regulated loans and struggled to transfer homesteaded properties to building cooperatives.[85]

LA LUCHA CONTINUA (1982–1999)

The hard-won gains in Loisaida were challenged throughout the '80s as the United States, under President Reagan (1981–1989), and the city, under Mayor Koch (1978–89), began to cut back on federal and municipal subsidies. Despite Loisaida's remarkable transformation, and partially because of it, the changing fiscal landscape dramatically affected the nature of organizing in this neighborhood. As capital began to flow back into the city, the once abandoned and neglected sites that had been transformed into the gardens, homesteads, and community centers in Loisaida were increasingly coveted by those with speculative interests. Whereas during the '70s community groups had focused on laying a physical claim to an unwanted neighborhood, the next decade was about preserving these gains and warding off new threats of dislocation as investors saw opportunities in a rapidly gentrifying landscape.

As federal money for energy initiatives, job training, and housing programs dried up, organizations that had come to rely on these benefits grew smaller and ultimately folded. This lack of fiscal support, combined with a change in leadership, led to the dwindling influence of AAB in the neighborhood. As the vocational training programs run by AAB drew to a close at El Bohio, CHARAS was left to run the center as a more arts-oriented community space. In 1984 El Bohio signed a fifteen-year lease with the city for the PS 64 building and hoped they would get more funding for pending renovation. After six full years of occupation, the building still lacked a functioning heating system, the roof leaked, and the top two floors of the building were mostly unusable. After repeated lobbying through supportive local politicians, El Bohio received a community development fund from the city to repair the roof and install a new heating system in 1984.[86] This money never went far enough, however, and new problems, such as a flood in the basement theater, kept management busy applying for construction grants and seeking new fiscal sponsorship.

Urban scholars and historians view the influx of educated white artists, galleries, clubs, and new cultural institutions into formerly poor and working-class neighborhoods as a contributing factor, if not a direct cause, of gentrification.[87] In the case of El Bohio, the new influx of artists, anarchists, and radicals was seen by CHARAS as a potential ally in the struggle against the city-developer coalition. To keep the building financially viable and socially vibrant, El Bohio rented the larger rooms to theater groups for rehearsals on an hourly basis and the smaller classrooms to artists for studio space. In the mid-'80s two well-organized art auctions brought some degree of fiscal solvency to the center as well as a new generation of contributors to the building.[88] The artists who donated their works for this auction helped subsidize the operations of the center, which continued to provide such basic services as computer classes, after-school programs, films, and theater spaces to local artists and residents at nominal fees (**Figure 3.18**).

Urayoán Noel, in his book on four decades of Nuyorican poetry, provides a nuanced perspective of the continuities and ruptures in the "counter-politics" of the Nuyorican poets movement, which is informative to the analysis of El Bohio's transformation.[89] In 1982 the Nuyorican Poets Café closed for repairs and went into a long hiatus. During this time, Noel writes, the homegrown Nuyorican poetic tradition, which was rooted in the politics of survival in Loisaida, was "canonized" within the context of the larger Chicano diasporic experience.[90] According to Noel, when the café reopened in 1989, a younger multicultural cast of characters performed within new formats that embedded the political struggles and anxieties of the older generation to offer a "global" resistance to new threats that commodified the authenticity of the older, more localized resistance. Similarly, in the later years, the Loisaida movement and, consequently, El Bohio opened to a wider audience in order to continue to provide vital resources at the local level. This culture was formed around several new identities that included the broader multiethnic Latino constituency as well as an emergent, anarcho-squatter-collectivity with links to a European, as well as a nascent American punk, search for a new identity. Added to this wide spectrum of outsiders was the escalating presence of the disenfranchised and homeless people that found, in the vacant lots and Tompkins Square Park, an odd camaraderie and tolerance. These disparate groups adapted the spatial struggles and counter-institutional stances of the previous decade of a Loisaidan struggle to the new modalities of police violence and the battle for urban space unfolding in the Lower East Side.[91]

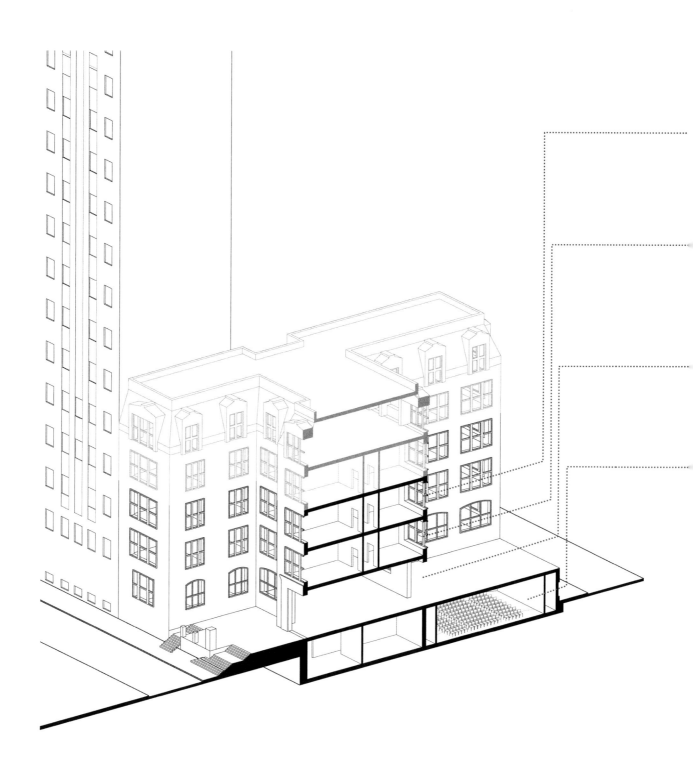

3.18
El Bohio Community Center. Sectional view with a select list of users and their
location within the building.
Illustration by Nandini Bagchee.

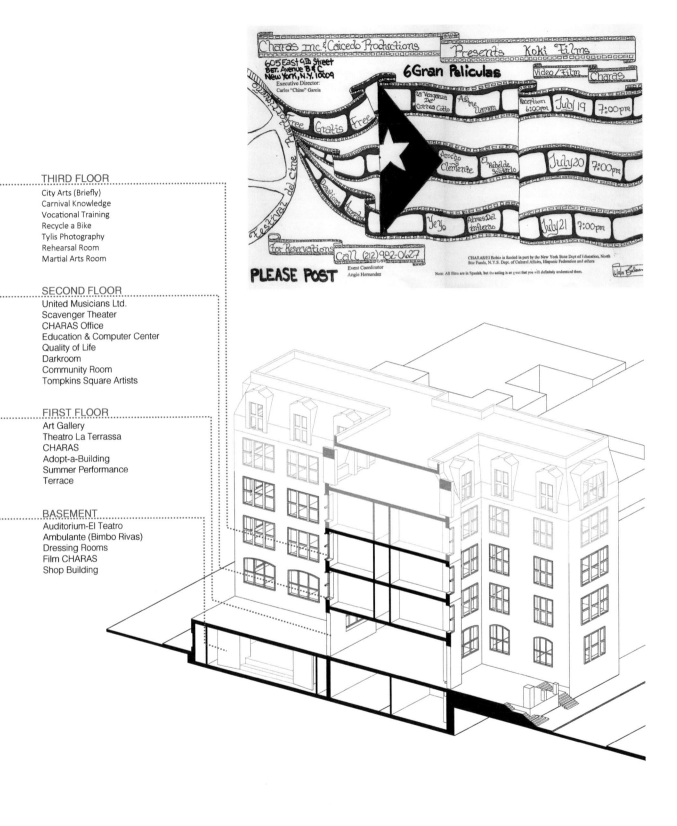

In 1985 a large-scale mural project sponsored by CHARAS, in collaboration with the arts collective Artmakers, celebrated this finding of common cause in La Plaza Cultural. This park, a decade after its creation, had once again deteriorated; parts of the chain-link fence were gone, and drug users encroached on the site, discouraging other residents from using La Plaza. In response to a call to paint the walls of buildings bordering La Plaza, trained artists worked with local collaborators to develop and execute a variety of murals along several linear feet of adjacent building party-walls that bordered the site's southern and western edges. Both local and global political perspectives determined the content of the new murals. Paintings of police brutality and the destruction of buildings in New York City were presented alongside images of popular uprisings in Latin America and anti-apartheid actions in South Africa. These works, designed and executed by different artists, varied stylistically but were linked in terms of thematic content. Dispossession, revolution, and community united an array of these global-political envisionings. Black-edged bands with white letters reading "La Lucha Continua" ("The Struggle Continues") visually tied these separate images executed by many artists into a fluid continuum.[92]

On a prominent exposed wall of the six-story tenement at Avenue C, Eva Cockcroft, founder of Artmakers, led a team of twelve artists in painting a crumbling tenement cityscape showing people struggling to fight demolitions and evictions with reconstructions, celebrations, and a dignified daily existence (**Figure 3.19**). Embedded in this image was a fragment of the mural depicting the Chinese contributions to the neighborhood, as first executed on this same wall by Freddie Hernandez in 1977. Also represented in this mural are the "Miracles of Loisaida"—a geodesic dome, a windmill, a solar roof array, and a street stand selling fresh produce. In the center is a crystal ball that evokes a bucolic landscape, or perhaps an urban garden, in which a circle of women are celebrating. Images of working women float on the surface of the glass globe, bringing into focus the contribution of women and an ecofeminist perspective of the struggle for self-sufficiency. These murals, with their many layers of references, brought together the experiences of people in Puerto Rico, New York, the Americas, and Africa, and displayed them on the disjointed walls of La Plaza Cultural. The flexibility of the syncretic aspects of the Puerto Rican culture, their complex identity, and the spatial politics of Loisaida were laced together and adapted in this instance to address a more global concern for social justice. This same mix of international artists, musicians, and environmentalists from all different backgrounds was also reflected in the tenants at El Bohio.

3.19
La Lucha Continua—murals on the
northern wall of La Plaza Cultural,
1985.
Photograph courtesy of the Artmakers Inc.

Urban development on the Lower East Side, beginning in the late '80s
and continuing into the next decade, was driven in large part by the
vast amount of real estate held by the city government. Many gardens
and community facilities with no leases were jeopardized as the city
sought to relinquish its role as the administrator of troublesome properties and preferred to hand them off to private developers. In the
vacuum left by AAB, other homesteading programs continued in the
area and were spearheaded by organizations such as the Lower East
Side Catholic Area Conference, United Homesteading Assistance
Board, and Rehabilitation in Action to Preserve Neighborhoods.[93] It
was through the concerted effort of these groups and the strong tenant
organizations that a lot of the remaining tenements were brought into
cooperative ownership (**Figure 3.20**). In 1986 the city officially ended
its homesteading program[94] and began a process of consolidating
smaller lots into bigger parcels and auctioning some of these larger,
more attractive properties to private developers. To contest these sales,
many housing advocates and politicized citizens' organizations in the
neighborhood gelled into a formidable opposition.[95] Signs of "Lower
East Side Not for Sale," "This Land is Ours," and "Speculators Keep
Away" appeared on buildings, in gardens, and in street demonstrations
(**Figure 3.21**).

HOMESTEADS

537 E 11TH STREET
B374 / L65
1976- City-Owned
2012- Transfers deed to HDFC

635 E 11TH STREET
B394 / L48
1981- City Owned
1992- Transfers deed to HDFC

304 E & 306 E 8TH STREET
B390 / L9
1978- City Owned
1992- HDFC

517 E & 519 E 11TH STREET
B405 / L7510 & L51
1974- City Owned
1990- 519 E Heartsone HDFC
Next to Windmill project where
cars were stripped for parts.

641 E 11TH STREET
B394 / L48
1977- City Owned
1988- Transfers deed to Florisol HDFC

191 E 3RD STREET
B399 / L41
1970- City Owned
1988- Transferred

522 E 6TH STREET
B401 / L21
Failed Homestead
1988- 522 E assoc.

239 E 2ND STREET
B384 / L24
1978- City Owned
1988- Transfers deed to
Joseph Card Memo
Currently HDFC

539 E 6TH STREET
B402 / L45

219 E 4TH STREET
B400 / L48

309 E 4TH STREET
B374 / L65
1978- City Owned
1987- Transfers deed to
All Peoples Homestead 309 HDFC

742 E 6TH STREET
B375 / L30
1978- City Owned
1985- Transfers deed to Habitat

66 AVENUE C
B374 / L6
1978- City Owned
1986- Transfers deed to HDFC

702 E 5TH STREET
B374 / L8
1978- City Owned
1986- Transfers deed to HDFC

507 E & 509 E 11TH STREET
B405 / L58
1974- City Owned
1976- Transfers deed to
507/509 ETAL

310 E 4TH STREET
B373 / L8
1976- City Owned
1979- Transfers deed to HDFC

320 E 4TH STREET
B373 / L13
1977- City Owned

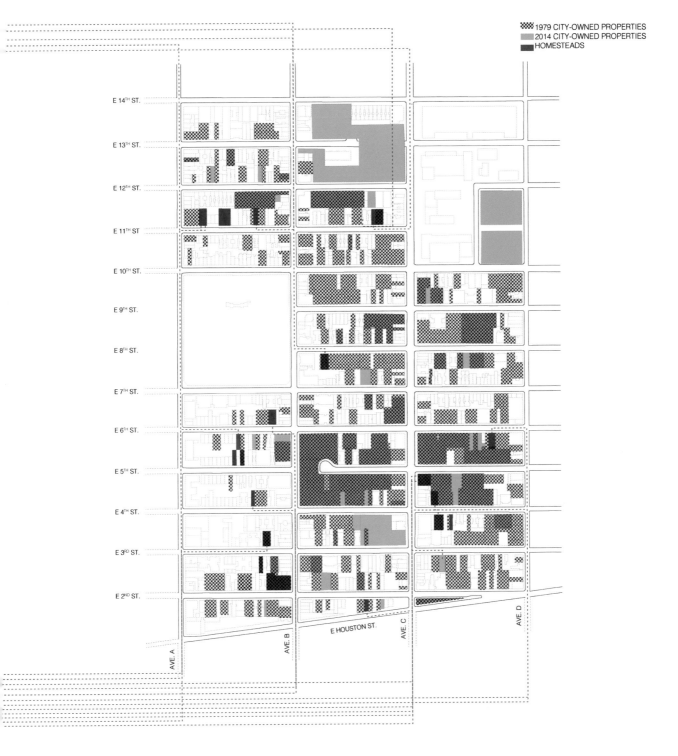

E 14ᵀᴴ ST.
E 13ᵀᴴ ST.
E 12ᵀᴴ ST.
E 11ᵀᴴ ST.
E 10ᵀᴴ ST.
E 9ᵀᴴ ST.
E 8ᵀᴴ ST.
E 7ᵀᴴ ST.
E 6ᵀᴴ ST.
E 5ᵀᴴ ST.
E 4ᵀᴴ ST.
E 3ᴿᴰ ST.
E 2ᴺᴰ ST.

AVE. A
AVE. B
E HOUSTON ST.
AVE. C
AVE. D

1979 CITY-OWNED PROPERTIES
2014 CITY-OWNED PROPERTIES
HOMESTEADS

3.20
Key homesteaded buildings in Loisaida, 1974–1991.
Illustration by Nandini Bagchee.
List compiled from different sources, including the research by Malve
von Hassell in *Homesteading in New York City, 1978–1993: The Divided
Heart of Loisaida* (1996).

3.21
Coalition protest march from East Fourth Street to Cooper Square, 1987.

Photograph by Marlis Momber.

By the end of the '80s, the Joint Planning Commission (JPC), a coalition of thirty-five housing advocates, block associations, and tenants on the Lower East Side, banded together and negotiated with the city to rethink its housing policy. In a deal brokered by the JPC, each unit of city-owned property auctioned for development was to be compensated by an equal amount of low-rent housing. This arrangement, dubbed a 50–50 subsidy, was equitable in theory but hard to monitor in practice. It created friction among the gardeners and homesteaders as the city selectively cleared gardens and evicted people to generate vacancies for new market-rate housing. JPC's initiative resonated poorly with some within the Puerto Rican community who felt that their struggle to build Loisaida was given short shrift, as the lottery for the new low-rent housing did not necessarily benefit the people who had toiled so long within the neighborhood.[96]

Beloved properties such as the recycling center, La Plaza Cultural, and El Bohio were also put on the auction block. A proposal to develop housing for the elderly (Casa Victoria) pitted La Plaza Cultural against a developer known for his unfair tactics.[97] This scheme was defeated with the help of district council member Margarita Lopez, a local organizer and homesteader-turned politician. The victory was bittersweet, however, as a series of smaller gardens and properties were bulldozed in exchange for La Plaza Cultural.[98]

In 1998, at the end of its fifteen-year lease, despite popular support and energetic fund-raising, El Bohio Community Center was sold to a private developer for $3.15 million (**Figure 3.22**). The sale of the center came as a shock to a neighborhood that saw other community groups attain ownership of their buildings. According to Armando Perez, codirector of El Bohio, this negative outcome was the result of the Giuliani administration's "vendetta" against the political rallying and specific importance of El Bohio to the Puerto Rican movement in Loisaida.[99] At the time of its sale, the building was being used by theater groups, Recycle-a-Bicycle, and several artists that rented studio space to produce and exhibit their work. Despite the continued dedication of El Bohio codirectors and CHARAS cofounders Chino Garcia and Armando Perez, there was a gradual shift in the user base as those that had initiated it as a center for Puerto Rican resistance twenty-two years ago moved away. The impending loss of the building, however, brought many of the older generation of the Puerto Ricans back to the building.[100] They joined arms with the white artists and their cohorts to participate in a collective campaign to maintain control of the building that many saw as a symbol of "cross-fertilization for white and Puerto Rican artists and activists."[101] On December 27, 2001, amidst chants of "Giuliani you are no good—you are destroying our neighborhood," the police in riot gear evicted the remaining occupiers of the building.[102]

ACTIVIST ESTATES—PROPERTY AS RESISTANCE IN LOISAIDA

In Loisaida, the conversion and transformation of vacant lots into gardens and of empty institutional buildings into community centers not only created public space but also produced an engaged public (**Figure 3.23**). Locally rooted activists did not outline a master plan in the conventional sense but generated a master narrative to create an urban ensemble that accommodated education, gardening, and cultural events and responded to the housing needs of an underserved neighborhood. The publicity skills of the organizers and the fruitful collaborations between disparate groups created a social momentum that captured the imagination of the people and generated a network of "activist estates" in Loisaida. Starting with the port-a-dome project, CHARAS broadened its knowledge to include youth engagement, environmentalism, and culture, making the troubled but increasingly

3.22
El Bohio for Sale. Save El Bohio, 1998-2001.
Illustration by Nandini Bagchee.

desirable neighborhood of Loisaida a model for self-organization. The grassroots work of AAB and their dexterous juggling of available resources allowed ordinary citizens to enthusiastically embrace the concept of sweat equity and led to the creation of affordable, cooperatively owned housing. Rich in its ideological dimensions (the de-commodification of labor, the hard work involved, and the grassroots DIY ethic) and in its practical benefits (warm apartments and community facilities), this movement attracted a large cast of characters. Carpenters, auto mechanics, concerned mothers, teenagers, housing advocates, grant writers, PhD students, poets, performers, artists, and alternative energy enthusiasts all contributed to the creation of a new urban imaginary anchored in the repurposing of physical space.

Poets and builders laid claim to the Lower East Side through the Loisaida movement, identifying it as a space of Puerto Rican resistance. This construction and political assertion over a disinvested territory within New York City brought into being a new type of urbanism. Jorge Brandon, the father of the Nuyorican poetry movement, not unlike the poet laureates of a nationalist Resistance-Neruda (in Chile), or Tagore (in Bengal), gave dignity to the degraded landscape in his incantations and presence as a street troubadour speaking a double tongue. This place-based construction of a communal identity was tactical in the struggle for political recognition. The renaming and remaking of places, such as El Sol Brilliante, La Plaza Cultural, and El Bohio, was driven by the need to contribute to the design and construction of a future city that was more inclusive and more radical in its use of space.

The Loisaida movement shared with other contemporary '70s grassroots urban movements unfolding in Spain, the west coast, and Latin America what sociologist Manuel Castells observed was a demand for access to the infrastructure of collective consumption—housing, education, art, and a clean environment.[103] The urban context of Loisaida, in its broken-down form, was simultaneously the facilitator and the object of collective action. By working outside the framework of electoral politics, residents connected the dots, filled in the holes, and founded a networked city. The series of properties in Loisaida, the "activist estates," functioned as a collective common held together by the thread of community action. As the city changed, so did the actions. The buildings brought under community control were not simply occupied but they were cultivated physically into places that constantly changed. The resulting change in material conditions for the participants from negative (disinvested, demolished, abandoned) to positive (cared for, rebuilt, enlivened) was the goal of their resistance.

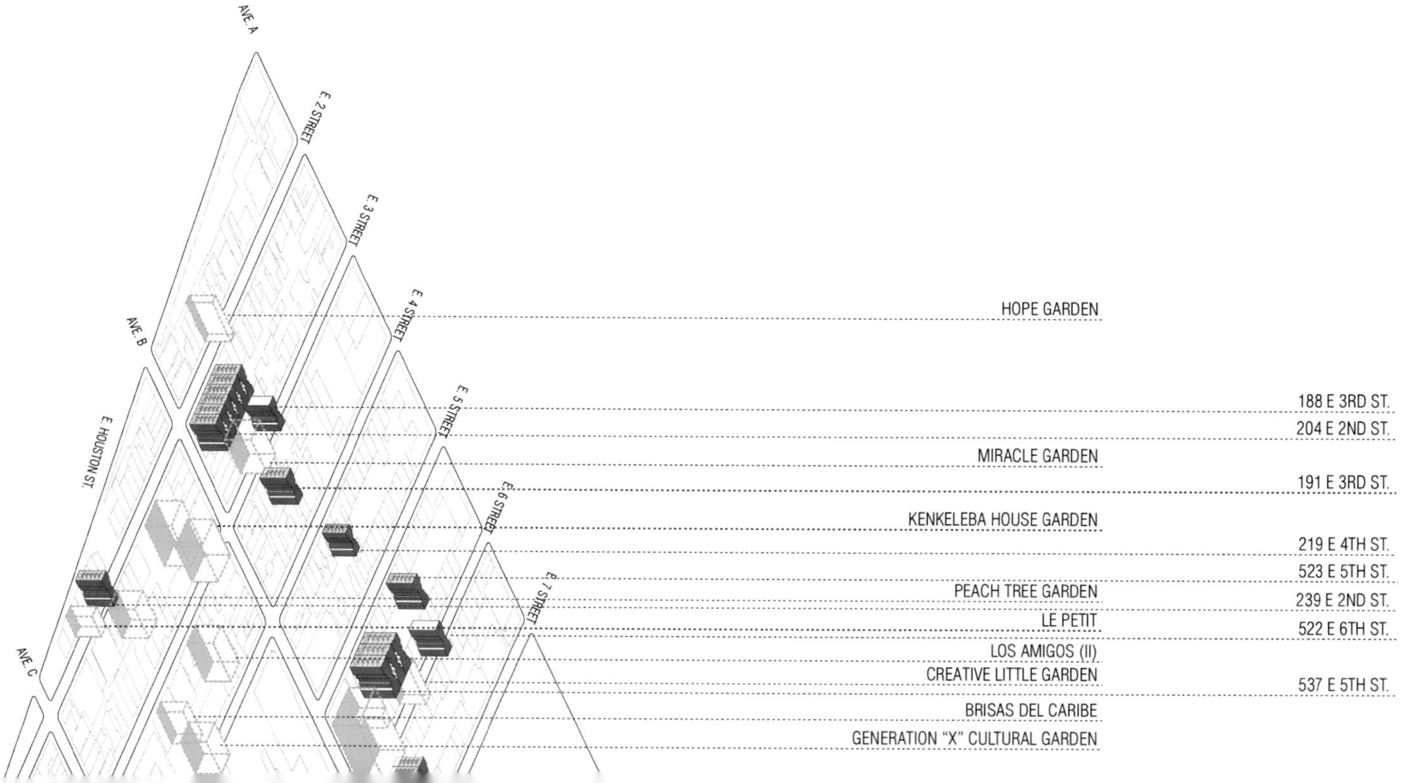

HOPE GARDEN

188 E 3RD ST.
204 E 2ND ST.

MIRACLE GARDEN

191 E 3RD ST.

KENKELEBA HOUSE GARDEN

219 E 4TH ST.
523 E 5TH ST.
239 E 2ND ST.
522 E 6TH ST.

PEACH TREE GARDEN

LE PETIT

LOS AMIGOS (II)

CREATIVE LITTLE GARDEN

537 E 5TH ST.

BRISAS DEL CARIBE

GENERATION "X" CULTURAL GARDEN

E. 7 STREET
E. 6 STREET
E. 5 STREET
E. 4 STREET
E. 3 STREET
E. 2 STREET

AVE. A
AVE. B
AVE. C

E. HOUSTON ST.

HOMESTEADS

GARDENS

SECRET GARDEN
ALL PEOPLE'S GARDEN
310 E 4TH ST.
320 E 4TH ST.
309 E 4TH ST.
66 AVE C
702 E 5TH ST.
EL JARDIN DEL PARAISO
304 E. & 306 E. 8TH ST.
507 E. & 509 E 11TH ST.
ORCHARD ALLEY
11 BC SERENITY GARDEN
517 E. & 519 E 11TH ST.
DE COLORES COMMUNITY GARDEN
EL BOHIO COMMUNITY CENTER
EL SOL BRILLANTE
537 E 11TH ST.
LA PLAZA CULTURAL
CHARAS RECYCLING CENTER
SAM AND SADIE KOENIG GARDEN
742 E 6TH ST.
DIAS Y FLORES
FIREMENS MEMORIAL GARDEN
CHILDREN'S GARDEN
EL SOL BRILLANTE JR.
VAMOS SEMBRAR
TOYOTA CHILDREN'S LEARNING GARDEN
GILBRT'S GARDEN
631 E 11TH ST.
9TH STREET COMMUNITY GARDEN
635 E 11TH ST.
641 E 11TH ST.
CAMPOS

E. 13 STREET
E. 12 STREET
E. 11 STREET
E. 14 STREET
E. 9 STREET
E. 8 STREET
AVE. D

3.23
Homesteads, gardens, and the legacy of CHARAS/El Bohio Community Center.
Illustration by Nandini Bagchee.

4

THE COLLECTIVE MAKING OF ABC NO RIO

(1980-2010)

CHAPTER 4: THE COLLECTIVE MAKING OF ABC NO RIO (1980-2010)

In December 1979 a group of artists broke into a city-owned property in the Lower East Side and installed an exhibit, the *Real Estate Show*. The works displayed by the artists expressed outrage at the exclusionary housing and land use policies that had destroyed neighborhoods and rendered many of New York City's poor homeless. The artists' manifesto announced their anti-institutional stance, but even as the police shut down the show, the Department of Housing Preservation and Development (HPD) of the city of New York offered the artists the use of an alternate space—a commercial storefront in a four-story tenement building in the same neighborhood. The artists accepted the offer and formed a volunteer-run art center at 156 Rivington Street, in a predominantly Latino neighborhood.[1] They named the place "ABC No Rio," in playful reference to a Spanish sign, "Abogado Notario," with partially erased letters directly across the street from the building.[2]

This chapter examines the changing form of this "counter institution" produced over a period of thirty years (1980–2010) by looking at the history of its occupation in a dilapidated four-story residential walk-up in Downtown Manhattan (**Figure 4.1**). The building and its community melded in a catalytic moment when the municipal government, despite its antipathy toward the renegade artists, saw an arts center as a temporary way to deflect negative media coverage and possibly enhance the value of a building depleted by years of neglect and mismanagement. ABC No Rio made the most of this opening and proceeded to develop the building as a venue for experimentation and exhibition for local artists, run by the artists themselves.[3] What began as an impromptu occupation of city-owned property and a critique of real estate speculation paradoxically crystallized into an institution in its own right. Over three decades, the constant reshaping of the idea of a volunteer-run art space by successive waves of politically committed countercultural collectives enabled this building to survive the constant pressure from the city to evict its tenants. The process of building collectivity in opposition to the bureaucracy of the city and the individuality embedded in the anarchic ethos of the many artists at ABC No Rio arguably generated a space that was guarded but open to different types of creative possibilities.

4.1
Street view, ABC No Rio, 2012.
Photograph © Jade Doskow.

The domestically scaled tenement building, located in an economically depressed and municipally neglected neighborhood in 1980s New York, facilitated a specific brand of DIY collectivity. The publicity garnered by the quick shows at this bootstrap undertaking in the first five years of its operation was consciously recorded in the book *ABC No Rio Dinero: The Story of a Lower East Side Art Gallery*.[4] This early period, which launched the careers of many of the artists involved in the shows, was followed by a contentious period of squatting, battling the HPD, and negotiating the right to occupy the building. The publicity garnered by the early shows and the space-based activism was instrumental in creating an oppositional institutional history for ABC No Rio that was subsequently leveraged to gain the support of a larger community and raise funds for the building. The survival of ABC No Rio was the outcome of a collective development of an institution that creatively used the space as a byproduct, a symbol, and finally as the goal of their social activism.

THE ART CONTEXT 1970–1980 NEW YORK

THE ALTERNATIVE SPACE

The emergence of the artists' collectives seeking social change through political art-actions was an outgrowth of an alternative art movement in 1970s New York.[5] This movement fomented opposition to the limitations of institutionalized art practices and focused on providing alternatives to artists excluded from museums and commercial galleries. This exclusion included prejudice against minorities and women and a process of weeding out work that was not salable based on the content and aesthetic parameters deemed valuable by the art market. In 1969 artists' collectives, such as the Art Workers Coalition (AWC) and Guerrilla Action Art Group (GAAG), targeted these inequities arising from established museum practices. The manifestos, picketing, and direct-action interventions called for the major New York museums (MOMA, Whitney, Guggenheim, and the MET) to change their discriminatory policies and to play a more active part in the political and social life of the city.[6] These actions did not directly transform the institutional policies of the targeted institutions per se but rather led to the foundation of alternative neighborhood museums and art centers in the Bronx, Harlem, Queens, and Downtown Manhattan. The process of challenging the art establishment also led artists to expand their practices of art making and to explore the role of the artist as a political and cultural agent. The opposition to the established art world represented by the museums and commercial galleries took shape in many different cities across the United States, where organized artist groups or curators set up nonprofit "alternative" galleries with funding from state and federal grants. In New York the pluralistic and often cross-disciplinary practices that included performance, video, music, and new media arts in addition to the traditional visual arts practices occurred in the context of a postindustrial city, where commercial lofts and vacant storefronts were co-opted by artists, curators, and gallerists to make and exhibit new types of work. The availability of affordable living, working, and exhibition spaces in locations such as the warehouse district of SoHo yielded a concentration of artist-run galleries (**Figure 4.2**).[7] The architectural quality of the SoHo lofts—industrial, unfinished spaces with big windows—invited artists to experiment with materials and methods to create expansive installations. The site specificity of these interventions made the work more connected to the place and foregrounded the relevance of the physical potential of the "alternative" space. This attention to the actual site, typically outside the gallery/museum context, led artists to challenge the norm of product or object-oriented art practices.

AN ALTERNATIVE TO ALTERNATIVES

Fueling these experimental practices in the mid-'60s and '70s was the availability of inexpensive living and working quarters for the small community of artists that sought out these situations. The Flux house project of Maciunas, discussed in Chapter 1, in effect tried to formalize and structure this process into a type of collectively controlled real estate. In reality the process was fairly ad hoc, and the presence of artists and the success of art galleries in former manufacturing locations quickly fueled speculation and, consequently, priced out the artists themselves.[8] By the late '70s, some artists felt that the alternate art spaces initiated in opposition to commercial galleries were compromised by the ever-expanding art and real estate market, which, once again, left very little control and agency to the artists themselves.

Critical of this setup, the artists' collective Collaborative Projects (Colab), a confederation of about forty artists, banded together in 1977 to create an alternative to the "alternative" institutions (**Figure 4.3**).[9] Their motivation was to circumvent the additional costs and attendant control of the alternative space administrations. Their goal was to apply for the same federal and state arts grants allocated to the established alternative spaces but use these funds to develop "collaborative works directed to the needs of the community at large."[10] The community for the Colab artists was a reference to themselves—a large heterogeneous artist collective that sought direct support and exposure for its members' work. The production of the work—a

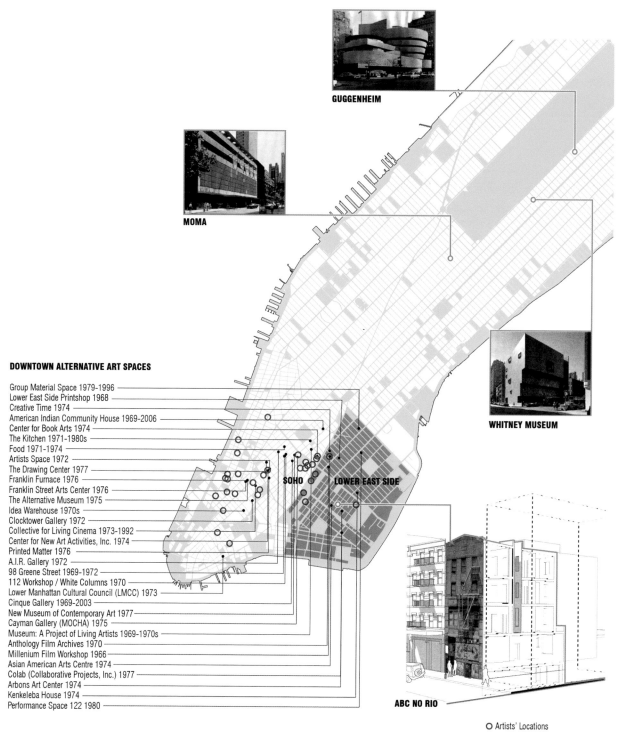

GUGGENHEIM

MOMA

WHITNEY MUSEUM

DOWNTOWN ALTERNATIVE ART SPACES

Group Material Space 1979-1996
Lower East Side Printshop 1968
Creative Time 1974
American Indian Community House 1969-2006
Center for Book Arts 1974
The Kitchen 1971-1980s
Food 1971-1974
Artists Space 1972
The Drawing Center 1977
Franklin Furnace 1976
Franklin Street Arts Center 1976
The Alternative Museum 1975
Idea Warehouse 1970s
Clocktower Gallery 1972
Collective for Living Cinema 1973-1992
Center for New Art Activities, Inc. 1974
Printed Matter 1976
A.I.R. Gallery 1972
98 Greene Street 1969-1972
112 Workshop / White Columns 1970
Lower Manhattan Cultural Council (LMCC) 1973
Cinque Gallery 1969-2003
New Museum of Contemporary Art 1977
Cayman Gallery (MOCHA) 1975
Museum: A Project of Living Artists 1969-1970s
Anthology Film Archives 1970
Millenium Film Workshop 1966
Asian American Arts Centre 1974
Colab (Collaborative Projects, Inc.) 1977
Arbons Art Center 1974
Kenkeleba House 1974
Performance Space 122 1980

SOHO

LOWER EAST SIDE

ABC NO RIO

○ Artists' Locations
• Alternative Art Spaces

4.2
A map of major art museums and alternative art institutions
in downtown Manhattan in the '70s.
Illustration by Nandini Bagchee.

combination of film, performance, and visual art—involved collective effort. Experimenting with new media technologies, and influenced by themes and visual presentations that bore the imprint of a populist yet marginal "punk" sensibility, Colab sought to move the discourse beyond the museums, galleries, and affiliated curatorial constraints of the new alternative art spaces to produce a more populist and collaborative artistic practice. Colab member and historian Alan Moore describes the populist punk inspiration of the group as follows: "This new mode of collectivity was vernacular and opportunistic. Rather than embracing the rationalized, programmatic 'new society' ideas of the organized left, the Colab artists drew on popular forms of grouping, such as the film crew and the rock and roll band."[11]

Although Colab made no formal effort to consolidate a singular artistic agenda, there was a desire on their part to publicize the collective effort and to create shows that were open to all and allowed for diverse participation. Early shows mounted in the downtown studio and loft spaces of founding Colab artists Coleen Fitzgibbon and Robin Winters were set up around seemingly random themes such as "Batman," "Doctors and Dentists," "Income and Wealth," "Manifesto Show," and "Library Show." The work produced for these shows rejected the

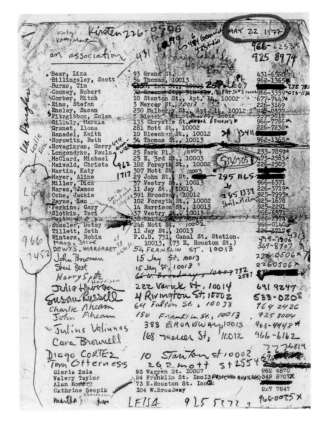

4.3
Colab contact list with artist's addresses, 1977. All listed addresses of Colab members are shown as red rings on downtown alternative art spaces map.

Document as printed in David Little, "Colab Takes a Piece, History Takes It Back: Collectivity and New York Alternative Spaces," *Art Journal* 66, no. 1 (2007), 60.

minimalist singularity of the artwork from the previous decade and instead gravitated toward the figural, expressive, and conceptually direct.[12] An interest in crime, sex, and drugs—pervasive realities in the downtown neighborhoods—were explored in the sensationalist style of a generation influenced by the oppositional punk culture popular in Downtown Manhattan. Work hung off ceilings and walls in a closely packed juxtaposition became a hallmark of these shows. Rather than respond to the expansive site of the loft and studio and the site-specific work of '70s artists, the Colab-themed shows generated a new site within the loft through accumulation and aggregation. The spatial collectivity was a product of proximity rather than agreement, consensus, or intentionality.[13]

The *Real Estate Show* (**Figure 4.4**), planned for the first two weeks of the New Year (1980) in a public venue by a few of the Colab cohorts, was an offspring of these open-participation, all-inclusive shows. The idea of using city-owned property as a community arts center was in the air.[14] The artists initially approached the HPD for permission to use the vacant city-owned property on 123 Delancey Street. When they received no response, they decided to move forward with an insurrectionary occupation instead. A small group broke into the building on December 29, 1979, with a pair of large bolt cutters and invited their colleagues to covertly install a show.[15] This show was themed around real estate. Unlike previous Colab shows, this one was a critical response to the interests of a city that had allowed hundreds of properties to lie vacant as displaced residents struggled to find accommodation. The building selected for this provocation was appropriately located at the corner of Delancey and Norfolk Streets, on a parcel of land cleared in 1967 to make way for an urban renewal project on the Lower East Side. The proposed mass-housing project, which was intended to provide moderate-income accommodation along Delancey Street, had displaced over two thousand families but failed to materialize thirteen years later at the time of the *Real Estate Show*. By targeting the city and the real estate industry, the artists felt like they were finding common cause with the residents in this, at the time, low-income neighborhood, and through the reclamation of public land. The exhibiting artists, in stated solidarity with resident citizens, pushed against the city's policy by attempting, in the words of participating artist Becky Howland, to create not just another art gallery but a "Citizens Center."[16] She mounted a seven-foot-long octopus on the façade of the building at Delancey Street (**Figure 4.5**) and made multiples of a poster for the show, also featuring the octopus grasping alternating tenement buildings and dollar bills in each of its tentacles. The artists installed their work inside the building, and the show opened on January 1, 1980, for barely a day before being shut down by

4.4
Flyer announcing the *Real Estate Show*, 1980.
Courtesy of ABC No Rio Archive.

4.5
Top: Artist Becky Howland wheat
pastes an Octopus to the façade,
1980.
Bottom: 123 Delancey Street—the
location of the Real Estate Show.
Top photograph by Ann Messner. Bottom
photograph by Alan Moore. Courtesy of
Becky Howland.

the HPD. The contents of the show were confiscated, the property was padlocked, and police were posted outside to prevent the artists from entering. This created a public outrage and the event was well reported in local newspapers.[17] The dexterity of the organizing artists lay in the way they successfully advertised the lack of spatial access and turned the failed exhibit into a political coup. The appearance of the visiting artist Joseph Beuys, photographed by the media at the barricaded exhibit, and seen milling around with the police and people, brought international attention and validation to the show.

A COMMUNITY OF ARTISTS IN SEARCH OF A COMMUNITY (1980–1983)

The HPD offered the artists the use of an alternative storefront space, at 156 Rivington Street, in an effort to stem the negative publicity generated by the closing of the *Real Estate Show*. In February 1980 Becky Howland, Alan Moore, and Robert Goldman, aka Bobby G, signed a monthly lease with HPD and took over the day-to-day running of an art gallery on the first floor at 156 Rivington Street. This storefront gallery, located a few feet above street level, was entered via a short flight of stairs and stoop shared with the residential tenants of the apartments above. A large plate glass window with the welcoming sign "Venga Ahora" was one left over from the days when the first floor had been used as a beauty salon. A deep backyard, which was connected to the first floor, allowed for the expansion of activities and projects into the outdoors during the summer months. The basement below, with direct access from the street, was also co-opted by No Rio shortly after their residency. The upper three floors of the narrow building configured as floor-through apartments, with a kitchen and bath at each floor, were occupied with residential tenants.

The early years of ABC No Rio's history[18] were marked by a flurry of short artist-curated shows built upon concepts of coming to grips with the living conditions and social realities of the neighborhood. This neighborhood, home to a working-class Puerto Rican, Dominican, and African American community, was severely impacted by the economic crisis in the '70s. The lack of jobs and the cycle of disinvestment, drugs, and violence caused all but the poorest families to stay on in the neighborhood. The remaining bodegas, street vendors, and people playing dominos on the streets were a mere fragment of what had once been a lively commercial and residential street. In the early '80s a *New York Times* article reported that a "multi-million-dollar heroin trade" was being run from the "215 city-owned tenements" of the Lower East Side. This same article on the drug trafficking in the

Lower East Side singled out Rivington and Eldridge Streets as "one of the busiest areas for drugs."[19] This and other types of issues arising from maintaining a large stock of old buildings made the city view the tenements it owned as liabilities. Not unlike the negligent private landlords, the city, in its role as landlord, deployed similar tactics like frequently cutting off the basic amenities—heat, water, and electricity—within their buildings in an attempt to drive out the remaining tenants.

The artists, having procured a month-to-month rental of the storefront from the city, earnestly desired to establish a relationship with the "local." In a 1980 article in the *Village Voice*, the writer Richard Goldstein labels ABC No Rio as an "Anti-Space"—one formed in opposition to the alternative galleries that responds directly to the social context of a city and a neighborhood in dire straits.[20] For the newcomers at ABC No Rio, the street and the storefront provided a potentially fecund context for the development of anarchist artistic practices. The ad hoc curation of themed shows by different artists foregrounded the deteriorating walls and ceilings inside ABC No Rio, and the gritty street outside provided a strong context that framed the brutal content and rough punk realism of some of the artworks. However, there was also a desire to engage with the place and include the community. This ambition for inclusivity was at the core of some early shows such as Christy Rupp's *Animals Living in the City* (1980), where artwork contributed by artists, scientists, and school children was displayed nonhierarchically in the long gallery space.[21] The storefront window was cordoned off from the main gallery with chicken wire to house a live hen, mice, pigeons, and even cockroaches in an attempt to explore the intersection of the animal world with the human one in the degraded environment of a neglected city (**Figure 4.6**). The exploitation of the authentic site of an ill-maintained tenement building led to art practices that were an odd combination of the domestic and the anarchic.[22]

The goal to create a citizen's center found traction with the neighborhood's children, but it proved harder to engage the adult population who were confronted with the hardships of survival and perhaps mistrustful of critical, white middle-class artists in their neighborhood. Despite the good intentions to create a nexus for the local community, the projects were unable to bridge the social divide between the artists and the working-class and poorer adult population at Rivington Street.[23] For instance, Tom Warren's *Portrait Show* (1981), envisioned as an icebreaker, brought people from the street to willingly pose for one-dollar portraits of themselves that were then enlarged by the artist and mounted in the gallery (**Figure 4.7**). The ABC No Rio book notes,

4.6
Bottom: Exterior view of ABC No Rio storefront. Top: Detail of same storefront with live hen and dog stencils by Anton van Dalen, *Animals in the City Show*, 1980.
Photographs courtesy of Anton van Dalen.

Installation by Tom Warren, *Portrait Show*, 1981.
Photograph by Tom Warren.

"These portraits, posed for by people who wanted to look good, show the enduring aspect of an Hispanic neighborhood often overlooked by those focusing on slum realities." This project, replicated in other settings by the artist with different participants, won acclaim but also received this comment from a fellow artist, Richard Armijo, who questions the political intentions as follows:

> Why do anonymous images of the so-called underclass elicit our interest and appreciation, even monetary patronage, while the people themselves are confined to ghettos, encouraged to concentrate in projects, restricted to mostly blue-collar jobs, their intelligentsia too late acknowledged, and their daily movements monitored by cops, sociologists, liberals and now artists?[24]

The desire to create a place—one that welcomed all manner of informal public participation—produced an energetic locus for artistic exchange for the young artists practicing, at the time, in the margins of the art and cultural world. There was a critical awareness on the part of the artists and outside critics that evaluated the situation in terms of the success or failure to create a solidarity with the "community." To

4.8
Installation by John Morton,
Murder, Junk, and Suicide Show,
1980.
Photograph by Tom Warren.

challenge the mores and preconceptions of established art world practices on the one hand, and to become a more accessible art center within a primarily low-income Latino neighborhood on the other, were sometimes irreconcilable impulses. The economic, cultural, and social differences between the artists and the many residents of the neighborhood were insurmountable. The open community art center, with its controversial art shows with themes such as "Murder, Junk, and Suicide" (**Figure 4.8**), was not a place that resonated with residents struggling to survive the intractable problems of a neighborhood that was plagued by these same problems while making a living, educating their children, and finding a way out of their misfortunes.

There was, in turn, wariness on the part of the artists, especially those who saw to the everyday running of the space. The gallery openings invariably followed by break-ins strained the resources of the gallery, recalled artist Bobby G.[25] Within the first few months of the gallery opening, he moved into the basement to be able to secure the building around the clock and to benefit from the rent-free accommodation. Other tenants within the building, at the time, included an extended Dominican family who occupied some of the apartments on the second and third floors. Maria Acosta (seen in many of the photographs from the time) and her brother, Manny, the children from this family, became regulars at the gallery and created artworks and participated in the shows. The children were always welcomed by the artists, but relations with some of the other family members associated with the drug dealing within the hallways of the building were somewhat strained. The flow of clientele, through the broken front door to the residential apartments, jeopardized the safety of the building as a whole and discouraged visitors to the gallery.[26] The ongoing maintenance issues stemming from the negligence of their landlord—the HPD—created hostilities between the various users of the building.

In the first three years of its existence at Rivington Street, the core users of ABC No Rio mainly consisted of a circle of exhibiting Colab artists and some of the local children curious about the happenings. The so-called gallery was, in fact, used as a workspace and a place of social gathering on a daily basis. Artist Christy Rupp remembers a period in her life when she would show up at the storefront space regularly to produce work and enjoy the camaraderie of whoever else might happen to be there (**Figure 4.9**).[27] The open interior, with the large street-facing storefront window, was more generous and communal than the cramped quarters of her own apartment in Downtown New York City. Weekly meetings on Monday, open to all, were a forum to pitch ideas about shows and to discuss grant proposals and other matters pertaining to the space itself. Gallery organizers did not formally vet the shows but accepted proposals on the understanding that the artists would take full responsibility to install their own shows. Although officially open to all, the meetings and the shows advertised by word of mouth tended to remain within the Colab network. Colab

4.9
Left to Right: Leonard Abrams, Christy Rupp and Layne Redmond at ABC No Rio, 1981.
Photograph courtesy of Marc Miller.

did not directly sponsor the storefront of ABC No Rio, but its connection to the larger collective kept it well used and vibrant.[28]

This situation at ABC No Rio began to change after about three years, as the success and notoriety of the Colab shows[29] presented new opportunities to the artists associated with the collective, and they moved on to explore new directions within their respective artistic practices. The founding members, though resolute in their desire to hold on to the space for future collaborators, felt that the managerial aspects of running the art center took too much time away from their own work as artists and art critics. As they looked for new types of programming to bring into the space, a new leadership sympathetic to the ambition of creating the "Anti-Space" presented itself.

BODIES IN CLUB SPACE AND THE INCORPORATION OF ABC NO RIO (1983–1990)

In 1983 the performance collective POOL (Performance on One Leg) proposed a week-long show entitled *Seven Days of Creation* in the gallery at ABC No Rio. This show, curated by dancers associated with the downtown club scene of 1980s New York, brought a new genre of performance to ABC No Rio. Staged inside the gallery during the month of April, at Easter, the seven-day, twenty-four-hour performance involved several different artists and their troupes.[30] A different group took charge of each of the seven days and choreographed and improvised the performances for that day. The varied perspectives and multimedia interests of the invited artists—film, painting, theater, sculpture, and dance—combined in this collective oeuvre. The biblical title of the show was allegorical because it celebrated the creativity of the artists and the birth of their ideas.[31] The project involved the participation of dancers trained in classical and modern balletic traditions as well as untrained performers. The POOL collective, influenced by German Expressionism and the theories of Bauhaus Total Theater, incorporated experimental body movements with words, images, props, and costumes.[32] The sets, like the performance, were prepared quickly and roughly from salvaged trash and readily available materials. The "screaming raw ruined and vibrant shelter"[33] that was ABC No Rio provided the performance with the unorthodox exuberance of the nightclub but remained, at its core, an artist-run collaborative space.

While poetry, music, and spoken word had always been a part of the earliest ABC No Rio visual art shows, the multimedia, collaborative production of the *Seven Days* performance created a different current within the space. On the heels of this performance, Jack Waters and

Peter Cramer of POOL took over running ABC No Rio. Like Bobby G before them, they moved into the basement in the mixed company of the ABC No Rio archive, the rats, and the smells of matzo from the factory next door. They lived here for two years while coordinating shows in the gallery and looking after the premises as the live-in co-directors of ABC No Rio. They continued the tradition of open Monday meetings and facilitated different artists to install shows and conduct poetry readings. Their own interests in performance, however, became the driver of ABC No Rio in the first years of their tenure as codirectors. Their performance circle at the Pyramid Club—a dance, music, drag venue on Avenue A—became a resource they exported to ABC No Rio. The *Extremist Show*, another long-durational event modeled after the *Seven Days* show, and choreographed by Kembra Pfahler, involved the same cortege of artists. The multimedia event was staged within the gallery and outside in the yard, and it provided a venue in which "Audience and performers merged in a series of mock ceremonies, some commencing at dawn, executed with orgiastic fervor."[34] Photographs document the bodies of the performers taking over the entire space in action (painting and engaging with the debris in the yard) and in repose (sleeping, examining, listening, and becoming a part of the physical space) (**Figure 4.10**).

4.10
Left: Peter Cramer and Jack Waters perform in the backyard. Center: Kembra Pfahler sleeps in storefront window. Right: Kembra Pfahler and Samoa seated on paintings. The Extremist Show, 1983.
Photographs by Toyo. Courtesy of Toyo Tsuchiya estate.

In comparing the politics of the performance artists to the previous Colab generation, Peter Cramer describes the artists as "less didactic, more amorphous," and the resultant atmosphere at ABC No Rio in the mid-'80s as more "clubby and colorful."[35] The concept of making do with very little, or whatever happened to be available, contributed to the ethical and aesthetic aspect of these performances. This concept, labeled "availabilism" by Pfahler,[36] was in part a reaction to the shrinking federal grant monies to art institutions and the censorship that

marked Reagan's second term in office. Having founded their own nonprofit performance "Allied Productions" in 1980' Waters and Cramer were well versed with the bureaucratic procedures needed to run an arts organization. They used this umbrella organization to apply for New York State–funded Cultural Council Foundation grants for ABC No Rio. With these grants, they instituted a residency program whereby the artists who exhibited at the gallery taught at the Marta Valle High School in the neighborhood. This collaboration with children in the neighborhood via the schools, first initiated by Colab artists Jody Culkin and Christy Rupp, became a cornerstone of community practice within ABC No Rio.

In 1983, still on a month-to-month lease with the city and with no formal structure for ABC No Rio, Waters and Cramer inherited the creative potential latent within the space as well as the combative relationship with their landlord—the HPD. HPD had reluctantly handed the keys over to the Colab artists in the aftermath of the *Real Estate Show* in 1980. The building at 156 Rivington was one among hundreds of such properties under the jurisdiction of the city.[37] Each passing year the city tried to evict its low-rent-paying tenants living in these old and hard-to-maintain buildings in order to demolish and/or sell them to private developers. It was in the interest of the city to have the flexibility of short-term leases. The monthly arrangement with ABC No Rio allowed the city to deny a renewal of the commercial lease and evict them with thirty days' notice.

After five years of being in the building, and with some advice from a pro bono housing attorney, ABC No Rio found a way to elude a series of near-evictions by going on a rent strike. They then leveraged the rent money to make much needed repairs to the building. Just a few steps ahead of their negligent landlord, through a combination of circumstance and strategy, the new management at ABC No Rio began a process of stabilizing their claim to the space. One basic strategy initiated by Waters and Cramer was to establish a board and begin a process of incorporating ABC No Rio as an official nonprofit organization.[38] This transformation of an informally run art space to a board-governed institution took several years,[39] during which time the demographic of the users at ABC No Rio changed from the visual arts–based first generation to a second generation of performance and multimedia-based artists.

In 1988, in the course of construction at the adjacent site, a bulldozer rammed into the eastern party wall of the building, and the city took this opportunity to serve an evacuation notice to the gallery and the residents upstairs. The few remaining residential tenants from the apartments above the gallery were hastily relocated into subsidized housing by the city. However, after verifying the structural integrity of the building from an independent professional, ABC No Rio refused to leave and forced HPD to rescind their evacuation notice. At this point, with the whole building empty, the entire facility became available to the ABC No Rio. In what had become an unofficial tradition at ABC No Rio, Lou Acierno, the new director of ABC No Rio, availed himself of this opportunity and moved into the fourth-floor apartment in the vacant tenement building.

Acierno was a videographer by training and liked the open-ended DIY attitude at ABC No Rio. He felt that this aspect allowed new and nonconforming radical interests to emerge.[40] In his capacity as the new director, Acierno was keen to explore new projects and build upon the international reputation of ABC No Rio. He viewed some of the efforts to engage with the "locals" as paternalistic and untenable, given the substantial sociocultural differences between the countercultural artists and the families striving to attain some normalcy in their everyday existence. In a period of mounting uncertainty about the building, Acierno saw the potential for ABC No Rio to become a part of a "global" community, with its radical history and its continuing role as a countercultural haven.[41] In pursuit of this idea, Acierno, along with artist Fly Orr, devised the idea of a touring ABC No Rio. To counter the attachment to one physical space as the driver for programming, they thought that ABC No Rio should become an itinerant institution and visit other cities nationally and internationally to widen its practices and create a global exchange.[42] The resultant Cult X Change project traveled, exhibited, and performed in different "sympathetic" locations and, in turn, invited out-of-town alternative institutions and collectives to curate shows at ABC No Rio. The first of these exchanges brought a small group of artists from the Purple Institution in Toronto to New York City. They installed the *Jungle Show* in the basement after spending a substantial amount of energy cleaning and emptying out the space. Old props, furniture from the past residencies, and all manner of junk surfaced from this effort and formed "a wall of trash" on Rivington Street.[43] Besides the exchange with Toronto, the ABC No Rio team, comprising Lou Acierno, Fly Orr, Jack Waters, and Peter Cramer, traveled to Bowdoin College in Maine and the Künstlerhaus in Hamburg in 1990. The multimedia presentation in Hamburg, titled "Ten Years, Seven Days," encapsulated ABC No Rio's short but vibrant organizational history. Performances, lectures, workshops, and exhibits from the ABC No Rio archive were a part of this itinerant operation, which attempted to create a future for No Rio that could distance itself from the ties to the property.

In the decade since the *Real Estate Show*, the physical structure of the building had deteriorated even further. The plate-glass storefront window that had made the gallery an inviting place for exhibition and exchange was broken and replaced with a piece of painted plywood. Within this windowless interior, there were ongoing problems with heat, water, electricity, and the interminable leaks. Outside, the increased drug trade made the streets and avenues around the building unstable and threatening to residents and visitors alike. The controversial "Operation Pressure Point," begun in 1984 on the Lower East Side, further exacerbated the situation by incarcerating small-time dealers and buyers in the streets. As the police purged one corner or block, the operators simply relocated their flexible businesses, moving further south or east in the geography of the Lower East Side, away from areas that were well policed. By the '90s, the block that housed ABC No Rio was a well-known market for all manner of illicit heroin. A *New York Times* article focused on a drug bust on Rivington Street reported, "Teams of eight officers have been working undercover, buying heroin and arresting sellers, while other officers on rooftops and in parked cars have been observing sellers and signaling for arrests."[44] The changing police tactics impacted buildings like ABC No Rio that were shabby, boarded up, and therefore fair game to sudden incursions by dealers, junkies, and armed undercover police in equal part.[45]

Under these precarious circumstances, the building had to be guarded 24-7. In 1990 Steven Englander joined Acierno as codirector and moved into the third floor at 156 Rivington Street. There were no official leases for any of these residential occupancies, but for a short period, the HPD was tolerant of the unauthorized living arrangements because it ensured that the building had free live-in caretakers. Englander recalls picking up trash bags at the HPD and taking care of the snow, and he realized that the city begrudgingly tolerated his presence in the building.[46] For the codirectors, the rent-free living in the building functioned as compensation for running the bootstrapped operation.[47] The '90s were a difficult time for art institutions. The budget cuts, censorship, and reevaluation of federal and state funding for the arts specifically impacted the smaller, more experimental art spaces all over the country.[48] The many nonprofit galleries, performance spaces, and venues that opened almost overnight a decade earlier closed or moved out of the neighborhood just as quickly. ABC No Rio, with its contentious politics, its resistant spirit, and its shifting cast of stakeholders, persisted but not without a degree of upheaval and turnover within its ranks.

ABC No Rio was finally incorporated in 1990. The first board of directors was comprised of first-generation Colab artists, former director Jack Waters, and other well-wishers of ABC No Rio. After ten years of existence and different ebbs and flows of artistic energy, the space needed fresh programming and vision. Monday night meetings, the previous forum for a local collective decision-making, became sporadic. The organizers of the day-to-day workings of the space struggled internally as the pressure of incorporating and battling with HPD and the hostile street conditions created what codirector Steven Englander described as a "fortress mentality."[49] The Cult X Change initiated by Acierno was short-lived and created a certain amount of friction between the people running the space daily and the board of directors. The board questioned the wisdom of a project that distanced itself from the building, and the management in turn felt the board was out of touch with the many crises affecting the space and its constituents. In 1991 Englander and Acierno resigned, leaving the building in the hands of the board.

PUNK/HARDCORE TO THE RESCUE (1990–1994)

In the '90s the Lower East Side, or the "East Village," as it was frequently being referred to by those hoping to cash in on its bohemian prestige, attracted large crowds of revelers from the different boroughs of the city; from the many suburban townships in Long Island, New Jersey, and New York; and from an international cortege of artists and students. Despite the substandard living conditions of many of its long-standing residents, the process of gentrification was under way in the Lower East Side. The dilapidated state of the buildings and performance venues seemed to add more cachet and brought larger audiences to the nightclubs and bars of the neighborhood. The open drug markets, the hyper-policing, and the resistant spirit made this a dangerous and exciting neighborhood for young people of all stripes to explore. Subcultures proliferated, mingled, and ultimately coalesced into "scenes" that catered to artists, musicians, and their audiences of young followers.

For a small but ardent group of fans, CBGB, the self-proclaimed birthplace of punk rock, was the place to be in New York City. The Sunday Punk Matinees at this venerable institution were prized events that attracted an enthusiastic audience of young adults. "These weekly moshathons," reminisces Jim Testa, in *Jersey Beats*, a fanzine covering punk and alternative music, "were hugely popular but plagued by violence—skinheads beating up suburban kids, straight-

4.11
Flyer for all ages, Saturday Matinee at ABC No Rio, 1990.
Flyer design by Java Dave, courtesy of Freddy Alva.

BAND: CITIZENS ARREST

THE MATINEE

ABC NO RIO
NEW YORK CITY'S ONLY NON-PROFIT, VOLUNTEER-RUN, ALL-AGES VENUE
SATURDAYS / 3PM / $5 / 156 RIVINGTON ST

09/29 - KRACK (MD) / STICKS & STONES (NJ) / NUTJOB / RON'S BETTER HALF

10/06 - SEIZURE (CT) / WUSSIES (CT) / DISRUPT (MA) / CASUALTIES

10/13 - SFA / NECRACEDIA (PA) / 23 MORE MINUTES (CA) / ANTIEM
        WORLD DISCRIMINATION (NJ) / STUPID AMERICANZ (TN)

10/27 - AFFIRMATIVE ACTION / WORD MADE FLESH / WRETCHED ONES (NJ) / +?

BOOKING: NEIL-718-782-6448 / FREDDY-718-672-2507(9-11 PM) / F. ALVA 35-18 83RD ST. JCK. HGTS. NY 11372
NO RACIST, SEXIST, OR HOMOPHOBIC BANDS WILL BE BOOKED

Design: Java Dave   Photo: Chris Boarts

edgers bashing drinkers, as well as the usual mayhem, fistfights, bloody lips, and black eyes that resulted as an inevitable consequence of NYC slamming."[50] The anti-authoritarian anarchic leanings and the rebellious sound associated with punk rock manifested itself in a variety of nuanced and oppositional social and political cliques across the country. Stephen Duncombe explains the group identity within punk culture as a kinship among the alienated. His work points out the many "divisions and subdivisions" that formed around identities—gay, Latino, feminist—as well as ethical positions—skinheads, straight-edge—all driven by the need to reconstruct a "community" of the disenfranchised.[51] The violence in clubs such as CBGB, often the result of a "macho posturing"[52] directed against gays, women, and other perceived minorities, was particularly repugnant to many who attended the shows. In 1989, following some particularly hair-raising incidents that involved guns and police, CBGB's owners decided to terminate their matinees.

The story goes that Mike Bullshit, the enterprising author of the fanzine *Bullshit Monthly*, an openly gay musician, in a simultaneous effort to keep the music and eliminate the homophobia, found ABC No Rio to be the right place to revamp the CBGB matinee tradition.[53] By 1990, Mike began booking bands regularly on Saturday afternoons at ABC No Rio. The show was open to all interested parties of all ages, but as the flyers stipulated, "no racist, sexist or homophobic bands will be booked" (**Figure 4.11**). The lyrics for the performing bands were screened in advance for these criteria, but almost all performing bands were generously allowed to play. The egalitarian politics, relaxed sociability and location of the venue in an old tenement in the Lower East Side brought forth a host of local and touring bands. Shows cost three to five dollars typically, and within a year, this event built a unique reputation within the circuits of the punk rock community.[54] The anarcho-punk camaraderie, minus the intimidation of the New York "hardcore social scene," was a relief to the regular and visiting audience at ABC No Rio. ABC No Rio also became a point of contact for the DIY punk culture, where bands and fans that distributed self-produced music, made zines, and communicated via mail had a place to meet in person.

This community is celebrated by Chris Boarts, a regular chronicler of the ABC No Rio punk scene in the early '90s and author of the fanzine *Slug and Lettuce* (S & L):

> A good show is a great way for this community to really be seen. To be sitting at ABC and have friends of mine come through; while I'm meeting people I've known through the mail; putting it all together can be a bit overwhelming at

times. I'm always blown away and astounded by the feeling of a community network. When all those things get working, and people are brought together, the energy is good, people are having fun, more acquaintances are being made, it makes me excited and happy seeing the way this community works.[55]

The importance of ABC No Rio, a known location where the "regulars" could interact with the transient but well-networked punk community, was prized by the many young punks who attended. Although the music itself could be experienced at other nightclubs or squats, the potential permanence and radical politics at ABC No Rio was something that the punk volunteers were keen to preserve. The ethos of anti-consumer entertainment as active production (making zines/making music) rather than passive consumption (getting wasted/feeling alienated) was the aspect of the punk movement that began to shape the spatial politics at ABC No Rio in the '90s. The hardcore/punk (HC/Punk) collective at ABC No Rio emerged as different people pitched in to organize the shows, print fliers, set up the sound system, man the door, and clean up after shows.[56] The larger group of volunteers fluctuated, but a core group of active "doers" remained attached to the place. The desire for collectivity that had always been at the core of previous practices at ABC No Rio (Colab and POOL) began to have a new direction in the early '90s within the hardcore punk model of organization. Over time, with the help of volunteers, the HC/Punk collective cleaned up the basement, constructed a stage, and installed a PA system.[57] In this subterranean space, with its steel columns and open wood joists, the energies of the punk crowd gathered momentum.

In addition to the HC/Punk Matinees, there were other regular ongoing events at this time: Poetry Readings on Sundays, followed by the long-standing Matthew Courtney's Wide Open Mike. The latter was an immensely popular event where Courtney, in his role as emcee, encouraged everyone to get up and perform. Spoken word, music, points of view, and "political raving and ranting" characterized this riotous and irreverent weekly event at ABC No Rio.[58] The punks, poets, and artists who were involved with the day-to-day activities at ABC No Rio from the early '90s were also actively involved in the political movements centered on housing, anti-war activism, and gentrification unfolding in the Lower East Side. In 1990 a subgroup from the punk matinee series initiated the local chapter of Food Not Bombs. This collective cooked vegan food in the makeshift kitchen in the second-floor apartment and served it on the streets and parks in the Lower East Side. These free meals were made with materials collected from dumpster diving, donations from restaurants, and slightly over-ripe produce from grocery stores. This vegan-anarchist version of charity joined the other soup kitchens that fed the homeless in Tompkins Square Park by drawing sustenance from the discarded surplus of the city.[59]

Although ABC No Rio was not technically a residential "squat," various individuals within the circle that organized shows were connected to the squatter movement unfolding in the Lower East Side in the late '80s.[60] This movement was centered on a series of buildings around Tompkins Square Park and was part of a larger and increasingly contentious homesteading movement in the Lower East Side. The squatters, like other organized homesteaders discussed in the previous chapter, aimed at occupying vacant buildings and converting them into housing by first occupying and then repairing them. Not unlike other homesteaders, most of them believed in the concept of sweat equity. The difference between the "homesteaders" and "squatters" was the anarchic leanings of the latter and their refusal to negotiate the process of their occupancies as per the mandate of the HPD. The heightened police presence in public spaces like Tompkins Square Park, initiated by the campaign against drugs, had by the late '80s mutated into an all-out battle against the homeless and the marginalized. In solidarity with the homeless and in a series of direct confrontations with the police, the squatters maintained a clearly anti-authoritarian stance.[61]

Many within ABC No Rio were directly connected to the squats or sympathetic to the squatters. The same bands that played at ABC No Rio often played concerts in the more makeshift spaces within the squats. Some buildings such as the C-Squat on Avenue C between Ninth and Tenth Streets had a dedicated space within the building for concerts. Other squats such as those on Thirteenth Street, between First Avenue and Avenue A, hosted punk art shows and performances on a more informal basis. The local anarchic network also cultivated a decisively "global" punk/political awareness with many divergent interpretations and understandings of their shared interests in anti-authoritarian, anti-consumer politics. Esneider, for example, immigrated from Colombia as a teenager and founded the band Huasipungo, named after a famous socialist novel by that name written by an Ecuadorian writer. Huasipungo performed regularly at ABC No Rio and had a connection to what Esneider describes as a thriving underground punk scene in Latin America.[62] Esneider, along with Freddie Alva, a Peruvian who also was intimately involved with the HC/Punk collective, brought a Latin American political consciousness to ABC No Rio. Having escaped from Colombia under adverse circumstances and living in New York City as an illegal immigrant, the politics of punk culture meant something different to him than, say, his colleague Neil Robinson, a London transplant with strong connections to the European squatter movement. This is just to register and cycle back to the point made earlier about the heterogeneity of the '90s punk culture, even within the anarcho-pacifist crowd gathered at ABC No Rio. In the early '90s, the HC/Punk collective at ABC No Rio hosted benefit concerts, Food Not Bombs, for the squatters and—with the outbreak of the first Gulf War in 1991—for the anti-war group from 339 Lafayette Street, the War Resisters League (**Figure 4.12**).[63] The ferment over housing within the neighborhood, the neocon politics of the nation, and the rebellious anti-consumer element of punk culture created a broad-based, post-modern, and charged political community at ABC No Rio.

The energy and creativity of the HC/Punk generation at the building kept the reputation of ABC No Rio alive, even as the directors (Lou Acierno and Steven Englander) quit and moved out of the building. The board struggled under the constant pressure from HPD to vacate the premises. In 1994, at the start of Mayor Giuliani's first term in office as Mayor of New York City, the HPD began a vigorous campaign to rid itself of its properties in a series of public auctions.[64] That same year, the HPD served a thirty-day eviction notice to ABC No Rio, following what it saw as a violation of certain "stipulations" that the board had signed to maintain the lease on the gallery space. The old board resigned for fear of being legally liable and left the management and organization of the building squarely in the hands of the HC/Punk collective.[65] The DIY solidarity, the connections to the squatters, and the antipathy toward authority were qualities that would serve ABC No Rio well as the HC/Punk collective confronted a city agency that was aggressively trying to force them out of the building. When the city stopped accepting rent from the gallery in 1994, a group of squatters moved into the empty apartments on the third and fourth floors to protect ABC No Rio from impending eviction. A cycle of squatting and eviction ensued for nearly three years. The city would confiscate the belongings and install new locks, and the squatters would respond by breaking in again and again. Steven Englander, who had resigned as codirector in 1991, returned at some point during these years to help the squatters. His experience with running the building, his understanding of its physiognomy, and his involvement with the anarchist-squatter movement made him a great resource.[66] A lawyer working for ABC followed an evasive tactic of getting each of the evictions dismissed on technical grounds. This

THE SATURDAY MATINEES AT
ABC NO RIO

15
R
IN
TO
NY

NEW YORK CITY'S ONLY NON-PROFIT, VOLUNTEER-RUN, ALL-AGES VENUE / 3PM-9

ORLANDO 88

JAN.12
GO!
PRESSUREHEAD
THE COMMONWEALTH (MD)
SITUATED CHAOS
HUASIPUNGO

JAN.19
BAD TRIP
DISRUPT (MA)
NUNCA MAS (MD)
UNLEASHED ANGER (MA)

JAN.26
RADICTS
THE CASUALTIES
NOBODY'S HEROES
THE WURST (RI)

FEB.2
WAR RESISTOR'S LEAGUE BENEFIT
SEIZURE (CT)
STICKS & STONES (NJ)
HEADSTRONG

OW INFO: 212-673-2743 / BOOKING: FREDDY-718-672-2507(9-11 PM) / 35-18 93RD ST. JCK. HGTS. NY 11372

O RACIST, SEXIST OR HOMOPHOBIC BANDS WILL BE BOOKED

strategy did not solve the problem but essentially delayed the HPD from taking more drastic actions.

Unable to oust the ABC No Rio by eviction notices and police interventions, the HPD came up with a new ruse. They offered the property to another neighborhood group, the Asian Americans for Equality (AAFE), as a potential site to develop new low-cost housing. This method of pitting one, more established nonprofit against the other was common practice as the city capitalized on rifts and conflicts of interest between community organizations. The relatively small size of the lot (twenty-three by one hundred feet) made the project of creating low cost on the site quite impossible. In January 1997 the ABC No Rio activists targeted the AAFE offices in Chinatown, accusing this once progressive civil rights organization of "greed," "profiteering," and "corruption."[67] These accusations in the media led AAFE to withdraw its interest in the property. That same year another smaller, more radical group of ABC No Rio activists snuck into the HPD commissioner's office in downtown and staged a sit-in. This act of civil disobedience, which they expected would get them arrested, got them a seat at the negotiating table with the HPD commissioner, Lillian Barrios. Following this more civil turn of events, the city stopped eviction proceedings in 1997 and agreed to transfer the ownership of the building to ABC No Rio for a dollar, provided they raise the funds to repair the building and remove all squatters from the premises.[68] With this turn of events, the eighteen-year trajectory of the counter-institutional history of ABC No Rio entered a new phase (**Figure 4.13**).

BARN RAISING (1998–2010)

The years of legal and semi-legal occupation, broad programming, and creative activism around saving the space created many supporters of ABC No Rio. These included the first generation of artists who petitioned on behalf of the building and other more recent participants who had stood on the frontlines, demonstrated, and temporarily squatted the building. This varied group perceived the outcome—potential ownership of the property with the city's blessing—with mixed feelings. With the many brutal evictions of squatted buildings still fresh on the mind of many, there could be no reconciliation with the city.[69] On the other side, from the city's perspective, the eight or so squatters had to vacate so that ABC No Rio could fully become what it claimed—a community arts center. The city was officially at war with the squatters, but was willing to tolerate a squat transformed into an art center with a clear program and mission.

STOREFRONT

1981

VISUAL ART   1980-1982

Artists For Survival   Murder, Suicide, & Junk   Animals Living in Cities   Portrait Show   Tube Show

PERFORMANCE   1981

Cardboard Band

1983-1985

Seven Days of Creation   Extremist Show

MUSIC/POETRY/
SPOKEN WORD   1982

Haunted Circus

1990-Present

ABC No Rio Hardcore/Punk Matinee

4.13
A selective time line of art, performance, music, and the
spoken word at ABC No Rio, 1980–1998.
Illustration by Nandini Bagchee.

1990

1991

1997

Island of Negative Utopia

1990   1991   1994   1995   1997   1998

4.14
Darkroom with red light, ABC No
Rio, 2012.
Photograph © Jade Doskow.

4.14
Darkroom with red light, ABC No
Rio, 2012.
Photograph © Jade Doskow.

In the first year, under the new agreement with the city, new uses
for the second, third, and fourth floor apartments were envisioned.
Relieved from the pressure of imminent eviction, ABC No Rio invited
all interested parties to a series of open meetings, where plans for the
future use of the building were debated. It was through these open discussions, rather than the closed board meetings typical of nonprofit
organizations, that the programs and the next phase mission of ABC
No Rio evolved. The resilient HC/Punk Matinee that had survived the
eviction phase moved into the first-floor gallery to comply with the
building code for assembly space. The ongoing Food Not Bombs collective commandeered the back room on the second floor and continued to prepare meals in what was once an apartment kitchen. The
computer room, screen print shop, and darkroom were introduced on
the upper floors as different people expressed their interests in setting

4.15
Zine Library, ABC No Rio, 2012.
Photograph © Jade Doskow.

up these facilities. A group of invested photographers adapted the bathroom plumbing on the third floor and turned it into a darkroom to develop film (**Figure 4.14**). Different people or groups of people organized each of these spaces initially, and the attendant programs run by interested volunteers grew into separate collectives. In 1998 ABC No Rio accepted a collection of zines that had traveled from an anarchist bookstore, Blackout Books, on Avenue B, to a Bronx squat and was eventually housed in a zine library in the front room on the second floor of the building. This room was once occupied by the artist and prolific zinester Fly Orr.[70] Her words "There is always something hanging above your head" boldly painted on the ceiling of this space portends the uncertainty that has always been the narrative at ABC No Rio (**Figure 4.15**).

A new board, comprising different generations of ABC No Rio artists and well-wishers, made decisions concerning the legal and fiscal matters of the institution, but the different collectives—HC/Punk, Print, Food Not Bombs, Zine, and others—ran the programming and the day-to-day operations within the newly established spaces in the building. In 1997 Steven Englander was the first squatter to move out of the building from the fourth floor. This apartment was converted into the Print Shop. Nine months later, Englander became the first paid administrative manager for ABC No Rio and began to organize a fund-raising campaign in conjunction with the board.[71]

After the extended battle against eviction and episodic squatting, ABC No Rio was the worse for wear. The apartment interiors were full of abandoned furniture and assorted trash—the debris of squatter domiciles. The walls were full of holes, the ceilings stained, and the floors encrusted with dirt. The whole place needed a thorough cleaning and an exhibit planned by the newly formed visual arts collective to launch the new arts center. Steven Englander and Scott Seaboldt coordinated the first installation of the *Ides of March* show in 1998. Seaboldt, like Englander, had lived in a squat and participated in the squatter movement on the Lower East Side and was enthusiastic about helping steer ABC No Rio in the post-squatter paradigm.[72] Conceived in the spirit of the "sweat equity" enterprise, they issued an open call for participation to artists who could invest some time cleaning up the space in order to participate in the show. This meant attending the planning meetings leading up to the show and carving out a bit of space for the display of the artworks by cleaning up a corner and painting a portion of the grimy walls.[73] This show, designed in the inclusionary tradition of ABC No Rio, was non-juried, but there was some dialogue among the participating artists about the relevance of their proposed installations within ABC No Rio.[74]

The first *Ides of March* opened on Friday, March 13, 1998, and included works by sixty-one artists (**Figure 4.16**).[75] The works were installed throughout the building, on the roof, and in the backyard. The first-floor gallery—the original leased storefront—was intentionally left empty to draw the visitors up the stairs through the apartments into the most domestic reaches of the tenement to discover works hidden in closets, lurking inside the broken plaster walls, and hanging from the ceiling of a former bedroom.[76] In response to the theme of the show *The Ides of March*, the artist Roberto Martinez drew a historic time line on the ceiling of the third-floor apartment of the events leading up to the assassination of Julius Caesar. Along the perimeter was a personal calendar of the artist's own life in the month leading up to the show. This work, according to the artist, spoke of the capacity of

1997   2008   2011   2012

ACME
B. Adler
Johanna Bartlet
Chris Benfield
Kim Bennett
Deborah Berkson
Angela Bocage
Matt Callinan
Eneas Capalbo
Caroline
Valerie Chirigos
Josephine Coniglio
Darren Corona
Kurt Dantzler
Okra P. Dingle
Anne Marie Farinacci
Jon Feinstein
Fly
John Fragala
Nancy Goldenberg
Charles Hancock
Steve Harrington
Thomas Jerold
John B. Johnson
Anikka Lachman/Andrew Stern
Victoria Law
Lindsay
Chris Lowery
Robert Martinez
Stacy Miller/Scott Scaboldt
Jason Moriber
Robert Nelson
Jan Nunn
Mark A. Randolph
Chris Rucker
Judy Tompkins
Victoria Veedell
Maria Yoon

Jon Allen
Aaron Auslender
Andre Barbosa
Kristin Cassidy
Mike Estabrook
Kevin Farley
David E. Franck
More Gardens!
John S. Hancock
Rob Horn
Robin Islam
Alex Khost
Rob Lecuyer
Hakim Maloum
Mac McGill
Tim McVicker
Stacy Miller
Jill O'Bryan
Oden
Nico Ramirez
Georgia Russell
Tom Sanford
Peter Stankiewicz
Laurie Stalter
Chris Thieke
Khan Vo
Erick Zuenskes

Osman Akan
Elaine Angelopoulos
Paul Biedrzycki
BOOKLYN
Frank Caprino
Christopher Cardinale
Rodrigo Chazaro
Brendan Coogan
Matthew Courtney
Doña
Jade Doskow
Matthias & Emily Duwel
Angel Garcia

Michel Bayard
Brock
Ernest Concepcion
Martin Dust
Exploitme.com
Kevin Farley
Lambert Fernando
A.P. Ferrara
Eugene Fiore
Kate Henderson
Peter Hofmiester
The Lower East Side Biography Project
Maya McCarthy
The Met Guard
Nineteenneighty
Scott Nobles

Dormafe Baluyos-fox
Andrew Baron
Suzanne Baron
Fabian Berenbaum
Alexander Bevington
Garry Boake
Lizxnn Bolger
Alexi Rutsch Brock/Chelsea Bruck
Michael Cataldi
Maureen Catbagan
Greg Cisneros
Peter Cree
Fei Cui
Sandy Edmonds
Stefan Eins
Meredith Gaydosh
Steve Harrington/ Miranda Edison
Anna Hutchings
Sarah Julig
Hyeon-Seok Lee
Jason Lujan
Isabelle R Lumpkin
Riza Manalo
Anna Marra
Moira McCaul
John Mejias
Anthony Meloro
Emmanuel Migrino
Judith Modrak
Pierre Obando
Lina Pallotta
Sara Parkel

Collective Gesture
Concepcion/Estabrook AKA
The Shining Mantis
Cueva & Wells
E.V.E. (Erase Your Ego)
Flux Factory
Harrah & Kipp
it/EQ Community Arts Collaborative
Justseeds Visual Resistance Artist Cooperative
PerfectEight
Shepperson/Stein/Radford
Subject To Change
Three Wise Goats
Zuvuya Collective

Cesar Arredondoa
Kevin Caplicki
Chris Clary
Peggy Cyphers
Charlotte Doglio
Joann Harrah
Rebecca Howland
Akiko Ichikawa
Julie McCabe
Alan Moore
Nsumi Collective
Olek
Douglas Einar Olsen
Dave Pugh
Vydavy Sindikat

● 1998   ● 2000   ● 2002   ● 2004   ● 2006   ● 2008   ● 2010

4.16
Ides of March time line, ABC No Rio, 1998–2010.
Illustration by Nandini Bagchee.
Source: *Ides of March* Catalogues (1998–2010).

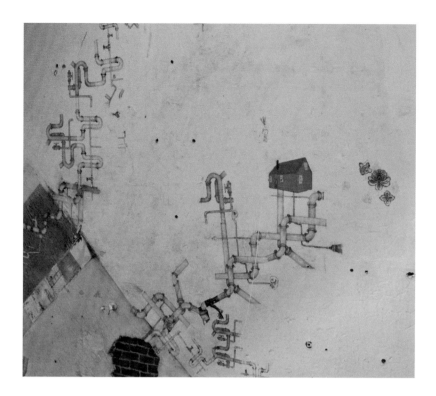

architecture to "unhinge time" and to juxtapose larger official histories
with the immediacy of the everyday life.[77]

Beginning with this first show, the *Ides of March* became a biennial
event in which artists would install works connected to the building
and its history of resistance. Lamberto Fernando began drawing in the
stairway for the annual *Ides of March* show in 2002 and continued to
develop his wall mural/relief over the course of eight years (**Figure
4.17**). The show's catalog in 2004 notes that "The Pipeline Project is a
mixed media collage that began with the creation of Brick Boy,
inspired by the youthful spirit of ABC No Rio."[78] Fernando, who
began this project while still in high school, found inspiration in the
existing brick as he scraped the plaster. Depicted in exquisite detail,
his renderings of the exposed plumbing "symbolize the interconnect-
edness of the subconscious. The addition of the houses made of plaster
explored the hidden connections of people in their private spaces."[79]
The private house, with its connection via plumbing to the subconscious in the work of the artist, seeks to connect to a larger public. The
squatter politics and reconciliation of the public agenda within a
semi-private realm made this and other works within ABC No Rio
particularly potent. The fragile materiality of the building was clearly
celebrated and exposed through these physical interventions and
political mobilizations.

The building became a living archive of these multifaceted undertakings. Artwork from past shows often remained on the interior stairwell, landings, and rooms within the building. The drawings, paintings, and reliefs that encrusted the walls felt like an extension of the exposed guts of the building. Questions of eviction, dispossession, and the "right to space" appear as themes within the artwork. Old symbols acquired new meanings as the political landscape of the country and the urban landscape of the city changed. Becky Howland's Octopus from the *Real Estate Show* peeked out from the peeling layers of wallpaper in the second-floor dining room. The wheat paste mural on immigration by the Brooklyn-based collective Justseeds (2008) incorporated the bolt cutter—a powerful symbol of squatter resistance—into the far-more perilous journey of an immigrant crossing a border (**Figure 4.18**). The quintessential representation of the labor movement, the garment worker in the Lower East Side, began at the edge of the fourth-floor window in a crumbling tenement on Rivington Street. The image enveloped the computer room, unfurling from the fabric of the garment workers' sewing machines.

These building-wide shows and the institution of programs in each of the rooms made the entire building more open, more public, more accessible. The print room, darkroom, and computer lab were available

4.18
Immigration Project by Justseeds collective in the ABC No Rio computer room.
Photograph by Nandini Bagchee, 2014.

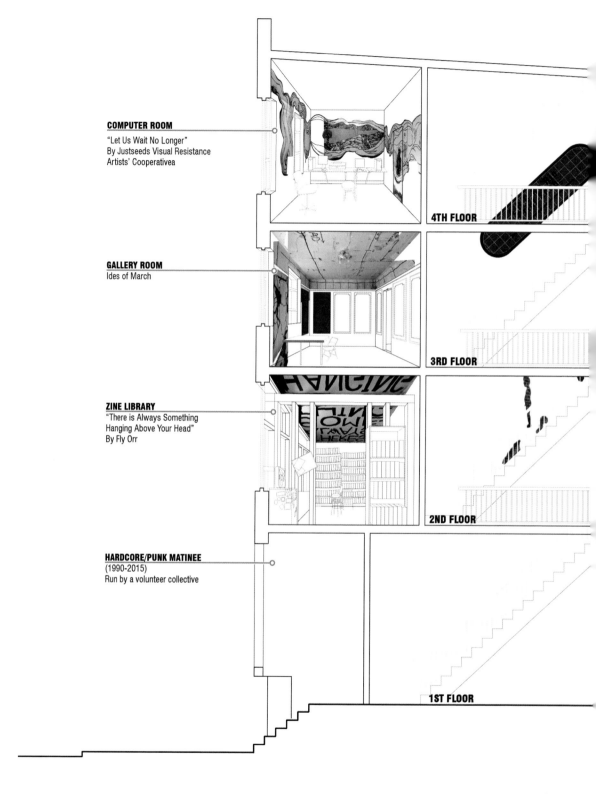

COMPUTER ROOM
"Let Us Wait No Longer"
By Justseeds Visual Resistance
Artists' Cooperativea

4TH FLOOR

GALLERY ROOM
Ides of March

3RD FLOOR

ZINE LIBRARY
"There is Always Something
Hanging Above Your Head"
By Fly Orr

2ND FLOOR

HARDCORE/PUNK MATINEE
(1990-2015)
Run by a volunteer collective

1ST FLOOR

4.19
Section through ABC No Rio showing wall paintings in
select locations, 2015.
Illustration by Nandini Bagchee.

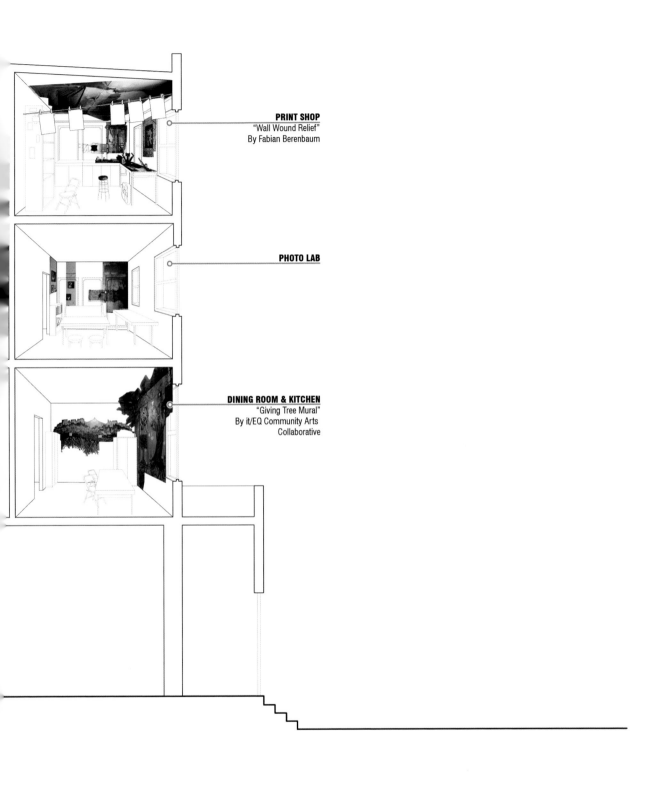

PRINT SHOP
"Wall Wound Relief"
By Fabian Berenbaum

PHOTO LAB

DINING ROOM & KITCHEN
"Giving Tree Mural"
By it/EQ Community Arts
Collaborative

for community use, and the zine library was open to browsers at scheduled times. Each of these facilities attracted new contingents of volunteers from different parts of the city who, like the others before them, cherished not only the sense of community but also the strong survivalist history of the space (**Figure 4.19**).

Alongside this sprucing up of the building and the establishment of new space-based community programs was the important task of fund-raising. An art center that had distinguished itself by its thrift and by its anti-capitalist self-sufficiency had to shift gears and approach donors and funders for help. By organizing in-house concerts, benefits, and auctions, the collective raised the agreed-upon sum of a hundred thousand dollars by the year 2000. Reconsidering the deteriorated condition of the building, HPD felt the collective needed more funds and a robust development plan to make sure the project moved forward.[80] This process took another six years as the board members reached out to the wider network of established artists and politicians who could invest in the future of the institution. A twenty-fifth-anniversary benefit held at "Mega dealer Jeffery Deitch's uber-hip exhibition space" in SoHo raised twenty thousand dollars auctioning off work by famous ABC No Rio alumni and other supportive members of the established art world. The reporter for this event hints at the paradox of the "defiantly downscale ABC No Rio, the Lower East Side's original 'anti-space' turning to help from the moneyed gallery scene."[81] The fight to acquire ABC No Rio had no holds barred and a place that had initially been a result of a subversive action (the *Real Estate Show*), and a part of an anarchist movement became an end in itself. In 2006 ABC No Rio, having raised $700,000 in private funds, was able to convince HPD to sell them the building. On June 26, 2006, ABC No Rio was the proud owner of 156 Rivington Street.[82] That same year, they began the process of planning a renovation of the building with Paul Castrucci, an architect who had been in the shows at ABC No Rio and was a part of the art/squatter movement in the Lower East Side.[83] The first feasibility study of the building revealed the building to be far less sturdy than imagined. The supporting walls of the building were made of an old wood frame infilled with brick. The foundations were precarious, and any effort to preserve the shell of the building would require substantial shoring and underpinning. This type of preservation work would make the project costly and inefficient. The architect advised a complete teardown to erect a brand-new building—one that would be better suited to the future mission of the institution and bring the structure into compliance with the building code. (**Figure 4.20**)

This revelation was difficult for the ABC No Rio community to process on two levels: First, the construction cost of a ground-up building was significantly more than the $700,000 it had raised. Second, the existing building, complete with all its defects, was a symbol of the resistance that fueled the spirit of this particular institution. How could a new building possibly embody the aspirations of the future ABC No Rio?[84]

The first problem of funding was eventually overcome as ABC No Rio, after several years of contention, found a sympathetic and generous partner in the Department of Cultural Affairs (DCLA) in New York City.[85] The DCLA is "the largest cultural funding agency in the nation." Among other types of spending, it also subsidizes construction and renovation at certain institutions that it sees "as providing cultural services to the citizens of New York City." This funding is given at the discretion of elected officials. In 2009 ABC No Rio received a combined $1.65 million grant from Manhattan borough president Scott Stringer and City Councilman Alan J. Gerson.[86]

The second problem of redesigning the building, without losing the spirit that had nurtured the organizations that had and would call it home, was tackled by working with the architect in consultation with a building design committee. The proposed new building design included a space for housing the existing programs (the kitchen, the darkroom, the zine library, and so on) with an enlarged gallery and performance space below. Envisioned with a façade composed of solar panels and green-walls, the building was designed to be 100 percent energy efficient. The organization saw the sustainable principles that dominated this architectural scheme as an appropriate symbol of the endurance of ABC No Rio (**Figure 4.20**). The architect's renderings showed a minimal white interior composed of galleries and artwork that sit neatly within its frame. The preservation the collective espoused was not that of the Lower East Side nostalgia for the punk-artifact but rather the social project of a volunteer-run arts center dedicated to exhibiting the works of young artists and providing a base for political mobilization. The future engagements will determine the actual shape and constitution of the new space.

ART, POLITICS, AND PLACE

Rosalyn Deutsche, in her book *Evictions: Art and Spatial Politics* (1996), wrote, "Social space is produced and structured by conflicts. With this recognition, a democratic spatial politics begins."[87] The conflicts arising from saving a building and making it meaningful have, in large

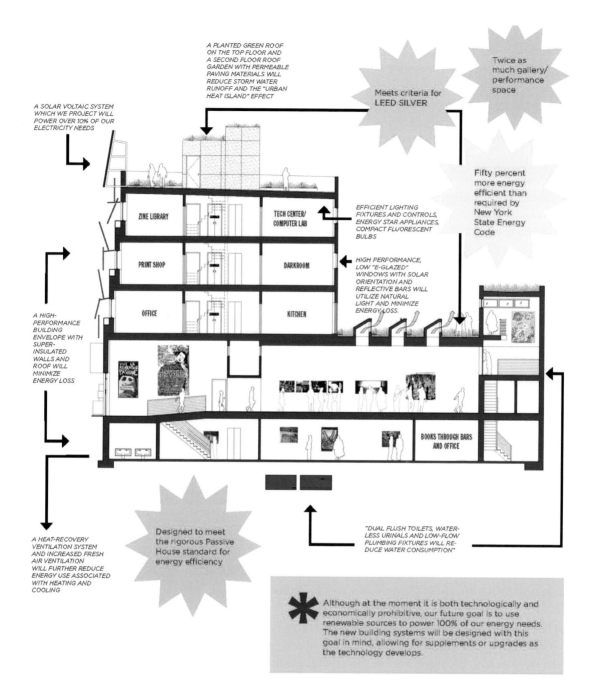

A SOLAR VOLTAIC SYSTEM WHICH WE PROJECT WILL POWER OVER 10% OF OUR ELECTRICITY NEEDS

A PLANTED GREEN ROOF ON THE TOP FLOOR AND A SECOND FLOOR ROOF GARDEN WITH PERMEABLE PAVING MATERIALS WILL REDUCE STORM WATER RUNOFF AND THE "URBAN HEAT ISLAND" EFFECT

Meets criteria for LEED SILVER

Twice as much gallery/ performance space

Fifty percent more energy efficient than required by New York State Energy Code

ZINE LIBRARY

TECH CENTER/ COMPUTER LAB

EFFICIENT LIGHTING FIXTURES AND CONTROLS, ENERGY STAR APPLIANCES, COMPACT FLUORESCENT BULBS

PRINT SHOP

DARKROOM

HIGH PERFORMANCE, LOW "E-GLAZED" WINDOWS WITH SOLAR ORIENTATION AND REFLECTIVE BARS WILL UTILIZE NATURAL LIGHT AND MINIMIZE ENERGY LOSS.

OFFICE

KITCHEN

A HIGH-PERFORMANCE BUILDING ENVELOPE WITH SUPER-INSULATED WALLS AND ROOF WILL MINIMIZE ENERGY LOSS

BOOKS THROUGH BARS AND OFFICE

A HEAT-RECOVERY VENTILATION SYSTEM AND INCREASED FRESH AIR VENTILATION WILL FURTHER REDUCE ENERGY USE ASSOCIATED WITH HEATING AND COOLING

Designed to meet the rigorous Passive House standard for energy efficiency

"DUAL FLUSH TOILETS, WATER-LESS URINALS AND LOW-FLOW PLUMBING FIXTURES WILL RE-DUCE WATER CONSUMPTION"

* Although at the moment it is both technologically and economically prohibitive, our future goal is to use renewable sources to power 100% of our energy needs. The new building systems will be designed with this goal in mind, allowing for supplements or upgrades as the technology develops.

4.20
New building proposal for ABC No
Rio showing passive design
principles, 2010.
Drawing courtesy of Paul A. Castrucci
Architect for ABC No Rio.

part, informed the practices of generations of patrons at ABC No Rio. The Real Estate Show artists who founded ABC No Rio saw it as an extension of their living situation and used its domestic shabbiness to mount a critique of the ways in which government failed to respond to the needs of its citizens. The second "performative" phase allowed for the development of multiple identities locally that moved ABC No Rio into a global orbit in search of that elusive "community." The last phase with the punk-squatter resistance was a return to the anarchic roots of the Lower East Side, where the building itself became the object of a more militant activism. After the stalwart occupiers of ABC No Rio finally won the battle for the building but lost the war of the neighborhood (**Figure 4.21**), their focus was redirected from the practices that resisted institutionalization to what Gerald Raunig calls "the process of instituting."[88] The broader ambition of this process, as Raunig sees it, was to move from "a belligerent critique of the state" to finding ways of self-governance.[89] By prioritizing its legitimacy as a *community center* that benefits from the ever evolving collectives of artists, ABC No Rio, in this phase, managed to distinguish itself from the alternative spaces that were pressed to return to the art institutional fold to survive. The constant renegotiation of the contours of that community was driven by the changing demographics of the neighborhood, the space, and its users in unison.

By the 2000s, the prohibitive rents in the neighborhood pushed both the Latino and younger artist communities that still visited ABC No Rio to live further and further away from the building. The crowd that gathered at the building for the HC/Punk Matinees and the *Ides of March* shows in 2010 was more than ever before a dispersed community of commuters. The institution thus stands at the cusp of this tenuous relationship between a past when space and politics were fiercely contested in this part of the city and a future where a resistance to consumerism still strives to hold a place in the cracks of the city, where it was injected with collective will and determination. The anarchic domesticity within the old building allowed generations of artists, activists, squatters, and performers to capture space and make it meaningful through the DIY approach that ABC No Rio celebrates. The proposed new space and functioning utilities will, no doubt, make the experience of being part of this building very different. The challenge of overcoming the odds will no longer be tied to the lack of amenities but rather to forming new criteria that address the question of the artist's response to civic agency in the shifting terrain of the new urban politics.

REAL ESTATE SHOW **TOMPKINS SQUARE RIOT**

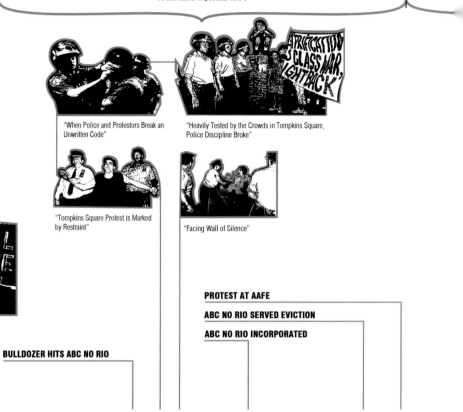

"When Police and Protestors Break an Unwritten Code"

"Heavily Tested by the Crowds in Tompkins Square, Police Discipline Broke"

"Tompkins Square Protest is Marked by Restraint"

"Facing Wall of Silence"

PROTEST AT AAFE

ABC NO RIO SERVED EVICTION

ABC NO RIO INCORPORATED

REAL ESTATE SHOW
"Artists Ejected In 'Occupation' Of a Storefront: Views of City Planning"

BULLDOZER HITS ABC NO RIO

ABC NO RIO OPENS

1980 | 1981 | 1982 | 1983 | 1984 | 1985 | 1986 | 1987 | 1988 | 1989 | 1990 | 1991 | 1992 | 1993 | 1994 | 1995

Ed Koch
January 1st, 1978
December 31st, 1989

David Dinkins
January 1st, 1990
December 31st, 1993

Rudy Giuliani
January 1st, 1994
December 31st, 2001

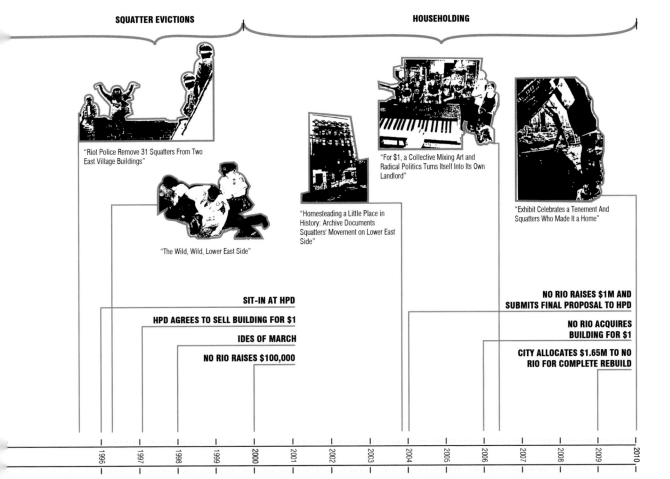

"Riot Police Remove 31 Squatters From Two East Village Buildings"

"The Wild, Wild, Lower East Side"

"Homesteading a Little Place in History: Archive Documents Squatters' Movement on Lower East Side"

"For $1, a Collective Mixing Art and Radical Politics Turns Itself Into Its Own Landlord"

"Exhibit Celebrates a Tenement And Squatters Who Made It a Home"

SIT-IN AT HPD

HPD AGREES TO SELL BUILDING FOR $1

IDES OF MARCH

NO RIO RAISES $100,000

NO RIO RAISES $1M AND SUBMITS FINAL PROPOSAL TO HPD

NO RIO ACQUIRES BUILDING FOR $1

CITY ALLOCATES $1.65M TO NO RIO FOR COMPLETE REBUILD

1996   1997   1998   1999   2000   2001   2002   2003   2004   2005   2006   2007   2008   2009   2010

Michael Bloomberg
January 1st, 2002
December 31st, 2013

4.21
A selective time line of mayors, squatting and ABC No Rio, 1980–2010.
Illustration by Nandini Bagchee.

EPILOGUE: TAKING STOCK
(2017)

EPILOGUE: TAKING STOCK (2017)

Today, property in New York City is a prized commodity. If an individual or a group owns a building, they hold onto it. The value of a building is determined by location, size, and potential for expansion, in that order. The perceived value gained through use is considered negligible and sometimes altogether ignored. A building, rooted to a place by virtue of its construction, is in fact entirely mobile as a commodity in the financial landscape. Investors build their portfolios and wait for opportunities to leverage one property to get another. The idea of amassing property holdings and building an estate is a time-honored tradition of business in New York. During periods of crisis, when property is suddenly devalued, its status as "real estate" is overturned. Crisis returns property, land, and the built environment back to the question of use and potentially back in the hands of its users. Such was the case in parts of New York City in the '70s as owners abandoned their properties and the city grudgingly took control of these devalued estates. Some of these city-owned, hence public buildings came to be at the center of the many right to city movements that challenged the authority of the city and the state.

The counter institution examined herein represents both a conceptual and a literal struggle to create a space for civic action in a city that is built upon real estate speculation. The actors described in this book—the war resisters, the Puerto Rican organizers, the housing activists, the punks, and the artists—all seized the opportunity to create what are seen here as Activist Estates, at a time and place where urban life was under attack. Whereas social movement organizing during the previous eras had focused on the right to participate and profit from the Fordist economy, in the '70s the shortcomings of this way of thinking, planning, and profiting were suspect. The '70s, a low point in the economic history of New York City, a moment when the city stood on the verge of bankruptcy, allowed various local groups to emerge and gain ground through a survivalist political ingenuity. The battles for community control were prompted by a removal of state resources and the availability of space. This confluence of negative factors in fact allowed for many different types of people with little cash in their pockets to insert different visions of "community" into the city.

These struggles for self-determination in the Lower East Side that defined the social movements of the '70s were followed by a second phase in the '80s in reaction to the austerity measures imposed by the central and municipal governments. Cutbacks in federal job training programs, low-cost housing projects, and small grants to community organizations whittled away at the public aspirations for "community control" and jeopardized the many small victories of the previous decade. The scope for social, collective undertakings was further diminished as the neighborhood became attractive to many new groups during the '80s, producing a culturally rich but politically fragmented institutional space within the Lower East Side.

By the '90s, the city's dominant project was to make the space under its control open and available for profit-based development. In the Lower East Side, it faced a formidable opposition as the many social groups that had gained power and momentum regrouped to contest the city's claim to the land under the gardens, community centers, homesteads, and squats in the neighborhood. Through collective action, some of these Activist Estates were "saved." Within the changing nature of the city at large, many of these "saved" buildings and properties had to transform to meet new expectations as the demographic of Manhattan drastically shifted and an upper middle class filtered back into a city transformed by the neoliberal policies of its municipal government. Meanwhile, the desired middle class that the city tried for years to insert into the poor neighborhoods of New York City never materialized, generating, instead, the now familiar landscape of extreme wealth disparity.

Despite the economic growth that the city has experienced in the first decade of the twenty-first century, there are still pockets of entrenched, socially active groups where islands of low-income space remain because of the vast tracts of public housing, rent-regulated apartments, and homesteaded buildings that came into the ownership of low-income families. Two maps of the Lower East Side, one from 1970 and the other from 2010, show the average and median[1] incomes from census tract data on the three quadrants around NoHo, Loisaida, and the Southern Lower East Side (**Figure 5.1**). In looking at the dots of household income, a few facts emerge. First, the population density in NoHo has doubled, whereas the other two areas have seen a more modest increase in population. Second, the number of residents above and below median income is a half and half mix. The maps seem to suggest that the sections of the Lower East Side close to the East River continue to house a mix of incomes, in large part due to availability of low-income housing built along the East River. In addition, the Lower East Side is populated with a large number of rent-

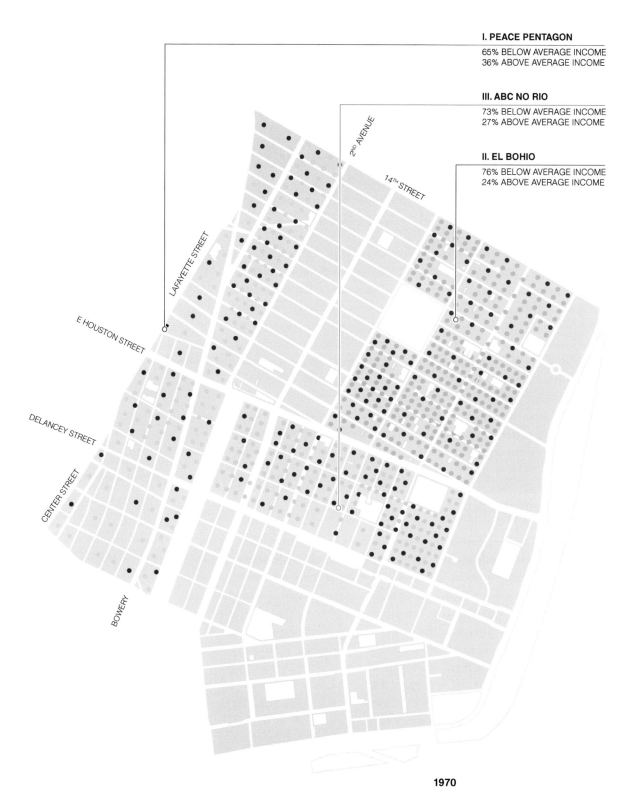

I. PEACE PENTAGON

65% BELOW AVERAGE INCOME
36% ABOVE AVERAGE INCOME

III. ABC NO RIO

73% BELOW AVERAGE INCOME
27% ABOVE AVERAGE INCOME

II. EL BOHIO

76% BELOW AVERAGE INCOME
24% ABOVE AVERAGE INCOME

2ND AVENUE

14TH STREET

LAFAYETTE STREET

E HOUSTON STREET

DELANCEY STREET

CENTER STREET

BOWERY

1970

5.1
**Comparison of Lower East Side "average" and "median"
income from 1970 and 2010.**
Illustration by Nandini Bagchee.
Source: U.S. Census Bureau.

I. PEACE PENTAGON

41% BELOW AVERAGE INCOME
59% ABOVE AVERAGE INCOME

III. ABC NO RIO

52% BELOW AVERAGE INCOME
48% ABOVE AVERAGE INCOME

II. EL BOHIO

50% BELOW AVERAGE INCOME
50% ABOVE AVERAGE INCOME

2ND AVENUE

14TH STREET

LAFAYETTE STREET

E HOUSTON STREET

DELANCEY STREET

CENTER STREET

BOWERY

2010

controlled apartments, a handful of converted squats, and several homesteaded buildings that are cooperatively owned. The very existence of such affordable options within the building stock of the Lower East Side is the legacy of decades of housing activism.

THE PEACE PENTAGON MOVES ON

In an interview Wendy Schwartz,[2] longtime member of the War Resisters League and executive director of the A. J. Muste Memorial Institute in the early '80s, spoke of the difficulty in dealing with a building full of dissenting radicals who had a disregard for any form of perceived authority or bureaucracy. The role of the Muste Institute as manager and landlord, while tremendously important to the "movement tenants," nonetheless created an unresolved tension within the building. A succession of executive directors and board members interested in providing grants and organizing for peace and justice, instead, found themselves mired in conflicts with, and about, the tenants. The responsibility of dealing with police, keeping the building insured, and dealing with a host of other unpleasant "nonmovement" issues was not fully appreciated by the more radical elements within the building and a board dedicated to furthering the cause of peace and justice.

By the '90s, as the Muste Institute paid off the remaining loan on the building, it shifted its focus toward the creation of grants for smaller peace and justice organizations and projects. The maintenance of a shoddy brick building in Downtown Manhattan was not a priority for an institution that wore the mantle of a movement far older than the building itself. By 2007, the eighty-five-year-old building at 339 Lafayette Street was in terrible shape. The roof had been leaking for years, the electrical wiring was shot, and the steel lintels over the large window openings were corroded from years of water damage. More alarmingly, a structural column had sunk to create a visible sag along the building's western façade on the Lafayette Street side (**Figure 5.2**). The structure, which was never quite as robust as some of its nineteenth-century neighbors, was an eyesore at the beginning of the twenty-first century, dwarfed by lush billboards and spruced-up, high-end development. With an ever-growing military presence in Iraq and escalating war in the Middle East, the Muste Institute, along with its movement tenants, tolerated the building's declining state with an air of resignation.

However, in 2007, outside bureaucratic forces came to bear upon the fate of the building. A project by the Metropolitan Transit Authority

(MTA) to begin a large-scale restructuring of the Bleecker Street subway station that abutted the building at the foundation level required the building owners to conduct a thorough analysis of the building's condition. An engineering investigation revealed that the building, though not an immediate danger to the occupants, was indeed structurally compromised.[3] To repair or rebuild the structure would be an extremely expensive undertaking. Murray Rosenblith, director of the Muste Institute at the time, advised the board to sell the building and move to a rented space. The institute tentatively put the building on the market and was offered $7 million for it. This amount, for a building initially purchased by the WRL for $60,000, seemed like a windfall to the Muste Institute. The prospect of selling the building, however, met with stiff opposition from the long-term tenants and concerned community members. A group called the Friends of 339 formed to publicize and assert the importance of this building.[4] Many people had been initiated into community organizing and civil disobedience within this building and viewed it as an active place of dissent in a neighborhood that had rapidly gentrified. This opposition stalled the sale for another eight years and created divisions among the building community as the prospect of losing the building suddenly made everyone reevaluate its worth. During this time, a sidewalk bridge was installed as bricks from the façade began to fall upon the sidewalk. Within the Muste Institute, a cloud of indecision hovered as options for keeping the building were weighed and discarded. In the meantime, the monetary value of the property tripled.

In the fall of 2015, unable to raise the money needed to repair the building, the board of the Muste Institute sold the building for $20.75 million.[5] They negotiated a six-month period to pack up, and in the summer of 2016, the Muste Institute, along with most of its existing tenants, relocated to a rented office space in Chinatown.[6] In an effort to rebrand the building, the new owner of 339 Lafayette Street, Aby Rosen, has named his corporation "337 Lafayette LP." Rosen, a well-known developer, has also invested in other prized properties along the Bowery-Lafayette Street corridor, including the women's shelter at 349 Lafayette Street, across the street from the former Peace Pentagon.[7] The transfer of these two institutions to a real estate tycoon known for his portfolio of high-priced real estate will definitively change the character of the section of Lafayette Street, where the fight against consumerism, war, and social justice once held sway.

5.2
Lafayette Street Facade of the Peace Pentagon, 2014.
Photograph © Jade Doskow.

CHARAS' EL BOHIO ON THE BARRICADES

PS 64, the onetime schoolhouse on East Ninth Street, has effectively been vacant for fifteen years. The imposing masonry structure, with its broken windows and elegant but damaged mansard roof, looms as an unresolved conundrum in a neighborhood where the property disputes from the contentious '90s have seemingly been put to rest (**Figure 5.3**). The building's Ninth Street wall is barricaded with plywood, and the blue tarp used to protect some parts of the roof has come undone, giving the monumental schoolhouse a derelict appearance more in keeping with the '70s rather than the present. Greg Singer, the developer who bought the building in 1999, was stopped in his tracks several times by a vigilant group of El Bohio supporters that have continued to canvass on behalf of CHARAS to regain control of the cherished community center.[8] A stipulation in the deed for the sale that states that the building and lot be "restricted and limited to a community facility use" has given El Bohio/CHARAS activists hope that the outcome will be favorable.[9] This clause, alone, prevented the developer from erecting a multistoried, high-end residential building on the large twenty-eight thousand–square-foot site. This stipulation has also kept the CHARAS/El Bohio "movement" alive and determined to regain possession of the building.[10]

To build profitable housing and to comply with the stipulation that the building be used as a community facility, Singer proposed tearing down the old schoolhouse and replacing it with a twenty-seven-story student dormitory. In 2006 a coalition of residents successfully lobbied to have the building designated as a city landmark and forced the developer to reconsider his plans. The lobbyists for El Bohio included the East Village Community Coalition, an organization formed by Michael Rosen, a developer who owns a penthouse in the adjacent Christodora House. The twenty-seven-story dorm would have blocked the views from the Christodora House and changed the quiet residential character of the few blocks to the east of Tompkins Square Park.[11] The landmarking of PS 64, despite what some saw as the dubious intentions of Rosen and his fellow Christodora residents, was nonetheless regarded as a victory for the community.[12]

More recent proposals for renovating the school building to house university students were stymied as the developer failed to get needed paperwork from the Cooper Union and the Joffrey Ballet School.[13] These new developments once again gave momentum for the community to persist in reclaiming the schoolhouse on East Tenth Street as a community center. Since their eviction from the building, a group that calls itself Save Our Community Center PS 64 (SOCC64) has

5.3
Mansard roof and gable at PS 64/
Charas El Bohio.
Photograph by Gilbert Santana.

exerted intermittent pressure on the city to have the building be returned to the community. The steering committee of SOCC64 hopes that, with the support of city officials, they can "restore ownership to an organization, like CHARAS/El Bohio, that will better the East Village, in lieu of having it become a useless eyesore as its current owners are content to have it."[14] On January 6, 2015, at the start of Mayor Bill De Blasio's first term in office, District Leader Anthony Feliciano, State Committeeman Michael Farrin, and Val Orselli of the Cooper Square M.H.A. dressed up as three kings for the holiday of "Three Kings Day" and rallied outside city hall. They respectfully requested that the new mayor "gift" the building back to the neighborhood.[15] The *Villager* reported that the event was attended by a crowd of supporters, and Councilwoman Rosie Mendez and Borough President Gale Brewer made statements requesting that the mayor take some action to restore the building back to the community. While little progress was made during De Blasio's first term in office, two years later, at a town hall meeting and in a bid for reelection, the mayor called the decision of the Giuliani Administration to sell PS 64 a "mistake" and announced his commitment in reacquiring the building.[16]

ABC NO RIO IN EXILE

The miraculous transformation of an insurrectionary group of artists, punks, and squatters into responsible arbitrators who bought a building from the city of New York for a dollar is the unlikely but true story of ABC No Rio. In addition to having acquired ownership of 156 Rivington Street, by 2016 ABC No Rio had received $6.45 million in grants from public officials and raised $1.6 million from private donors to replace the squalid three-story residential building with an energy-efficient arts center. This grant came with the predictable bureaucratic restrictions. The group was required to have the city serve as the construction manager and select a contractor via the vetting process set up by the city. ABC No Rio went through a series of unsuccessful bidding processes through the city's Department of Design and Construction, each time coming in over budget and having to return to the drawing board. This process of revising and resubmitting plans created a stalemate that lasted more than five years.

Fate, ever the friend of ABC No Rio, intervened when the adjoining Streit's matzo factory was sold to a private developer to build new residential condominiums. The razing of the factory's four buildings, which span half the block, brought the frail ABC No Rio building down with it. And so the sluggish processes of the city bureaucracy were nudged along by the demolition required for this private development. In the summer of 2016 ABC No Rio hosted a final exhibition and then vacated the premises after thirty-six years of continuous occupancy. The new owners of the matzo factory site have helped them jump-start the project for the new building. However, at the end of 2017, even as construction moves along at an even pace at the new residential development site, a hole barely visible from above marks the site of ABC No Rio. Meanwhile, ABC No Rio remains in exile at the nearby Clemente Soto Velez Cultural and Educational Center (**Figure 5.4**).[17]

MOVEMENT SPACE

The buildings discussed in this book are not simply elements of an inert backdrop in front of which important events unfold. They are an active component of the practices of the groups that they support. The buildings move from being merely convenient to being crucial to the social movements they house. These spaces, spread throughout the city, collectively counteract the exclusion and marginalization that are ingrained in the current cityscape. These spaces became operative through a complex process, one that reflects Henri Lefebvre's contention that space is not simply there for the taking but is produced through conscious participation and embodied action. This framework helps one understand how the Peace Pentagon generated a presence beyond the confines of its sagging exterior walls and its lopsided interior to create a collective space for active resistance. This process of participation produces both new representations of space and new forms of knowledge that can be used to modify and define new uses. The building at 339 Lafayette Street, embedded with layers of internationally or nationally oriented activist practices, sat at the center of this buildup of knowledge and practice. The building itself was seen by the users as a by-product, sometimes in a positive way and other times as a waste of time, a place that needed continuous upkeep and maintenance. However, the succession of groups inheriting space from one another and pursuing the legacy of A. J. Muste over time accumulated a power base in the city. The last decade of the internal struggle within the board, involving both the tenants and the broader peace and justice community, allowed the Muste Institute to potentially realize that building a movement space—virtual, physical, and institutional—is critical to the survival of the beleaguered peace and justice movement.

The neighborhood-based activities of CHARAS and associates at El Bohio, within the blocks and streets of Loisaida, were specifically about claiming space and were a part of a global right to city movement. This struggle for community space encompassed all aspects of life—economic concerns, housing, arts, and education. This movement was inherently ecological in its re-use and salvage of waste—locally as well as in its search for broader alternative energy resources. The existence of a community was not a given but one that was consolidated in the territory of Loisaida as a strategy to manage the available resources. The production of identity—Puerto Rican, Latino, and artistic—emerged from the sense of being a part of a landscape of spaces in need of repair and restoration. The quest for community control of city properties by marginalized groups was part of a nationwide movement in the '70s. The existence of a broader network of support and solidarity is what made the local efforts relevant and effective.[18]

In *The Death and Life of Great American Cities*, Jane Jacobs provides a critical perspective on how urban space can thwart or foster the life of an urban community.[19] Her understanding of the neighborhood as a space that is knit together by people who know and recognize one another is pertinent to understanding the locally grounded but conceptually global Loisaida community. The intimate knowledge of each block and the choreography of spaces and actors within its boundaries created a strong place-based opposition such as one advocated by Jacobs. This same structure, and the somewhat narrow focus on neighborhood, was ultimately also the cause of internal fragmentation in the '80s and '90s as the lots and properties that had once formed the basis of community cohesion became contested assets that the city sought to auction off.

ABC No Rio (vacant site)

Streit's Matzo Factory Site
(Residential Condominiums
Under Construction)

Clemente Soto Velez

5.4
Aerial view of the ABC No Rio neighborhood with Clemente Soto Velez Cultural and Educational Center in the foreground and condominium construction at the former Streit's matzo factory site, 2017.
Photograph by Gilbert Santana.

The larger properties such as El Bohio were targeted for sale to private developers. However, the contract of sale of El Bohio, which had been a school and a community center, used loosely worded language calling for continued "community use." The language of self-reliance was thus co-opted by fuzzy terminology in a series of codifications that destroyed the political potential for such terms. These pressures from above led to a reconfiguration of movement groups. Those that survived have had to come to terms with the new processes of becoming more professional and engaged with the city through intermediaries such as the community boards and local elected officials. This gradual institutionalization of "community" to negotiate the gardens, community centers, and housing put various properties at risk as various groups argued for an authentic claim to Loisaida.

As many of the people who actually ran and were a part of the community center moved out of the neighborhood, El Bohio acquired the status of a symbolic space. Its ruined appearance and its exalted status as a landmark protected it and kept it in an iconic limbo. The need for a community center such as El Bohio, with large and small spaces and a mixture of programmed and unprogrammed activity, seems vital to the functioning of a city that grows more exclusionary with each passing year. As the income map discussed earlier reveals, this neighborhood full of homesteaded buildings and low-income housing remains a bastion of resistance. If the SOCC64 succeeds in its campaign, the question of who the "community" is and what its members desire will once again be open for debate.

The situation of ABC No Rio, a project inspired by El Bohio, is very different not merely because of its slow but, so far, seemingly successful outcome. Perhaps one could argue that the building and the site were so small and the resistance so persistent that the city in this instance had more to gain by being generous to an arts institution than by continuing to dismantle what it saw, ultimately, as a cultural asset in the new, gentrified neighborhood in the southern half of the Lower East Side. The importance of the space to an older generation of artists, some with established careers, also contributed to ABC No Rio's successful fund-raising campaigns, which in turn brought more official support. The status of this institution is one in which the earlier conflicts brought a broader social acceptance that could potentially and ironically transform ABC No Rio from a rebellious squatter enclave into a viable community-run art center. Once again, though, the community is not a fixed entity but one built upon old and future networks that most often transcend the immediate neighborhood to generate greater stability.

COUNTER INSTITUTION

> *To be modern is to live a life of paradox and contradiction. It is to be overpowered by the immense bureaucratic organizations that have the power to control and often to destroy all communities, values, lives; and yet to be undeterred in our determination to face these forces, to fight to change their world and make it our own. It is to be both a revolutionary and a conservative: alive to new possibilities for experience and adventure, frightened by the nihilistic depths to which so many modern adventures lead, longing to create and to hold on to something real even as it melts.*
> —Marshall Berman, *All That Is Solid Melts into Air*

The gleaming metallic space volumes of the New Museum hold center stage on the Bowery, siphoning in tourists and shoppers along Prince Street, from SoHo to the Lower East Side. This erstwhile counter institution, founded in 1977 by the young curator Marcia Tucker, was the quintessential alternative museum, one that provided a venue in which a more diverse group of living artists could exhibit their work.[20] The institution still performs this function, but it is no longer a renegade downtown museum. The organization has expanded, changed, and in 2000 accumulated enough support from donors and foundations to build a new facility on the Bowery between Stanton and Rivington Streets. This block still retains a little of its old Skid Row character, notably because of the survival of the two remaining Bowery shelters—the Sunshine Hotel at the corner of Stanton Street and the Bowery Mission in the middle of the block. Tired and disheveled homeless men and women line up for the free hot meals offered at the Bowery Mission alongside the energetic, mainly touristic, museum-going crowd.

A view from the seventh-floor terrace of the New Museum overlooking Chrystie Street on the eastern edge of the Lower East Side encapsulates a large part of the world described in this book. The strip of median-turned-park between Chrystie and Allen Streets serves as a multipurpose play area that incorporates basketball courts, a children's playground, a soccer field, and a skating rink as well as the lush M'Finda Kalunga and Hua Mei Bird Gardens. This seven-block-long open space, named Sara D. Roosevelt Park in 1934, after President Roosevelt's mother, was the result of an unfinished slum clearance and housing development scheme. Dense blocks of tenements were acquired and demolished in 1930 to make way for new housing, characterized by housing historian Richard Plunz as "the first casualty of the public housing era."[21] This same piece of land is now a boon to the many sporting and relaxing residents in the neighborhood. Its efficient shotgun-style allocation of recreational "rooms," from Canal Street in the south to Houston Street in the north, allows a multigenerational and multilingual group of people to peaceably coexist. In the early morning elderly Chinese residents gracefully practice Tai Chi, and by the evening soccer enthusiasts race around the median and shout out in several different languages.

From the vantage point of the New Museum's terrace, a block east of this park, one can also see the original University Settlement building where resident "settlers" once lived. This building was modified in 1966 into a childcare center. It continues to serve this function, providing an all-day facility for toddlers with working parents for a nominal fee based on income. The smaller rooms have been combined to make larger classrooms for play, and modest interior transformations have brought the building into compliance for its current use. The building retains its grand institutional character with its large brick fireplaces in each room and the light-filled interior spaces. The current staff speak English, Spanish, Mandarin, Fujianese, and Taiwanese to better communicate with the parents and children they serve.

The chief executive officer of University Settlement, Michael Zisser, attributes the survival of this institution to its willingness to accept a more pragmatic business model, forming partnerships with local schools, colleges, and other nonprofit organizations in the neighborhood and working with both the city and private foundations.[22] The settlements are also part of a larger umbrella organization, the United Neighborhood Houses, that provides the support that most smaller organizations lack. University Settlement and the Henry Street Settlement are the go-to institutions in the Lower East Side when the city seeks to implement a neighborhood program, or a developer seeks community approval. Foundations trust their record, and their website lists multiple programs and sites of engagement in the Lower East Side as well as farther afield in other boroughs. The settlement houses, the boys' and girls' clubs, and some of the churches mentioned in the first chapter have weathered many economic and political crises to hold on to their buildings while adjusting their programs to meet new demands.

Institutions such as the Judson Church on Washington Square continue to provide space to community groups for meetings, events, and fund-raisers. They proudly hold on to their tradition of "Justice, Art and Worship."[23] A cursory look at their calendar reveals that this institution remains a place for political action. However, to maintain control and repair the main sanctuary, Judson had to sell their parish buildings along Thompson Street to New York University's Law School in 1999. The Judson House and the parish were demolished amid controversy to accommodate the eleven-story Furman Center. The continuing expansion of New York University around Washington Square Park and the lack of a comprehensive city plan to protect the smaller residential and commercial interests have community groups concerned.

The tall blocks of NYCHA housing lining the East River still provide low-income housing to 120,000 residents. Despite the poor maintenance within these buildings and the continuing financial problems of this institution, resulting from the withdrawal of federal resources, the waiting lists for these apartments is always long. As part of a strategy to add to this stock of low-income housing while seeking a solution to its financial problems, NYCHA has launched a controversial "Next Generation" plan.[24] Under this plan, the agency would lease the open spaces in between its housing towers to developers and allow them to build moderate-income housing. If this densification plan moves forward, the income demographics of the Lower East Side, which thus far have been less uneven than in other parts of the city, will certainly change.

This book reveals a partial view of this landscape of modernity, a landscape in which the paradox of both revolutionary and conservative forces continue to converge to form the melting city described by Berman. The connections to networks of people, ideas, and places are key elements that help energize and ultimately stabilize urban institutions. The "counter institution," in positioning itself against the established power of the "institution," leads to social practices that have the potential to challenge the status quo and call for a redistribution of resources. In the case of the buildings discussed in this book, there was a specific attempt to disrupt the cycle of commodification of property that was partially successful. Reading between the lines of what is superficially seen as a monolithic process of gentrification, this account seeks to consider some of the inherent contradictions involved in sustaining counter-institutional practices and negotiating the public domain. The outcome is far from perfect. But within the recognition of these imperfections and the ambiguous intentions of counter-institutional practices lie the possibilities for future interventions. In the writing of this micro-history of Activist Estates in the Lower East Side, this book aims to create an awareness of the potential for activism and the need to build more relevant spaces for insurgent action.

ACKNOWLEDGMENTS

The account of the events, actions, and analyses recounted in this book is based on conversations and interviews with many activists, organizers, artists, and advocates who used the spaces examined in the book. I am grateful to all the people who have spoken to me over the past four years about their projects and who have provided me with research material. In particular, Maureen Shea, who collaborated with me on "Peace Pentagon: A Call to Action"; Ed Hedemann, who recounted the actions of the War Resisters League; Linda Cohen, Chino Garcia, and Marlis Momber, who shared their memories of Loisaida; and Steven Englander, who made ABC No Rio and its dynamic community accessible to me. I thank them and the many other inspiring activists, artists, and organizers for trusting me with their stories and photographs.

Preliminary research was supported by grants from the Professional Staff Congress–City University of New York Research Awards Program. Colleagues at the Spitzer School of Architecture at City College provided intellectual support and collegiality. I wish to thank Marta Gutman and June Williamson for inviting me to participate in collaborative lectures, reviews, and symposiums that provided a testing ground for early research and writing. I also thank Michael Sorkin for championing the Peace Pentagon. My interest in architecture and urban history as part of a broader thinking about global politics benefited from the mentorship of Professor Nasser Rabbat as well as the cosmopolitan cadre of scholars and friends I met during my studies at the Aga Khan Program at the Massachusetts Institute of Technology in Cambridge. I thank many wonderful teachers, including the late Diane Lewis and Raimund Abraham, and classmates Charles Stone and Cagla Hadimi at the Cooper Union, who shared a belief that the roadmap to the center lies in the margins.

Insightful comments on the manuscript by Mariana Mogilevich and editing by Jackie Braun, Constance Rosenblum, and Oksana Mironova shaped my writing. Reviews from Clara E. Irazabal-Zurita and Maurice Isserman influenced the final revision. The technical support and overall enthusiasm from the board and staff at Fordham University Press made this book a reality. The design and graphic content of the book greatly improved with assistance from my students Midori Tanabe and Jeremy Iannucci. Martin Perrin guided the design of the book cover and interior. I am much obliged to these designers for putting their skills and talents toward crafting a beautiful book.

Finally, I want to thank the Bagchee-Schmerbeck clan for exercising patience and support for this undertaking. The curious and adventuresome spirit of my parents, Sudeep and Padmini Bagchee, moved us from the valley of Dehra Dun to the metropolitan environs of New York via the cities of Kano, Kaduna, and Minna. Without the keen eye and constructive input of my husband, Philip Schmerbeck, and the generosity of my parents-in-law, Gayla and Steve Schmerbeck, this book would not have come to fruition. Many family vacations were infiltrated by talk of the Activist Estates. I also wish to thank my extended family of friends, Janna Israel, Ralph Ghoche, Patrick Foster, and Cesare Birignani, who have graciously read and edited excerpts of the manuscript over the years.

NOTES

CHAPTER 1

1. Mario Maffi, *Gateway to the Promised Land: Ethnic Cultures in New York's Lower East Side* (New York: New York University Press, 1995), 50.

2. For an account of the cyclical nature of real estate speculation in the Lower East Side see Neil Smith, Betsy Duncan, and Laura Reid, "From Disinvestment to Reinvestment: Mapping the Urban 'Frontier' in the Lower East Side," in *From Urban Village to East Village: The Battle for New York's Lower East Side,* ed. Janet L. Abu-Lughod (Cambridge, Mass.: Blackwell Publishers, 1994), 149–167.

3. James F. Richardson, "Wards," in *The Encyclopedia of New York City*, ed. Kenneth T. Jackson (New Haven, Conn.: Yale University Press, 1995), 1237. The description of wards in the *Encyclopedia of New York City* establishes that 80 percent of New York's total population was housed in these four wards—Ten, Eleven, Thirteen, and Seventeen—within the geographic parameters of what is referred to later as the Lower East Side.

The website http://www.demographia.com/db-nyc-sector1800.htm, accessed September 15, 2015, calibrates the population density of this area in 1900 at 314,931 per square mile. This meant that more than three times as many people lived in this neighborhood as the rest of Lower Manhattan.

4. Jacob A. Riis, *How the Other Half Lives: Studies Among the Tenements of New York* (New York: Charles Scribner's Sons, 1890). This piece of writing raised awareness of the poor. His famous exposé first appeared as a long, illustrated essay in an 1889 edition of *Scribner's Magazine*.

5. Maureen A. Flanagan, *America Reformed: Progressives and Progressivisms, 1890s–1920s* (New York: Oxford University Press, 2006).

6. The concept of the settlement house originated in England with the still extant Toynbee Hall (1884) in East London. The movement was tremendously influential in the United States, and by 1910 there were well over four hundred settlement houses in the United States. Most of these were in major cities along the east and west coasts—targeting immigrant populations. For an overview of the settlement house movement, see Allen F. Davis, *Spearheads for Reform: The Social Settlements and the Progressive Movement, 1890–1914* (New York: Oxford University Press, 1967).

7. The chapter "Jewtown," by Riis, focuses on the dismal living conditions in this ward. The need to not merely aid the impoverished community but to transform the physical city became a part of the settlement work.

8. Stanton Coit, *Neighbourhood Guilds: An Instrument of Social Reform* (London: Sewan Sonnenschein and Co., 1891). Coit had visited Toynbee Hall and later published his ideas of the "guild," a unit of a hundred families that could function as a unit capable of self-sufficient organization.

9. Jeffrey Scheuer outlines a brief history of University Settlement in his essay *Legacy of Light: University Settlement's First Century* (New York: University Settlement, 1986).

10. Scheuer, *Legacy of Light*.

11. Ibid. The purchase of the site and construction were funded by some of the wealthiest families of New York.

12. Robert A. Woods and Albert J. Kennedy, eds., *Handbook of Settlements* (New York: Russell Sage Foundation, 1911), 177–248. This handbook lists the settlements across the country and provides a brief description of their activities.

13. Mina Carson, *Settlement Folk: Social*

Thought and the American Settlement Movement, 1885–1930 (Chicago: University of Chicago Press, 1990). Carson provides insight into the broader history of the settlement houses, with a focus on the early leaders who shaped the movement. Christopher Mele, "Different and Inferior," in *Selling of the Lower East Side: Culture, Real Estate, and Resistance in New York City* (Minneapolis: University of Minnesota Press, 2000), 31–77, emphasizes the patriarchal imperative within the charitable impulse.

14.   For a discussion of the shaping of the ideology of the settlement workers in urban policy reform, see Carson, "The Settlers Look Outward: Housing, Health, and Labor," in *Settlement Folk: Social Thought and the American Settlement Movement, 1885–1930* (Chicago: University of Chicago Press, 1990), 69–84.

15.   See Davis, "The Settlement Movement and Municipal Reform," *Spearheads for Reform*, 170-193.

16.   Carson, "Settlers Look Outward," 153–160.

17.   "Protesting Women March in Mourning," *New York Times*, September 30, 1914, 11.

18.   Wald was elected the first chairperson of AUAM, a New York City–based organization with fifteen thousand members. Accessed August 15, 2015, http://newyorkhistoryblog.org/2015/06/24/new-yorks-long-history-of-peace-activism/#sthash.t8VtWXaN.dpuf.

19.   Wald, along with settlement colleague Jane Addams of Hull House, remained committed to the anti-war efforts through their membership in the Women's Peace Party (later renamed the Women's International League of Peace and Freedom [WILPF]). Their criticism of the country's decision to enter the war, however, put them at odds with many former supporters, both within and outside the government circles. See Carson, *Settlement Folk*, 153-160.

20.   In 1924 the Johnson-Reed Act, an immigration law, created quotas that allowed immigration visas to 2 percent of the total number of people of each nationality in the United States as per the 1890 national census, accessed October 9, 2015, https://history.state.gov/milestones/1921–1936/immigration-act. This excluded many minority national groups and had the effect of decreasing the continuous influx of immigrants to the Lower East Side.

21.   Robert A. Woods and Albert J. Kennedy, eds., *Handbook of Settlements* (Arno Press and the *New York Times*, 1970). First published in 1911, the Russell Sage Foundation, Philadelphia, 1–5. The handbook lists a total of 415 settlements in the United States and describes the collaborative effort.

22.   For an account of Hall's participation and statement before the House Ways and Means Committee, see Helen Hall, *Unfinished Business* (New York: Macmillan Company, 1971), 53–58.

23.   Hall, *Unfinished Business*, 30.

24.   Ibid., 29–39. Hall speaks of the impact of "The New Deal Initials" in Chapter V.

25.   The Housing Act stipulated that its funds be used for slum clearance, followed by low-income housing. Given the high cost of land in Manhattan—even on the Lower East Side—this area was slated for slum clearance and then developed with privately funded middle-income housing. The availability of money from the federal government and the lobbying by reformers and construction unions changed the course of this development into low-income housing under the aegis of NYCHA. See Joel Schwartz, "Redevelopment and Public Housing," in *The New York Approach: Robert Moses, Urban Liberals, and Redevelopment of the Inner City* (Columbus: Ohio State University Press, 1993), 25–60; and Ann L. Buttenwieser, "Shelter for What and for Whom? On the Route Toward Vladeck Houses," *Journal of Urban History*, vol. 12 (August 1986).

26.   Hall, *Unfinished Business*, 145–157. Hall qualifies her position in support of the need for the new public housing by pointing to the studies and reports developed by Henry Street Settlement volunteers based on interviews and opinion polls of the residents. The

titles of the reports ("Can We Renovate the Slums?," "What Some Slum Dwellers Want in Housing," and "Rooms of Their Own") indicate the focus of the settlement workers on the residents.

27. The board chairman, Langdon Post, was the head of the Tenement House Commission; the vice chair, Mary Simkhovitch, founded the Greenwich House Settlement; and other members included Charney B. Vladeck, veteran socialist and general manager of the *Jewish Daily Forward*; Louis Pink, a former settlement house worker and lawyer on the State Housing Board; and Monsignor E. Roberts Moore of the Catholic Charities of the Archdiocese of New York.

28. Buttenwieser, "Shelter for What and for Whom?," 12. Buttenwieser reports that a sixth of the people who moved into the Vladeck Houses were from the neighborhood.

29. Helen Hall quoted in Joel Schwartz, "Tenant Unions in New York City's Low Rent Housing, 1933–1949," *Journal of Urban History* 12 (August 1986): 424.

30. Schwartz, "Redevelopment and Public Housing," 25–60.

31. Buttenwieser, "Shelter for What and for Whom?," 12.

32. After World War II, large numbers of Puerto Ricans began migrating to the United States. In 1953 Puerto Rican migration to New York reached its peak when 75,000 people left the island. By 1960, the U.S. census showed that there were well over 600,000 New Yorkers of Puerto Rican birth or parentage. See Christopher Mele, "Neighborhood 'Burn-out': Puerto Ricans at the End of the Queue," in *From Urban Village to East Village*, ed. Janet L. Abu-Lughod, 128-131.

33. Buttenwieser, "Shelter for What and for Whom?," 12.

34. Hall, *Unfinished Business*, writes about the concerns of growing gang violence and drugs within the neighborhood. For gang warfare, see 219–225; for narcotics abuse, see 245–253.

35. Henry Heifetz, "Introduction," in *Individual and Group Services in the Mobilization for Youth Experience*, ed. Harold H. Weissman (New York: National Board of Young Men's Christian Associations, 1969), 19.

36. Noel A. Cazenave, "Professional Turf Battles in the Planning of the Mobilization for Youth Project," in *Impossible Democracy: The Unlikely Success of the War on Poverty Community Action Programs* (Albany: State University of New York Press, 2007), 19–31. Cazenave convincingly articulates the different tactics of the settlement versus the MFY administrators.

37. Beverly Luther, "Group Service Programs and Their Effects on Delinquents," in *Individual and Group Services in the Mobilization for Youth Experience*, ed. Harold H. Weissman, 126.

38. Cazenave, *Impossible Democracy*, 117–118.

39. Daniel Soyer, "Landsmanshaftn and the Jewish Labor Movement: Cooperation, Conflict, and the Building of Community," *Journal of American Ethnic History* 7, no. 2 (1988): 22–45.

40. Stanley Nadel, *Little Germany: Ethnicity, Religion, and Class in New York City, 1845–1880* (Urbana and Chicago: University of Illinois Press, 1990), 29–46. Germans migrating to New York in the 1840s settled in the Tenth, Twelfth, Thirteenth, and Seventeenth Wards in the Lower East Side. Nadel maps the territory of Kleindeutschland (Little Germany) in New York.

41. For a description of the many different types of German social organizations and the attendant architectural typologies in the Seventeenth Ward, see Mathew Kuhnert, *Building Community in Kleindeutschland: The Role of German Immigration in Shaping New York City's Seventeenth Ward* (master's thesis, Columbia University, 2012), 65–101.

42. Nadel, *Little Germany*, 104–118. Nadel provides an account of the many associations revolving around drinking, sports, singing, theater, and political organizing that proliferated in Kleindeutschland. For the social landscape of the German anarchist movement, see Tom Goyens, *Beer and Revolution: The German Anarchist Movement in New York City,*

1880–1914 (Urbana and Chicago: University of Illinois Press, 2007).

43. Soyer, "Landsmanshaftn." Soyer's article provides an account of the complicated relationship between the more academic Marxist intelligentsia and the Landsmanshaftn (local Jewish benefit societies) in creating a labor-power base in the Lower East side.

44. Ibid.

45. John M. Okinson, "The Public Halls of the Lower East Side," in *Year Book of the University Settlement Society of New York* (1899), 31-J.

46. Tom Goyens, *Beer and Revolution*, 34-51.

47. New York City Landmarks Preservation Commission, Webster Hall and Annex Designation Report, LP-2273, March 18, 2008.

48. For an overview of Judson Church's History, see http://classic.judson.org/Historical-Overview, accessed July 25, 2016.

49. Richard P. Poethig, "Charles Stelzle and the Roots of Presbyterian Industrial Mission," *The Journal of Presbyterian History* (1997–) 77, no. 1 (1999): 29–43.

50. Ibid., 39.

51. For Hughan's role as a leader of the Pacifist movement and founder of the War Resisters League, see Scott H. Bennett, "Jessie Wallace Hughan and the WRL," in *Radical Pacifism: The War Resisters League and Gandhian Nonviolence in America, 1915–1963* (New York: Syracuse University Press, 2003), 1–22.

52. Jo Ann Ooiman Robinson, "The Pharos of the East Side, 1937–1940: Labor Temple Under the Direction of A. J. Muste," *Journal of Presbyterian History* 48, no. 1 (1970): 18–37.

53. Muste's long career as a pastor and radical leftist is indicative of his struggle to find the right approach to nonviolence, labor issues, and social justice. His life, which spanned three wars (World War I, World War II, and the Vietnam War), is described in Leilah Danielson, *American Gandhi: A. J. Muste and the History of Radicalism in the Twentieth*

Century (Philadelphia: University of Pennsylania Press, 2014).

54. Scott H. Bennett, "Toward Direct Action: The WRL and the CO Revolts in CPS and Prison 1940–1945," in *Radical Pacifism: The War Resisters League and Gandhian Nonviolence in America, 1915–1963* (New York: Syracuse University Press, 2003), 98–133. Bennett provides a detailed account of the situation of the COs as well as the key actors of the dissent.

55. Marion Mollin, *Radical Pacifism in Modern America: Egalitarianism and Protest* (Philadelphia: University of Pennsylvania Press, 2006). Mollin lists federal prisons in Pennsylvania, Kentucky, Virginia, Michigan, and Arizona.

56. Bennett, *Radical Pacifism*, 98–114. Bennett points to the small number of men (12,000) involved as COs during World War II. Of these, only about half (approximately 6,000) went to jail, serving sentences of two to three years. He notes that about 100 members of the WRL were among those jailed. The Danbury strike involved 18 COs, who began a 135-day work strike.

57. Ibid., 113–133. Bennett provides a detailed account of the strikes in Danbury and Lewisburg and the Ashland Correctional Facilities and the involvement of WRL members Jim Peck, William Sutherland, Bayard Rustin, David Dellinger, and Ralph DiGia that led to these actions.

58. An unlikely duo, Peter Maurin was a Catholic Philosopher, and Dorothy Day was a journalist with strong ties to the labor movement in New York City. The quote is a part of the tenets for the Catholic Worker, enumerated by Maurin in the column "Easy Essays in the *Catholic Worker*."

59. James J. Farrell, *The Spirit of the Sixties: The Making of Postwar Radicalism* (New York: Rout-ledge, 1997), 28.

60. In 1976 they purchased a second building, the Third Street Music School, and converted it into the Mary House. These two institutions are still in existence as of 2017. For more about the Catholic houses in New

York City, see Gary Dorrien, *Social Ethics in the Making: Interpreting an American Tradition* (Boston: Blackwell Publishing Ltd., 2008), 368.

61.   For the contribution of the pacifist (WRL and FOR) to the formation of the new left, see Van Gosse, *Rethinking the New Left: An Interpretive History* (New York: Palgrave Macmillan, 2005), 55–57.

62.   Bennett, *Radical Pacifism*, 134.

63.   Farrell, *Spirit of the Sixties*, 23.

64.   Bennett, *Radical Pacifism*, 195–203

65.   Ibid., 222–223.

66.   "31 Flouting Test Seized by Police: 29 Taken in City Hall Park Claim to Be Pacifists—Woman Disrupts Court," *New York Times*, June 16, 1955.

67.   Judith Malina, *The Diaries of Judith Malina, 1947–1957* (New York: Grove Press, 1984), 441–462. Malina notes her experience in jail and encounter with Dorothy Day.

68.   Malina, *The Diaries of Judith Malina,* 368.

69.   See Bradford D. Martin, *The Theater Is in the Street: Politics and Performance in Sixties America* (Amherst and Boston: University of Massachusetts Press, 2004), 52–62. Martin describes the couple's distaste for the "stylized realism" of Broadway. In a deliberate break from the stylized theatrics of commercial performance, Artaud proposed a more improvisational form in which the audience encounters the actor's emotions and physicality more directly.

70.   Ibid., 55–56. Dissent, as noted earlier, was unpopular during the Cold War. The House Un-American Activities Committee (HUAC), formed in 1947, specifically targeted artists. The visual artists, particularly the Abstract Expressionists, were not eager to risk their newfound successes in museums and galleries to take on a more radical political position. Later, in the '60s, the civil rights movement and the Vietnam War changed this attitude within the arts community with the emergence of groups like Art Workers Coalition and the Guerilla Art Action Group (125–159). See also Lucy Lippard, "Biting the Hand that Feeds," in *Alternative Art New York, 1965–1985*, ed. Julie Ault (Minneapolis: University of Minnesota Press, 2002).

71.   Martin, *Theater Is in the Street*, 60–63. See also Allan Antiff, "Poetic Tension, Aesthetic Cruelty: Paul Goodman, Antonin Artaud, and the Living Theater," *Anarchist Developments in Cultural Studies*, no. 1 (2015). Antiff discusses the problematic aestheticizing of cruelty.

72.   Douglas Robinson, "The Show Goes on Despite Ban," *New York Times*, October 20, 1963, 1, 41.

73.   Richard J. H. Johnston, "Jury Finds Beck Guilty in Tax Case: Living Theater Faces Fines and Jail Terms," *New York Times*, May 26, 1964, 45.

74.   See Phyllis Eckhaus Pasternak and Judith Mahoney, "An Interview with Grace Paley, 'Every Action was Essential,'" *Non Violent Activist: The Magazine of the War Resisters League* (March–April 2000).

75.   For a description of the urban landscape that defined the character of Greenwich Village in the '60s, see Sally Banes, "Another Space," in *Greenwich Village 1963: Avant-Garde Performance and the Effervescent Body* (Durham: Duke University Press, 1963), 13–32.

76.   See, Robert E. Haywood, "Heretical Alliance: Claes Oldenburg and the Judson Memorial Church in 1960s," *Art History* 18, no. 2 (1995), 185-212.

77.   George Maciunas, "Manifesto," circa 1963. Sohm, "Happenings and Fluxus," quoted in Sally Banes, *Greenwich Village 1963*, 63.

78.   Roslyn Bernstein and Shael Shapiro, "1967: George Maciunas The Father of Soho," in *Illegal Living: 80 Wooster Street and the Evolution of SoHo* (Vilnius, Lithuania: The Jonas Mekas Foundation, 2010), 35–71.

79.   Aaron Shkuda, *The Lofts of SoHo: Gentrification, Art, and Industry in New York, 1950–1980* (Chicago: The University of Chicago Press, 2016), 53–58. Shkuda, under the subheading "Paying for a loft," provides a clear account of the illegality of the financial arrangements and co-operative itself.

80. Bernstein and Shapiro, *Illegal Living: 80 Wooster Street and the Evolution of SoHo*, 76. Bernstein and Shapiro discuss the friendship and shared vision of Maciunas and Mekas.

81. An article in the *New York Times*, March 15, 1992, calls Maciunas "The Irascible 'Father' of SoHo." The article suggests that Maciunas left because of failing health, disagreements with shareholders, and physical threats to his safety by unpaid workmen. In a response to the *Times* article, his sister Nijole Valaitis wrote that her brother had an intense dislike for bureaucracy and that he was not about to negotiate with them, unlike his fellow artist shareholders.

82. Sharon Zukin, *Loft Living: Culture and Capital in Urban Change,* 23–57. Zukin, in her critical study about loft living, argues that the eventual legalization of the SoHo lofts for living pushed out the remaining small-scale industry in this area and paved the way for big business and real estate development.

CHAPTER 2

1. Hannah Arendt, *On Revolution* (New York: Viking Press, 1963), 142.

2. Arendt, *On Revolution*, 126. The body politic is a metaphor that refers to the governing state as a corporeal entity. I refer to it in the sense proposed by Arendt, as a new constellation of people with a shared political awareness and civic agency.

3. Arendt, *On Revolution*, 166. Arendt, in her discussion of the American Revolution, celebrates the concept of the New England town hall as a Jeffersonian ideal.

4. Hannah Arendt, *The Human Condition* (Chicago: University of Chicago Press, 1958), 199–212.

5. The A. J. Muste Memorial Institute, founded in 1974, was named after A. J. Muste, onetime member of the War Resisters League and a key leader of many pacifist organizations. For a current description of this organization and its mission, visit their website, accessed June 15, 2016, http://www.ajmuste.org/.

6. Arendt, "The Public and the Private Realm," in *The Human Condition*, 22–78.

7. See Henri Lefebvre, *The Production of Space*, trans. Donald Nicholson-Smith (Oxford: Blackwell Publishers, 1991), 24.

8. See Chapter 1 for a brief history of Abraham Johannes Muste and the pacifist movement in New York City.

9. The WRL had been located at 5 Beekman Street since World War II. For a brief history of the WRL at Beekman Street, see Chapter 1. For a comprehensive history of the WRL from its beginnings in 1923 until 1963, see Scott H. Bennett, *Radical Pacifism: The War Resisters League and Gandhian Nonviolence in America, 1915–1963* (New York: Syracuse University Press, 2003).

10. David McReynolds (WRL) and Brad Lyttle (Committee for Nonviolent Action) were both a part of the office at the time of the raid. David McReynolds, interview by author, New York City, June 20, 2013. Brad Lyttle, phone interview by author, July 6, 2013.

11. McReynolds, interview by author, New York City, June 20, 2013.

12. The Overton Commission (1919) and the later House Un-American Committee (1939) specifically targeted the members of pacifist movements and maintained a file on the War Resisters League. See Susan Frances Dion, "Pacifism a Subversion: The FBI and the War Resisters League" (master's thesis, Marquette University, 1980).

13. As stated on the Certificate of Occupancy from 1922, accessed June 14, 2015, http://a810-bisweb.nyc.gov/bisweb/CofoJobDocumentServlet.

14. A large body of scholarship discusses the role of artists in SoHo—setting the precedent for industrial spaces to be converted into living lofts. Most of the conversions in SoHo began illegally in the '60s and culminated in their legalization in 1975. Sharon Zukin provides a critical account of the commodification of the industrial loft in *Loft Living: Culture and Capital in Urban Change* (Baltimore, Md.: Johns Hopkins University Press, 1982). A more current study by Aaron Shkuda

focuses on SoHo artists and looks at the parallel forces of urban renewal and the precedent set by artists in the change from industrial to residential in the rezoning of SoHo. See Shkuda, *The Lofts of SoHo: Gentrification, Art, and Industry in New York, 1950–1980* (Chicago: University of Chicago Press, 2016). The same was true of the neighborhood just north of Houston Street, or NoHo—the neighborhood in which the Peace Pentagon was situated.

15. In quoting the sum of sixty thousand dollars and the date of this transaction, this research relies on the deed of the 1971 property transaction records from the New York City Department of Finance.

16. Details of the move are gathered from David McReynolds, who, along with WRL members Ralph DiGia, Norma Becker, Bernice Lanning, and Igal Roodenko, was instrumental in setting up the new office. McReynolds, interview by author, New York City, June 20, 2013.

17. Information courtesy of Joanne Sheehan, a staff member of WRL who was part of the Catholic Peace Fellowship at 339 Lafayette Street. Joanne Sheehan, phone interview by author, September 11, 2013.

18. This account of the setting up of the Muste Institute as a legal "front" is gathered from McReynolds, interview by author, New York City, June 20, 2013. Over time, the Muste Institute developed its own independent programming and institutional agenda.

19. WRL mission statement, accessed May 15, 2016, at https://www.warresisters .org/about-us. Some within the WRL saw the Vietnam War as an unfortunate event that also detracted from the revolutionary potential of the civil rights movement. This point of view was articulated by McReynolds, interview by author, June 20, 2013. A similar sentiment was expressed by Grace Paley in "An Interview with Grace Paley, 'Every Action Was Essential,'" interview by Phyllis Eckhaus and Judith Mahoney Pasternak, *Nonviolent Activist: The Magazine of the War Resisters League*, March/April 2000.

20. Information about this walk is derived from Vickie Leonard and Tom MacLean, eds., *The Continental Walk for Disarmament and Social Justice* (New York: The Continental Walk for Disarmament and Social Justice, 1977).

21. Leonard and MacLean, *Continental Walk*, 23.

22. For an account of the Shoreham power plant and its contentious history, see Kenneth F. McCallion, *Shoreham and the Rise and Fall of the Nuclear Power Industry* (Westport, Conn.: Praeger, 1995).

23. John Breitbart, interview by author, New York City, July 10, 2015. Breitbart was part of SHAD and also the "Bookmobile Project" that distributed political literature at rallies and other events. He organized both projects at 339 Lafayette Street.

24. Paul L. Montgomery, "Throngs Fill Manhattan to Protest Nuclear Weapons," *New York Times*, June 13, 1982, sec. A1.

25. Paul L. Montgomery, "1,600 Are Arrested in Nuclear Protests at 5 U.N. Missions," *New York Times*, June 15, 1982, sec. A1.

26. Breaking with this thirty-year practice, in 2013 the Nuclear Regulatory Commission issued a permit for the Virgil C. Summer Nuclear Generating Station in South Carolina. The United States remains the world's largest producer of commercial nuclear power.

27. This information is based on a list compiled by Ed Hedemann, a member of the War Resisters League and an active participant in most of these actions since 1972. My selective time line singles out demonstrations with more than a thousand participants and is by no means comprehensive.

28. Leonard and MacLean, *Continental Walk*, 41.

29. A 1970 Certificate of Occupancy records this conversion, accessed May 15, 2016, http://a810-bisweb.nyc.gov/bisweb/ CofoJobDocumentServlet. The building was later converted into transitional housing for women suffering from mental illness. It remained as such until its sale in 2015.

30. Kim Hopper, a sociologist who spent more than a decade working at this shelter,

tells of the overwhelmed staff members and people in need of more serious care. He cites the de-institutionalization of patients suffering from mental heath problems between 1965 and 1977 and the subsequent release of 125,000 patients by the state as the cause of the surge of the homeless population. See also Kim Hopper, *Reckoning with Homelessness* (Ithaca, N.Y.: Cornell University Press, 2003), 77.

31. Hopper, *Reckoning with Homelessness*, 93. The large lobby of the shelter served as a makeshift shelter, where men slept on chairs, couches, and the floor while waiting for a more suitable placement by social service agencies.

32. Ed Hedemann, interview by author, New York City, June 28, 2013.

33. Chapter 1 discusses Dorothy Day and the relationship to the anti-war, pacifist movement. For a broader discussion, see James J. Farrell, "Catholic Worker Personalism," in *The Spirit of the Sixties: The Making of Postwar Radicalism* (New York: Routledge, 1997).

34. See Frida Berrigan's article, "A Place Where It's Easier to Be Good," *Waging Nonviolence* (May 2013) for a sense of what it meant to live at and contribute to the Mary House Community, accessed August 30, 2014, https://wagingnonviolence.org/feature/a-place-where-its-easier-to-be-good/. Although it's a more recent account, the article conveys the practice well.

35. Igal Roodenko, "60 Years on the Frontlines Against War," *Philadelphia Inquirer* (November 9, 1983).

36. Lyttle, phone interview by author, August 1, 2013.

37. Ibid.

38. Joanne Sheehan, phone interview by author, September 9, 2013.

39. Ibid.

40. There is a body of writing on artists and their impact on real estate values. For an account of the metrics of gentrification in the Lower East Side, see Neil Smith, *The New Urban Frontier: Gentrification and the Revanchist City* (New York: Routledge, 1996), 3–29.

For a discussion of the influx of art, culture wars, and gentrification in the East Village, see Christopher Mele, *Selling the Lower East Side: Culture, Real Estate, and Resistance in New York City* (Minneapolis: University of Minnesota Press, 2000), 220–254. For a history of artists and galleries in SoHo, see Shkuda, *Lofts of SoHo*. For the later proliferation of galleries eastward, see Walter Robinson and Carlo McCormick, "Slouching Toward Avenue D," *Art in America* (Summer, 1984).

41. Gallery 345, Karen DiGia's short-lived project, is featured in the context of the broader alternative art movement. See Julie Ault, ed., "A Chronology of Selected Alternative Structures, Spaces, Artists' Groups, and Organizations in New York City, 1965–85," in *Alternative Art New York, 1965–1985* (Minneapolis: University of Minnesota Press, 2002), 55.

42. Karen DiGia, interview by author, New York City, August 15, 2013.

43. Quote from the manifesto of the group published in their newsletter, *PAD/D: First Issue* (February 1981). All issues of this newsletter are accessible at www.darkmatterarchives.net.

44. Gregory Sholette, *A Collectography of PAD/D: A 1980's Activist Art and Networking Collective*, Groups and Spaces E-Zine, 2001. Sholette, an artist and historian, was a member of PAD/D and REPOHistory. Both organizations operated from offices at 339 Lafayette Street, accessed September 20, 2015, http://www.gregorysholette.com/wp-content/uploads/2011/04/14_collectography1.pdf.

45. Editorial, "Fanning the Spark," *Upfront: PAD/D*, no. 5 (1983): 2.

46. See Chapter 1 for the reference to the Bread and Puppet Theater working within the pacifist movement.

47. See Gregory Sholette, *Snip, Snip, Bang, Bang: Political Art, Reloaded* (2008) for artists' participation in El Salvador March in 1980, accessed September 20, 2014, http://www.gregorysholette.com/wpcontent/uploads/2011/04/SnipSnipBangBang.1.pdf. See also report in *PAD/D: First Issue,* no. 1 (1981).

48.   See *PAD/D: First Issue*, no. 1 (1981) for the call for submissions.

49.   Ed Hedemann and Ruth Benn, eds., *War Tax Resistance: A Guide to Withholding Your Support from the Military*, 5th edition, War Resisters League (February 2, 2003).

50.   According to Ruth Benn and Ed Hedemann, the creators of this chart. Since the Vietnam War, the chart issued by the U.S. government includes social security, a citizen's trust fund, which is shown as a tax allocation. Information gathered from Ed Hedemann and Ruth Benn, interview by author, June 28, 2013.

For a detailed analysis of the current fiscal budget and previous charts, visit the WRL website at https://www.warresisters.org/federalpiechart.

51.   For a description of the projects and artists' statements, see *PAD/D: First Issue: Political Art Documentation/Distribution*, no. 2 (1981).

52.   For an overview of the Alternative Art movement in New York, see Ault, *Alternative Art*.

53.   An observation by McReynolds, who was on the board of the Muste Institute at the time. McReynolds, interview by author, New York City, June 20, 2013.

54.   Ibid.

55.   The Freedom of Information Act allows for a partial disclosure of all previously unreleased information and documents controlled by the U.S. government. This act, passed in 1966, has been amended to the point whereby any actions deemed a threat to national security (aka "terrorism") are exempt from disclosure.

56.   Angus MacKenzie, *Secrets: The CIA's War at Home* (Berkeley and Los Angeles: University of California Press, 1997), 153.

57.   Video accessed 5 June, 2016, http://papertiger.org/?s=buitrago.

58.   Schiller was an influential educator and a vociferous critic of the corporate control of the media. He wrote several books that cautioned against the dangers of the control of public space by corporate media. See Herbert Schiller, *Mass Communications and American Empire* (Boulder, Colo.: Westview Press, 1969).

59.   Details gathered in an interview by the author with DeeDee Halleck on July 12, 2013. The PTTV videos, accessed June 5, 2016, are archived at http://papertiger.org/video-archive/image-archive/.

60.   For a discussion of Paper Tiger TV in relation to other media activism, see Jesse Drew, "The Collective Camcorder in Art and Activism," in *Collectivism after Modernism: The Art of Social Imagination after 1945*, ed. Blake Stimson and Gregory Sholette (Minneapolis: University of Minnesota Press, 2007), 95–113.

61.   DeeDee Halleck, "The Camcorder Goes to War: Making Outrage Contagious—A Chronology of the Gulf Crisis TV Project with Texts and Testimonies," in *Hand-Held Visions: The Impossible Possibilities of Community Media* (New York: Fordham University Press, 2002), 169–187.

62.   For information about the series see their website, accessed May 5, 2016, http://papertiger.org/war-on-the-home-front/.

63.   Deedee Halleck, "Camcorder Goes to War," 172

64.   Muste Newsletter, 2001, accessed May 5, 2016, http://www.ajmuste.org/notes-fall2001.htm.

65.   David Graeber, "Occupy Wall Street's Anarchist Roots," *Al Jazeera*, November 30, 2011, accessed May 15, 2014, http://www.aljazeera.com/indepth/opinion/2011/11/2011112872835904508.html.

66.   Sean Captain, "Wired Threat Level: Inside Occupy Wall Street's (Kinda) Secret Media HQ," November 16, 2011, accessed December 14, 2013, http://globalrevolution.tv/in-the-press/125.

67.   Information from member of Global Revolution TV, Vlad Teichberg, interviewed by author, New York City, Jan. 14, 2015. Also see Graeber, "Occupy Wall Street's Anarchist Roots" for the OWS ideals of the "leaderless movement."

68.   Teichberg, interviewed by author, New York City, Jan. 14, 2015. Teichberg sees

the continuing engagement of GRTV as a continuation of ideas developed during OWS.

69.   Saskia Sassen, "Seeing Like a City," in *The Endless City: The Urban Age Project by the London School of Economics*, ed. Ricky Burdett and Deyan Sudjic (London: Phaidon, 2007), 276–289.

70.   Jeffrey Hou, "Beyond Zuccotti Park: Making the Public," *Places Journal*, September 2012, accessed May 30, 2016, https:// placesjournal.org/article/beyond-zuccotti-park-making-the-public. See also Andrew Merrifield, *The New Urban Question* (London: Pluto Press, 2014).

71.   Bennett, "Present at Creation: The WRL, Direct Action, Civil Disobedience, and the Rebirth of the Peace and Justice Movements (1955–1963)," in *Radical Pacifism*, 204–246. Bennett suggests that by integrating a Gandhian strategy of "nonviolent direct action" with a more homegrown tradition of pacifism, the WRL has been tremendously influential in shaping various resistance movements in the United States. The civil rights movements and the Vietnam War resistance in the '60s saw the more widespread acceptance and formulation of these practices. Chapter 1 discusses the roots of the movement.

72.   In looking at correspondence from the A. J. Muste Memorial Institute as well as talking to some of the WRL women staffers, the question of combatting "sexism"—a subject also embedded in the WRL mission statement—comes up often. Marian Mollin's book *Radical Pacifism in Modern America: Egalitarianism and Protest* (Philadelphia: University of Pennsylvania Press, 2006) discusses the machismo within the pacifist movement after World War II.

73.   Ali Issa, interview by author, New York City, January 20, 2015.

74.   Ibid.

75.   See Dan Barry, "As Wars Come and Go, Ralph Keeps Protesting," *New York Times*, March 22, 2003. Ralph DiGia's perseverance and humility were legendary and came up in conversations with long-term members and colleagues at the WRL (Ruth Benn, Ed

Hedemann, and David McReynolds). Bennett, *Radical Pacifism*, 131–132, describes Ralph DiGia's imprisonment during World War II and his role in the Danbury and Lewisburg parole strikes.

76.   Gregory Sholette in a phone conversation with author, June 2013. REPOHistory (1989–1999), was a collective whose mission was to reclaim forgotten histories. They took over the third-floor office from PAD/D. Sholette was part of both PAD/D and REPOHistory.

77.   Formation of PAD/D recounted by Gregory Sholette, *A Collectography of PAD/D: A 1980s Activist Art and Networking Collective* (2001): 2.

78.   Arendt, *On Revolution*, 248–255.

79.   Judith Butler, "Bodies in Alliance and the Politics of the Street," Lecture in Venice, September 7, 2011, as part of the series, "The State of Things," organized by the Office for Contemporary Art Norway, accessed May 15, 2016, published online at http://www.eipcp .net/transversal/1011/butler/en.

80.   Jeffrey Hou, "Beyond Zuccotti Park: Making the Public."

CHAPTER 3

1.   Ruth Nazario, phone interview by author, April 8, 2015. Ruth and Roberto Nazario, codirectors of Adopt-a-Building (AAB) at the time, were responsible for getting permission to use the building for their organization.

2.   This three-part agenda, as stated in the bylaws of CHARAS, "Article II—Purposes." Document in CHARAS Box 10, Centro Archives, Center for Puerto Rican Studies, Hunter College, CUNY.

3.   See Chapter 1 for the connection to this history.

4.   For a history of the building, see Landmarks Preservation Commission Designation List 377 LP-2189, June 20, 2006.

5.   This account of the foundation of El Bohio Community Center is based on conversations with Ruth Nazario, codirector of AAB, phone interview by author, April 8, 2015; and

Chino Garcia, founder of CHARAS, interview by author, New York City, April 9, 2015. The time line of abandonment of PS 64 varies in different written and oral accounts of this building's history, but the description of the state of the building is consistent.

6. Interfaith Adopt-a-Building, "Loisaida: Strategies for Neighborhood Revitalization and Self-Determination," HUD Contract 4376, New York, December 18, 1979, 78–92. This territory is the focus of AAB's work, as per the HUD report.

7. See Christopher Mele, *Selling of the Lower East Side: Culture, Real Estate, and Resistance in New York City* (Minneapolis: University of Minnesota Press, 2000), 123–126, for a summation of the dynamics of Puerto Rican migration to the United States. After World War II, Puerto Ricans began migrating to the United States in larger numbers. In 1953 Puerto Rican migration to New York City reached its peak when 75,000 people left the island. By 1960, the United States Census showed that there were well over 600,000 New Yorkers of Puerto Rican birth or parentage.

8. Bimbo Rivas, "Loisaida," in *Aloud: Voices from the Nuyorican Poets Café,* ed. Miguel Algarín and Bob Holman (New York: Holt, 1994), 361. The name was popularized in "Loisaida," a poem written by Bimbo Rivas in 1974, and simultaneously adopted more consciously by activists and community organizers in the Lower East Side.

9. For an account of the naming and construction of identity through space, see Liz Ševčenko, "Making Loisaida: Placing Puertorriqueñidad in Lower Manhattan," in *Mambo Montage,* ed. Augustín Laó-Montes and Arlene Dávila (New York: Columbia University Press, 2001), 293–318.

10. Carmelo Quinones, "Loisaida," *Quality of Life in Loisaida,* March–April 1979, 15.

11. Syeus Mottel, *CHARAS: The Improbable Dome Builders* (New York: Drake Publishers, 1973), 123–124. Chino Garcia describes the spontaneous creation of Real Great Society at a meeting with friends in the Lower East Side.

In 1964 President Lyndon B. Johnson introduced his concept for the Great Society in which America ended poverty and promoted equality. The channeling of federal funds in the form of grants to community-based organizations was the way to implement a series of education, housing, health, and environmental initiatives. In New York City, the low-income neighborhoods of the South Bronx, East Harlem, and the Lower East Side were the recipients of this aid. The difficulty in monitoring and holding groups accountable ultimately led to criticism and partial failure of this well-intentioned program.

12. Roger Vaughan, "The Real Great Society," *Life Magazine* 63, no. 11 (1967): 76. Vaughan describes the gang affiliations of the various leaders of Real Great Society. The article features Chino Garcia, Angelo Gonzalez, Papo Giordini, Armando Perez, and Rabbit Nazario (who was later instrumental in Adopt-a-Building) as the leaders of this movement. He also highlights Fred Good, who helped write grant applications and—though an outsider in terms of his background—was a vital part of the organization.

13. "'A University' Is Opened Up by Former Street-Fighters," *New York Times,* June 27, 1967, 23. This *New York Times* article reports the grants from the Astor Foundation and the opening of the University of the Street.

14. See Fred Good, "Origins of Loisaida," in *Resistance: A Radical Social and Political History of the Lower East Side,* ed. Clayton Patterson (New York: Seven Stories Press, 2007), 21–36. Fred Good, a member of the Real Great Society, was instrumental in founding the University of the Street. He describes the initial formation and the later development of this institution.

15. Peter Kihss, "Ex-Gang Leaders Obtain U.S. Funds," *New York Times,* February 27, 1968, 53. The *New York Times* reported a $258,447 grant from the federal Office of Economic Opportunity. The article noted that the university was operating at five locations: three on the Lower East Side and two in East Harlem.

16. The grant from the Office of Economic Opportunity stipulated job training and accountability that was hard to sustain and created some friction within the organization. For a more critical version of the rift between Real Great Society members and the university, see Good, "Origins of Loisaida," 21–36.

17. For an account of this initiative, see Luis Aponte-Parés, "Lessons from El Barrio—The East Harlem Real Great Society/Urban Planning Studio: A Puerto Rican Chapter in the fight for Urban Self-Determination," in *Latino Social Movements: Historical and Theoretical Perspectives*, ed. Rodolfo D. Torres and George Katsiaficas (New York: Routledge, 1999), 43–78.

18. Gathered in conversations with Chino Garcia, interview by author, New York City, November 11, 2015. This connection to Outward Bound continued over the next twenty years, where CHARAS regularly sent young men and women from the Puerto Rican community to Outward Bound expeditions. This encounter with nature, along with the extreme physical challenges, was part of the idea of building a strong "youth corps."

19. Felicity D. Scott, "Fluid Geographies: Politics and the Revolution by Design," in *New Views on R. Buckminster Fuller*, ed. Hsiao-Yun Chu and Roberto G. Trujillo (Stanford, Calif.: Stanford University Press, 2009), 160–176. Scott argues that Fuller was more interested in the structure and geometry of the domes than their practical applications to help solve a postwar housing crisis, and so the 1968 embrace by countercultural rural communities such as Dropout City was unexpected but welcome.

20. Mottel, *Improbable Dome Builders*, 24.

21. Ibid., 27.

22. "Building Geodesic Domes Tests Skills of Students," *New York Times*, November 4, 1972, 53.

23. Mottel, *Improbable Dome Builders*, 60–63.

24. This parcel of land extending along the East River, from the Manhattan Bridge to Corlears Hook, was one of the last remaining parcels to be slated for Urban Renewal. Built by a private developer under the Section 8 criteria for affordable housing, this project, begun in 1972, took until 1997 to complete. See http://www.twobridges.org/about-us/history, accessed January 15, 2015, for a brief description of the neighborhood council's role in its planning.

25. Garcia, interview by author, New York City, November 11, 2015. According to Chino Garcia, CHARAS set up boarding facilities for many "hundreds" of volunteer youth. "CHARAS was big," said Garcia. "The organization operated in the South Bronx, Harlem as well as in Puerto Rico."

26. Marlis Momber, prod., "Viva Loisaida," Gruppe Dokumentation, 1978, DVD, Center for Puerto Rican Studies at Hunter College, CUNY. "Viva Loisaida" visually chronicles the neighborhood. The film, with a German voiceover, was aired on German TV in 1978.

27. Garcia, interview by author, New York City, November 11, 2015.

28. The inauguration of the Young Lords Party in the Tompkins Square Park band shell was emphasized in this manner at an exhibit at the Bronx Museum of the Arts and the local art space Loisaida Inc. called "¡Presente! The Young Lords in New York" (2015). For a larger political history of the park, see Marci Reaven and Jeanne Houck, "A History of Tompkins Square Park," in *From Urban Village to East Village: The Battle for New York's Lower East Side*, ed. Janet L. Abu-Lughod (Cambridge, Mass.: Blackwell Publishers, 1994), 81–98.

29. Matthew Gandy, "Between Borinquen and the Barrio," in *Concrete and Clay: Reworking Nature in New York City* (Cambridge: MIT Press, 2003), 153–186. Gandy examines the contribution of the Young Lords and the Puerto Rican political legacy within the environmental movement in New York City.

30. Gandy, "Between Borinquen and the Barrio," 164–177. A series of articles in the *New York Times* show the amount of attention these events received in the press; see: "Puerto

Rican Group Seizes Church in East Harlem in Demand for Space," December 29, 1969; "Young Lords Give Food and Care at Seized Church," December 30, 1969; "Young Lords Defy Takeover," January 3, 1970; and "105 Members of Young Lords Submit to Arrest, Ending 11-Day Occupation of Church in East Harlem," January 8, 1970. In addition, the Young Lords produced their own bilingual newspaper, *Palante* (1969–1973), to galvanize support within the neighborhood and to raise support for these actions.

31. For a collection of writings from this movement, see Young Lords Party and Abramson, *Palante: Voices and Photographs of the Young Lords, 1969–1971,* photographs by Michael Abramson, introduction by Iris Morales (Chicago: Haymarket Books, 2011). For the history and specific ideology and decolonial praxis of the Young Lords, see Darrel Wanzer-Serrano, *The New York Young Lords and the Struggle for Liberation* (Philadelphia: Temple University Press, 2015).

32. Published in the first issue of *Palante*, June, 1970. See also, the Sixties Project, sponsored by Viet Nam Generation Inc. and the Institute of Advanced Technology in the Humanities at the University of Virginia at Charlottesville, accessed February 15, 2016, http://www2.iath.virginia.edu/sixties/HTML_docs/Resources/Primary/Manifestos/Young_Lords_platform.html.

33. Garcia, interview by author, New York City, April 9, 2015. Chino also explained that he was closely connected to the Young Lords movement and that the many strands of the Puerto Rican Resistance, though varied, were overlapping and interconnected.

34. WIN collective, "Loisaida," *WIN*, December 20, 1979, 5. Articles by several participants from the "Loisaida movement," 4–25.

35. Mele, *Selling of the Lower East Side*, 181–182, discusses how the symbolic representations of the neighborhood in decline created a "contagion of abandonment." However, there were other systemic forces at play—such as the urban renewal schemes that targeted low-income neighborhoods and the redlining that caused property values to drop.

36. See Ronald Lawson, with the assistance of Reuben B. Johnson III, "Tenant Responses to the Urban Housing Crisis, 1970–1984," in *The Tenant Movement in New York City, 1904–1984*, ed. Ronald Lawson (New Brunswick, N.J.: Rutgers University Press, 1986), 209–271. This book is available at the following website, accessed July 17, 2014: http://www.tenant.net/Oversight/50yrRentReg/history.html. Lawson points to several causes for the disinvestment in real estate and the success of a tenant movement between 1970 and 1984. He writes, "The system of rent regulations, the central features of which had been in place since 1943, was suddenly challenged and undermined: a law enacted by the state legislature in 1971 provided that the bulk of apartments with regulated rents would be decontrolled within a few years, while a measure passed by the City Council the previous year introduced annual rent increases for apartments that remained rent controlled." Lawson reports that from July, 1971, through December, 1973, approximately 300,000 rent-controlled units were decontrolled and approximately 88,000 rent-stabilized apartments were destabilized. This measure was withdrawn again three years later, only adding to the instability and chaos.

37. Lawson, "Tenant Responses." The rent strike has a long history in New York City. Tenants can legally withhold rent in an escrow account if the landlord fails to provide basic services and maintain a building. In the '70s, as landlords abandoned their buildings, some tenants used a provision in the real estate law known as Article 7A to "self-manage" their buildings.

38. Ibid.

39. This was a precursor to the Housing Development Corporation (HDC).

40. In 1974 the federal Department of Housing and Urban Development (HUD) officially recognized homesteading of city-owned properties through Section 810 of the Housing Law. In 1981 New York City put out

its first call for requests for proposals. The program came to an end in 1994 as no new properties were put up for homesteading. UHAB, *The Urban Homesteading Assistance Board, 1974–1984: A Retrospective Report and Review* (New York: UHAB, 1985), provides a good description of the program.

41.   For a thorough analysis and critical account of homesteading in the Lower East Side, see Malve von Hassell, *Homesteading in New York City, 1978–1993: The Divided Heart of Loisaida* (Westport, Conn.: Bergin and Garvey, 1996).

42.   Over the years, many other such organizations worked with tenants on sweat equity projects and homesteading citywide. In the Bronx, the People's Development Corporation played an important role. Other early groups included Los Sures and Pueblo Nuevo (on the Lower East Side), Banana Kelly (in the South Bronx), and the Harlem Renegades (in East Harlem). Hassell, *Homesteading in New York City*, 150–160, compares a few of these organizations.

43.   Christopher Mele, "Urban Malaise, Community Abandonment, and Underground Subcultures of Decay," in *Selling of the Lower East Side: Culture, Real Estate, and Resistance in New York City* (Minneapolis: University of Minnesota Press, 2000), 180–219. Mele discusses how the disinvestment and abandonment disproportionately impacted the Puerto Rican community in the Lower East Side.

44.   Description of organization gathered from Ruth Nazario, phone interview by author, April 8, 2015; and Brent Sharman, interview by author, New York City, September 22, 2015.

45.   Interfaith Adopt-a-Building, "Loisaida: Strategies for Neighborhood Revitalization and Self-Determination," HUD Contract 4376, New York, December 18, 1979, 45.

46.   Nazario, phone interview by author, April 8, 2015.

47.   Certificate of Occupancy in 1969 lists the number of rooms per floor. In 1973 it was sold to a private owner who, by the early '80s, developed it into "luxury" condominiums. This building, notes Marlis Momber through her photographs, represented one of the first signs of gentrification on Avenue C. Momber, interview by author, New York City, September 2015.

48.   *Quality of Life in Loisaida*, March 1978, 2

49.   Michael Freedberg, "Self-Help Housing and the Cities: Sweat Equity in New York City," in *Resettling America: Energy, Ecology, and Community*, ed. Gary J. Coates (Andover, Mass.: Brick House Publishing Company, 1981), 263–281. Freedberg provides an account of the logistics of this project, notably the financial and legal arrangements that led to the successful completion of this project in the record time of two years. The conversion into the limited-equity model took longer, as the tenants had to provide evidence of fiscal solvency.

50.   Luz Rodriguez, interview by author, New York City, September 22, 2015.

51.   Brent Sharman, interview by author, New York City, September 22, 2015.

52.   ABB received a Comprehensive Employment and Training Act (CETA) grant. This program was enacted by the Congress in 1973 to consolidate a number of federal job training programs to help unemployed, underemployed, and disadvantaged individuals.

53.   See Linda Cohen and Brent Sharman, "Garden of the Sun," *Quality of Life in Loisaida*, (June–July 1978), 6.

54.   The story of this sweat equity project was covered incrementally by the *New York Post*, January 24, 1974; *Daily News*, January 25, 1974; *New York Times*, May 11, 1975; November 13, 1976; and May 6, 1977.

55.   *No Heat, No Rent: An Urban Solar and Energy Conservation Manual*, the Energy Task Force, U.S. Government Printing Office, 1977.

56.   *The MacNeil/Lehrer Report* filmed a segment on the roof of the building, and Senator Edward Kennedy referred to the building as "the little windmill that could." See *New York Times*, August 3, 2008. Also see Shaya Love, "The Almost Forgotten Story of the 1970s East Village Windmill," *Gothamist*, September 29, 2014.

57. *Washington Star*, October 7, 1978. The story of the sweat equity project was also covered incrementally by the *New York Post*, January 24, 1974; *Daily News*, January 25, 1974; *New York Times*, May 11, 1975; November 13, 1976; and May 6, 1977.

58. Daniel Chodorkoff, *Un Milagro de Loisaida: Alternate Technology and Grassroots Efforts for Neighborhood Reconstruction on New York's Lower East Side* (PhD thesis, New School for Social Research, 1980), 3–4.

59. Murray Bookchin and Eirik Eiglad, "The Communalist Project," in *Social Ecology and Communalism* (Oakland, Calif.: AK Press, 2007), 77–117.

60. Linda Cohen, interview by author, New York City, April 8, 2015. Cohen, who was a key participant of El Sol Brilliante, met some of the architects in Vermont. Bookchin's ideas on ecology were influential for Cohen and other participants of the Eleventh Street movement.

61. Daniel Chodorkoff, phone interview by author, November 8, 2015.

62. Image of the Vermont Dome published in Janet Biehl, *Ecology or Catastrophe: The Life of Murray Bookchin* (New York, N.Y.: Oxford University Press, 2015), 165–166. Photograph by Josie Rolon shows dome at nuclear protest with World Trade Center towers in the background. See "Loisaida," *WIN*, December 20, 1979, 12.

63. Miguel Algarin, *Aloud: Voices from the Nuyorican Poets Café*.

64. Algarin, *Nuyorican Poetry: An Anthology of Puerto Rican Words and Feelings*, ed. Miguel Algarin and Miguel Piñero (New York: William Morrow and Company, 1975), 15. The Renegades and Dynamites were reformed gangs that became involved in the East Harlem homesteading movement. There are many parallels and links between the East Harlem and Lower East Side communities that are important but beyond the scope of this work.

65. Garcia, interview by author, New York City, April 9, 2015.

66. Chodorkoff, *Un Milagro de Loisaida*, 130. Chodorkoff names six of the core CHARAS

members at the time of his research in 1978–1980. However, the structure of the organization fluctuated over the span of forty years, with Chino Garcia as the one constant founding member and key organizer.

67. Garcia, interview by author, New York City, April 9, 2015. Garcia mentions "hundreds" of CHARAS volunteers. The fluid structure of the organization makes it difficult to establish its contours.

68. Miriam Rivas, "Dancing from the Heart and Soul," *WIN*, December 20, 1979, 20–23. Rivas describes *La Bomba* as a dance music that was an assertion of the irrepressible spirit of the plantation slaves. Rivas explains the politics of the "Bomba" performance tradition, a struggle against the landed Spanish gentry, and notes "song, dance and performance as a part of the resistance and liberation movements" of Puerto Rico.

69. Chodorkoff, *Un Milagro de Loisaida*, 151–158. Chokdorkoff describes the project in detail. See also *Quality of Life in Loisaida*, February–March 1979, 7.

70. *Quality of Life in Loisaida*, March–April 1979, 6.

71. For a fuller history of the building, see Landmarks Preservation Commission Designation List 377 LP-2189, June 20, 2006.

72. Comprehensive Employment and Training Act (CETA) was enacted by Congress in 1973 to consolidate a number of existing federal job training programs to help unemployed, underemployed, and disadvantaged individuals.

73. Nazario, in a phone interview by author, mentioned that their organization of two staff members and a handful of volunteers grew to a hundred as a result of the CETA grant. See also Lawson, *The Tenant Movement in New York City, 1904–1984*, 222. Lawson reports of the meteoric rise in the budget of AAB that went from an unpaid staff of three in 1975 to 2.7 million in 1977–1978 because of the CETA grants. By 1980–1981, its budget had surpassed $4 million.

74. The Loisaida Townhouse, a privately-owned property, was one of the first buildings

in Loisaida to be converted into market-rate housing and advertised in 1984 as "luxury" condominiums. Marlis Momber has a photograph of this building advertising "luxury" apartments. Automatic City Register Information System records verify this.

75. Barbara Newsom and Adele Silver, eds., *The Art Museum as Educator: A Collection of Studies as Guides to Practice and Policy* (Berkeley and Los Angeles: University of California Press, 1978), 212–216. Seven Loaves was a nonprofit arts coalition that included several smaller arts organizations.

76. Conversation with Chino Garcia, December 7, 2015. Picture the Homeless and Recycle-a-Bicycle are still active in 2017 in East Harlem and Brooklyn respectively.

77. Doris Cornish, interview by author, New York City, September 4, 2015.

78. Cornish, interview by author.

79. Information from conversations with Alan Moore (Founding Member, ABC No Rio) and Greg Sholette (Member PAD/D). Other locations for this show included the branch library on Eleventh Street as well as in the newly formed ABC No Rio. Alan Moore and Marc Miller, *ABC No Rio Dinero: The Story of a Lower East Side Art Gallery* (New York City: ABC No Rio and Colab projects, 1985), 70–71.

80. Anton Van Dalen, interview by author, January 24, 2016.

81. Josh Gosciak, *East Village Eye*, June 1982, 2–3.

82. Biehl, *Ecology or Catastrophe*, 169–170. Biehl refers to CHARAS as the "poster child of ecological self-reliance" and describes the many exchanges between the Institute for Social Ecology and Loisaida.

83. Gosciak, *East Village Eye*, 3.

84. Algarin, *Nuyorican Poetry*, 12.

85. Hassell, *Homesteading in New York City*, 101–107.

86. *El Bohio Community and Cultural Center Report*, 1st Draft, March 1986, Centro Archives, Center for Puerto Rican Studies, Hunter College, CUNY. They received a sum of $60,000 for Phase 1 from the New York City Department of General Services. In this report they estimated that they would need another $177,600 to do a more integrated Phase 2 upgrade.

87. Rosalyn Deutche and Cara Gendal Ryan, "The Fine Art of Gentrification," October, Vol. 30 (Winter 1984): 91–111; Sharon Zukin, *Loft Living: Culture and Capital in Urban Change* (Baltimore, Md.: Johns Hopkins University Press, 1992); Neil Smith, *The New Urban Frontier: Gentrification and the Revanchist City* (New York: Routledge, 1996), 18–20.

88. Interview with Mary Ann Monforton, November 9, 2015. Monforton organized the art auctions at El Bohio in 1986 and 1887.

89. Urayoán Noel, *In Visible Movement: Nuyorican Poetry from the Sixties to Slam* (Iowa City: University of Iowa Press, 2014), 66.

90. Ibid., 82. Davila and Agustín also discuss the progression from Nationalist to pan-Latino solidarity movements within the United States. See Arlene Dávila and Laó-Montes Agustín, "Culture in the Battlefront: From Nationalist to Pan-Latino Projects," in *Mambo Montage: The Latinization of New York City* (New York: Columbia University Press, 2001), 159–82.

91. Clayton Patterson, "Section Three: Tompkins Square," in *Resistance: A Radical Social and Political History of the Lower East Side*, ed. Clayton Patterson (New York: Seven Stories Press, 2007), 289–415, provides a multi-authored perspective on the resistance that fomented in and around Tompkins Square Park at the end of the '80s.

92. For an account of *La Lucha Continua* project by Artmakers Inc., see Mike Alewitz, "1985–1988," in *On the Wall: Four Decades of Community Murals in New York City*, ed. Janet Braun-Reinitz and Jane Weisaman (Jackson: University Press of Mississippi, 2009), 89–97.

93. Hassell, *Homesteading in New York City*, provides a rich history and critical analysis of the homesteading movement in the Lower East Side. The book focuses on the efforts of one organization, the Lower East Side Catholic Area conference, which was active in the

'80s and '90s. The movement came to an end in the early '90s.

94. The task of homesteading and creating tenant-managed buildings, however, continued into the '90s. The Tenant Interim Lease Program (TIL) provided renters that lived in city-owned buildings the opportunity to own those units as a cooperative. This program is still in existence in 2017. See http://furman center.org/institute/directory/entry/tenant-interim-lease-program, accessed May 7, 2017.

95. Mele, *Selling of the Lower East Side*, 220–310.

96. Ibid., 258–262.

97. Steven A. Holmes, "A Neighborhood Battle: Apartments or a Park," *New York Times*, December 18, 1989, sec. LB3.

98. Eric V. Copage, "La Plaza 1 Used, 8 to Go," *New York Times*, May 9, 1999.

99. CHARAS leader Armando Perez accuses Giuliani of the vendetta in Amy Waldman, "Separate Fates for Two Hispanic Cultural Centers," *New York Times*, July 26, 1998, sec. CY5. This *New York Times* article points to how arbitrary or biased the sales were. Another building (Soto Clemente Velez) managed to convince the city to give them their building for one dollar at the same time as CHARAS, perhaps due to its active, politicized campaigning, lost its building.

100. For a nuanced reading on the complexities of the Puerto Rican versus "Non–Puerto Rican" activist relationships in the struggle to save El Bohio as well as the garden Bello Amanecer Borincano see Miranda Martinez, *Power at the Roots: Gentrification, Community Gardens and the Puerto Ricans of the Lower East Side* (Plymouth, UK: Lexington Books, 2010), 15–126.

101. Bill Weinberg, "Looking Back on the Tompkins Square War," in *A Radical Social and Political History of the Lower East Side*, ed. Clayton Patterson, 372.

102. See the news report of the eviction. Robert F. Worth, "East Village Community Group is Evicted: Chants and Arrests as Charas is Evicted from its Home of 22 Years," *New York Times* December 28, 2001, sec. D3.

103. Manuel Castells, *The City and the Grassroots* (Berkeley and Los Angeles: University of California Press, 1983), 94-96.

CHAPTER 4

1. The neighborhood at large was predominantly Puerto Rican, as discussed in Chapter 3. However, in pockets, especially by the '80s, there was a strong presence of Dominicans. There are no clear statistics on this matter, so I use the designation Latino—further research is needed on establishing the nuance of this difference. For a larger discussion about the Dominican experience and questions of Latino, see José Itzigsohn and Carlos Dore-Cabral, "The Manifold Character of Pan-ethnicity: Latino Identities and Practices Among Dominicans in New York City," in *Mambo Montage: The Latinization of New York City*, ed. Augustín Laó-Montes and Arlene Dávila (New York: Columbia University Press, 2001), 319–36.

2. The account of the show and the founding of ABC No Rio is documented in Alan Moore and Marc Miller, eds., *ABC No Rio Dinero: The Story of a Lower East Side Art Gallery* (New York City: ABC No Rio and Colab Projects, 1985). An excerpt of an interview by Shelly Leavitt with founding members (Bobby G, Becky Howland, and Alan Moore) on page 66 outlines the means by which ABC No Rio was founded. This interview was originally published in *BOMB Magazine*, vol. 1, no. 2 (1982): 40–41.

3. Shelly Leavitt, "ABC No Rio Interviewed," *BOMB Magazine*, vol. 1, no. 2 (1982): 40–41. Mission is as stated in this interview by *BOMB Magazine*.

4. Alan Moore, founding member, compiled the book with Marc Miller in 1985.

5. See Julie Ault, ed., *Alternative Art New York, 1965–1985* (Minneapolis: University of Minnesota Press, 2002). The book examines the many dimensions of various artists' collectives and alternative art spaces in New York. For a closer look at artists' collectives in New York between 1969 and 1985, see Alan Moore,

Art Gangs: Protest and Counterculture in New York City (Brooklyn, N.Y.: Autonomedia, 2011).

6. See Lucy Lippard, "Biting the Hand: Artists and Museums in New York since 1969," in *Alternative Art New York, 1965–1985*, ed. Julie Ault (Minneapolis: University of Minnesota Press, 2002), 79–120. See also pp. 88–89, where Lippard examines the actions of the broad-based protests of artists in AWC and GAGG.

7. The chronology of these spaces is listed in Ault, *Alternative Art New York, 1965–1985*, and the more updated version is listed in Lauren Rosati and Mary Anne Staiszewski, eds., *Alternative Histories: New York Art Spaces 1960 to 2010* (Cambridge, Mass.: Exit Art and MIT Press, 2012).

8. The effective organization by the artists and the promotion of preservation contributed to the speculation and led to the ultimate gentrification of many former industrial neighborhoods. See Aaron Shkuda, "Real Estate and SoHo Politics: Loft Promotion and Historic Preservation in Lower Manhattan," in *The Lofts of SoHo: Gentrification, Art, and Industry in New York, 1950–1980* (Chicago: University of Chicago Press, 2016), 131–157.

9. David Little, "Colab Takes a Piece, History Takes It Back: Collectivity and New York Alternative Spaces," *Art Journal* 66, no. 1 (2007): 60–74. Little provides a description of the early history of Colab 1977–1979. Some of the main founding members left the organization in 1979, but the organization continued until 1984. For the later history of Colab and artists' collectives, see Alan Moore, "Artists' Collectives: Focus on New York, 1975–2000," in *Collectivism After Modernism: The Art of Social Imagination After 1945*, ed. Blake Stimson and Gregory Sholette (Minneapolis: University of Minnesota Press, 2007), 193–221.

10. Moore, "Artists' Collectives," 64. Moore quotes from an early document the Colab group put together.

11. Moore, *Art Gangs*, 81.

12. See Moore, *Art Gangs*, 92–93, for a short account of these shows. The shows were reported in the *Village Voice* and *SoHo Weekly* news.

13. Ibid.

14. El Bohio Community Center, discussed in Chapter 3, was a point of reference. Alan Moore, interview by author, New York City, September 23, 2015. In addition, most of the artists were aware of the successful negotiations by curator Alana Heiss for temporal art events in the Brooklyn anchorage, as well as the leasing of PS 1 under her direction in 1976. These precedents were all indications to the arts community that the city was open to leasing space to arts organizations.

15. Stephen Zacks, "Where Can We Be? The Occupation of 123 Delancey Street," *Places Journal*, August 2015, accessed February 6, 2016, https://placesjournal.org/article/where-can-we-be-123-delancey-street/. Zacks provides an account of this occupation with firsthand interviews with participants of the show.

16. Artist quote from Lehmann Weichselbaum, The Real Estate Show, *East Village Eye*, 1980. Republished in Moore and Miller, *ABC No Rio Dinero*, 53.

17. Oliver, *New York Post*, January 3, 1980; Weichselbaum, *East Village Eye*, January 17, 1980; Barbanel, *New York Times*, January 9, 1980.

18. Accounts of the early shows are from the documentation of them in Moore and Miller, *ABC No Rio Dinero*.

19. Marcia Chambers, "City Seeks to Dislodge Drug Trade by Demolishing Tenement Havens," *New York Times*, July 18, 1982, 1.

20. Richard Goldstein, "Enter the Anti-Space," *Village Voice*, 1980, also published in Moore and Miller, *ABC No Rio Dinero*, 64–65.

21. For a description of the show, see Jerry Taimer, "'Peaceable Kingdom,' *New York Post*, 1980," in *ABC No Rio Dinero: The Story of a Lower East Side Art Gallery*, ed. Alan Moore and Marc Miller (New York City: ABC No Rio and Colab projects, 1985), 78.

22. Alan Moore, "Punk Art," in *Protest and Counterculture in New York City* (Brooklyn, N.Y.: Autonomedia, 2011). Moore elaborates

on the "anarchic" and "opportunistic" aspects of the Colab artists in relationship to a larger art/music/club culture.

23. These irreconcilable differences are noted by ABC No Rio directors over the years:
1. Alan Moore, Becky Howland, and Bobby G, (directors from 1980–1983) speaking in a collective voice, come to terms with the fact that there is little participation from the Hispanic community of the neighborhood. "ABC No Rio Interviewed," *BOMB Magazine*, vol. 1, no. 2 (1982).
2. Jack Waters, Peter Cramer, and Lou Acierno (directors of ABC No Rio) in 1991 discuss this in detail, along class and racial lines, in a candid interview with Kathrin Wildner, "ABC No Rio: An Alternative Space in the Lower East Side," Autumn 1991, accessed July 25, 2016, http://www.abcnorio.org/about/history/wildner_91.html
3. Steven Englander, director of ABC No Rio, in a later interview speaks of the same issue but "is not in favor of art as a proselytizing tool" and is comfortable not trying to reconcile those differences. Steven Englander, oral history interview with Liza Kirwin, Archives of American Art, Smithsonian Institution, September 7–October 10, 2007.

24. R. R. Armijo, "Afterword," in Alan Moore and Marc Miller, *ABC No Rio Dinero: The Story of a Lower East Side Art Gallery* (New York City: ABC No Rio and Colab projects, 1985), 99.

25. Bobby G, interview by author, New York City, December 13, 2016.

26. Ibid.

27. Christy Rupp, phone conversation with author, October 5, 2015.

28. Alan Moore, conversation with author, September 19, 2015.

29. *The Times Square Show* in June 1980, organized by Colab in a large building in Times Square, was tremendously influential. In addition, related undertakings such as the Fashion Moda gallery in the Bronx proved more fruitful in breaking down the cultural/racial divisions. For the interconnected history of these undertakings see Moore, "Punk Art," 80–108.

30. Peter Cramer and Jack Waters, oral history interview with Lisa Kirwin, Archives of American Art, Smithsonian Institution, September 6–October 9, 2007. Cramer and Waters (of POOL) discuss their performance collective and name Arlene Schloss, George Moore, Eric Bogosian, Steve Buscemi, and Michael Keene as some of the participants.

31. Ibid.

32. Peter Cramer and Jack Waters, interview by author, January 14, 2015.

33. Quoted from Carl George, Peter Kramer, Brad Taylor, and Jack Waters, "Seven Days of Creation," in Moore and Miller, *ABC No Rio Dinero*, 142.

34. Moore and Miller, *ABC No Rio Dinero*, 144.

35. Cramer and Waters, interview by author.

36. See Georgina Cardenas, "Rocky Horror Stage Show," *Miami New Times*, July 11, 1996, accessed May 14, 2016, http://www.miaminewtimes.com/music/rocky-horror-stage-show-6361422.

37. Ronald Lawson, with the assistance of Reuben B. Johnson III, *The Tenant Movement in New York City, 1904–1984* (New Brunswick, N.J.: Rutgers University Press, 1986), 240. Lawson and Johnson examine the reason that properties in tax remission (in REM) ended up in the ownership of the city; and Chapter 3, "No Heat, No Rent: Adopting Buildings (1970-1975)," looks at the impact of this citywide phenomenon in Loisaida.

38. Cramer and Waters, oral history interview with Liza Kirwin.

39. As per state department records, ABC No Rio was officially incorporated in 1990.

40. Jack Waters, Peter Cramer, and Lou Acierno, interview with Kathrin Wildner.

41. Ibid. Acierno articulates his position clearly in the joint interview.

42. Fly Orr, interview by author, New York City, January 2016. Fly articulated her connection to an international art/punk/political scene and the presence of other autonomous spaces in Europe and the United States that had much in common with ABC No Rio.

43. Vikki Law, *Enter the Nineties: Poets, Punks, Politics at ABC* (New York: ABC No Rio, 2005), 2, access to zine courtesy of the author.

44. Joseph B. Treaser, "Police Comb Neighborhood for Source of Fatal Heroin," *New York Times*, September 1, 1994.

45. Steve Englander, interview by author, New York City, April 16, 2015. Englander mentions his terrifying encounters with police trying to break into ABC No Rio in the course of their raids.

46. Fly Orr and Steve Englander, along with Lou Acierno, lived within the building between 1989 and 1991. Englander, oral history interview with Liza Kirwin.

47. This is discussed by Waters, Cramer, and Acierno, interview with Kathrin Wildner.

48. See Brian Wallis, "Public Funding and Alternative Spaces," in *Alternative Art New York, 1965–1985*, ed. Julie Ault (Minneapolis: University of Minnesota Press, 2002), 161–181.

49. Steve Englander, interview by author.

50. Jim Testa, "The Rise and Fall (and Rise Again) of NYC's Only All-Ages Non-Racist, Non-Sexist, Non-Homophobic Punk Scene," *Jersey Beats*, no. 56 (Spring 1996).

51. See Stephen Duncombe, "Let's Be Alienated Together: Zines and the Making of Underground Community," in *Generations of Youth: Youth Cultures and History in Twentieth-Century America*, ed. Joe Austin and Michael Kevin Willard (New York: New York University Press, 1998), 427–451. For a more specific history of anarcho-punk culture in the Lower East Side, see Ben Nadler, *Punk in NYC's Lower East Side, 1981–1991*, Scene History series, vol. 1 (Portland, Oreg.: Microcosm Publishing, 2015).

52. Esneider, a Colombian immigrant and longtime organizer of the HC/Punk collective at ABC No Rio, described the specific politics of the New York City Punk scene in the '90s. According to Esneider—unlike other parts of the country where the violence was racially directed—in New York City, given the strong presence of Black and Latino punks, the aggression was not exclusively racially directed but rather "macho" and "homophobic." Esneider, interview by author, New York City, January 17, 2016.

53. "Rockbeat: Boneheads Need Not Apply," *Village Voice,* December 1990.

54. Ibid. ABC No Rio Punk performances were written up in *Maximum Rock and Roll, Village Voice*, and *Jersey Beat* magazines.

55. Chris Boarts, *Slug and Lettuce*, no. 27 (September–October, 1992).

56. Ibid.

57. Esneider, interview by author.

58. Englander, oral history interview with Liza Kirwin. Englander views this event as the "signature event" at ABC No Rio. It was his point of entry to the space.

59. Many different charities—the churches and community centers in the neighborhood as well as the Catholic Peace Worker—also ran soup kitchens and served food in Tompkins Square Park as the homeless population there grew in the mid-'80s.

60. For a brief history of squatter resistance in the Lower East Side, see Sarah Ferguson, "The Struggle for Space: 10 Years of Turf Battling on the Lower East Side," in *Resistance: A Radical Political and Social History of the Lower East Side*, ed. Clayton Patterson (New York: Seven Stories Press, 2007), 148–163.

61. The resulting tension between the homesteaders, the "squatters," and the homeless is discussed in Malve von Hassell, *Homesteading in New York City, 1978–1993: The Divided Heart of Loisaida* (Westport, Conn.: Bergin and Garvey, 1996), 121–135. For a longer narrative of the squatter movement in New York City, see Amy Starecheski, *Ours to Lose: When Squatters Became Homeowners in New York City* (Chicago: University of Chicago Press, 2016).

62. Esneider, interview by author.

63. Dave Powell, member of HC/Punk collective, booked the concert for WRL. He speaks of his high school colleagues that were previously apathetic being politicized by this event. He is quoted in Law, *Enter the Nineties*, 26.

64. See Christopher Mele, *Selling of the Lower East Side: Culture, Real Estate, and*

Resistance in New York City (Minneapolis: University of Minnesota Press, 2000), 258–262.

65. Englander, oral history interview with Liza Kirwin.

66. Ibid. Englander had been a part of the Anarchist Switchboard, an informal center for the people involved in the 1988 Tompkins Square Park police riots.

67. Andrew Jacobs, "What a Difference Two Decades Make: Asian Americans for Equality Is Attacked as the Establishment It Once Fought," *New York Times*, January 17, 1997.

68. Englander, interview by author. There was no signed or written agreement, but there was a verbal understanding between HPD and ABC No Rio.

69. See Ferguson, "Struggle for Space," 157–158, 186.

70. Orr, interview by author.

71. Englander, interview by author.

72. Scott Seaboldt, phone interview by author, January 20, 2016. Seaboldt lived in the East Thirteenth Street squats for nine years and was a part of the resistance that got a lot of media coverage, even as they were evicted in 1995. It made front-page news in the *New York Times*. See "Riot Police Remove 31 Squatters from Two East Village Buildings," *New York Times*, May 31, 1995.

73. Seaboldt, phone interview by author.

74. Ibid.

75. See catalog *The Ides of March,* A Building-Wide Exhibition, March 13–March 27, 1998, ABC No Rio Archives.

76. Ibid.

77. Roberto Martinez, phone interview by author, February 2016.

78. See catalog *The Ides of March,* The 4th Biennial Building-Wide Exhibition, March 19–April 15, 2008, ABC No Rio Archives.

79. Ibid.

80. Colin Moynihan, "Avant-Garde Cultural Center Isn't Quite Home Free Yet," *New York Times*, November 12, 2000, reports the changing criteria of the HPD.

81. Sarah Ferguson, "Punk Rock to Riches: Rio Raises Big Bucks," *Villager*, vol. 75, no. 23 (October 26–November 1, 2005).

82. Colin Moynihan, "Punk Institution Receives City Money for New Building," *New York Times*, June 29, 2009.

83. Paul Castrucci, conversation with author, August 2014. Paul was involved in the Bullet Space Squat and lived in the neighborhood, participating and providing his expertise to many of the neighborhood homesteading efforts.

84. Castrucci, conversation with author. Castrucci spoke of how they looked into "preserving" the building—the façade and the interior wall—because of the emotional attachment people (including himself) have to the place.

85. See http://www.nyc.gov/html/dcla/html/funding/funding.shtml, accessed May 3, 2016.

86. Moynihan, "Punk Institution."

87. Rosalyn Deutsche, *Evictions: Art and Spatial Politics* (Cambridge: MIT Press 1996), xxiv.

88. Gerald Raunig, "Instituent Practices: Fleeing, Instituting, Transforming," accessed May 2, 2014, http://eipcp.net/transversal/0106/raunig/en.

89. Ibid.

EPILOGUE

1. The U.S. Census from 1970 uses the term "average," and that from 2010 uses the term "median."

2. Wendy Schwartz, phone interview by author, New York City, July 15, 2015.

3. Colin Moynihan, "Structural Flaws Found in a Building That's Known as the Peace Pentagon," *New York Times*, September 4, 2007, sec. B6.

4. Members of the PTTV collective opposed to the sale made the documentary *Peace Pentagon*, accessed July 2017, http://papertiger.org/portfolio/the-peace-pentagon/. The Friends of 339 organized an architectural competition to reimagine a new Peace and Justice Center at 339 Lafayette Street. See Nandini Bagchee, "Building for Peace in New York City," *Journal of Architectural Education* 69, no. 1 (2015): 73–85.

5. Colin Moynihan, "The 'Peace Pentagon,' an Activist Office in NoHo, Is Forced to Move," *New York Times*, April 12, 2016, sec. B4.

6. Ibid.

7. Ibid.

8. The property, with 152,000 square feet of usable space, was reported to be valued at $78 million in 2015. Tanay Warerkar, "Redevelopment of East Village School Is in Turmoil Again," *Curbed New York*, December 31, 2015, accessed July 18, 2016, http://ny.curbed.com/2015/12/31/10850432/redevelopment-of-east-village-school-is-in-turmoil-again.

9. Deed of Sale between the City of New York and Ninth and Tenth Street LLC, July 21, 1999.

10. Chino Garcia, interview by author, New York City, November 15, 2015.

11. Christodora, a former settlement house, was one of the first buildings in the Lower East Side to be developed as a high-end condominium. Its tall profile and adjacency to Tompkins Square Park has made it a target of anti-gentrification protests since the late '80s. These protests, continuing in 2008, often end up in front of the Christodora, with their anthem "Die Yuppie Scum."

12. For the controversial role of Michael Rosen, the founder of East Village Community Coalition, see Maria Luisa Tucker, "Michael Rosen Fights Back Over East Village Rezoning," *Village Voice*, August 13, 2008.

13. For dorm proposal, see Sarah Ferguson, "Scaled-Down Dorm Pitched for Embattled CHARAS Site," *Villager*, April 25, 2013, accessed May 23, 2016, http://thevillager.com/2013/04/25/scaled-down-dorm-pitched-for-embattled-charas-site/.

14. Quoted from the mission statement of the Save Our Community Center PS 64 (SOCC64), accessed May 28, 2016, https://soccc64.wordpress.com/about/.

15. For an account of this rally, see Lincoln Anderson, "Kings and Politicians Ask Mayor for Best Gift of All: The Old PS 64 Back," *Villager*, January 8, 2015, accessed May 23, 2016, http://thevillager.com/2013/04/25/scaled-down-dorm-pitched-for-embattled-charas-site/.

16. Levar Alonzo and Lincoln Anderson, "City Is 'Interested in Reacquiring' Old P.S. 64, Mayor Tells Town Hall," *Villager*, January 8, 2015, accessed November 23, 2016, http://thevillager.com/2017/10/13/city-interested-in-reaquiring-old-p-s-64-mayor-tells-town-hall/.

17. See Colin Moynihan, "ABC No Rio Gears Up for a Razing and a Brand-New Home," *New York Times*, May 16, 2016, sec. C3.

18. For this larger picture of community control, see Susan Fainstein and Norman I. Fainstein, *Urban Political Movements* (Englewood Cliffs, N.J.: Prentice Hall Inc., 1974).

19. Jane Jacobs, *The Death and Life of Great American Cities* (New York: Random House, Inc., 1961).

20. Marcia Tucker was dismissed from her job as a curator of painting and sculpture at the Whitney Museum of Art and set up the New Museum in Downtown Manhattan as a counterpoint to what she saw was the exclusionary culture of the established art museums that allowed no room for new and contemporary art practices. See also Julie Ault, ed., *Alternative Art New York, 1965–1985* (Minneapolis: University of Minnesota Press, 2002), 49–50.

21. Richard Plunz, *A History of Housing in New York City* (New York: Columbia University Press, 1990), 209.

22. Michael Zisser, conversation and building walk-through with author, February 22, 2016.

23. Accessed July 5, 2017, http://www.judson.org/.

24. New York City Housing Authority, *NextGeneration NYCHA* (New York: NYCHA, May, 2015), http://www1.nyc.gov/nextgeneration.

INDEX